MW00986558

The Last Slave Ships

The Last Slave Ships

New York and the
End of the Middle Passage

———————————————

JOHN HARRIS

Yale

UNIVERSITY PRESS

New Haven and London

Yale University Press books may be purchased in quantity for educa-
tional, business, or promotional use. For information, please e-mail sales
.press@yale.edu (U.S. office) or sales@yaleup.co.uk (U.K. office).

Set in Janson type by Tseng Information Systems, Inc., Durham, North
Carolina.
Printed in the United States of America.

Library of Congress Control Number: 2020935692
ISBN 978-0-300-24733-6 (hardcover : alk. paper)

A catalogue record for this book is available from the British Library.

This paper meets the requirements of ANSI/NISO Z39.48-1992 (Perma-
nence of Paper).

10 9 8 7 6 5 4 3 2

Contents

Acknowledgments

Many people helped me write this book. I conducted early research at Queen's University Belfast, where Catherine Clinton, Brian Kelly, and Antony Stanonis welcomed me into the Master's program in American history. The following summer Catherine supervised my thesis on the voyage of an illegal slave ship, the *Echo*, shaping it into a piece that helped me gain entry into a doctoral program in the United States. She has been a stalwart supporter ever since. Thank you, Catherine, for your encouragement and wise counsel.

At Johns Hopkins University, Phil Morgan was the faculty adviser I needed, pushing me to think through challenging issues, giving incisive but constructive criticism, and allowing me to work at the right pace for myself and my family. Whatever has rubbed off, I am the better for it. Thanks also to Toby Ditz, François Furstenberg, Jessica Marie Johnson, Michael Johnson, Pier Larson, and Gabriel Paquette, who all shaped my research, thinking, and writing. The Atlantic Seminar at Johns Hopkins was an excellent place to present my work and receive feedback. Thanks, especially, to fellow doctoral candidates Joe Clark, Christopher Consolino, Meredith Gaffield, Stephanie Gamble, Alexey Krichtal, Lauren MacDonald, Nathan Marvin, Dexnell Peters, Nicholas Radburn, Oriol Regué-Sendrós, Katherine Smoak, and Jennie Williams. It is a joy to follow your ongoing work and growing accomplishments.

Many other individuals and institutions provided support. Archivists at the national archives in Britain, Cuba, Spain, and the United States, and librarians Chella Vaidyanathan and Sara Morrison at Johns Hopkins and Erskine College, respectively, helped me locate key documents. Marial Iglesias Utset smoothed the path into the archives in Havana. The National Maritime Museum in London, the Program in Latin American Studies at Johns Hopkins, and Duke University all provided funding for research trips. Invitations to speak at the Gilder Lehrman Center at Yale University, Queen's University Belfast, and the University of Havana enabled me to engage with experts in the field and refine my ideas. David Eltis, Roquinaldo Ferreira, Ada Ferrer, Leonardo Marques, and Randy Sparks have offered particularly helpful conversation and correspondence. Special thanks also to Alan and Catherine Cottney, Neil and Tahmineh Hendron, Olwyn and Pete Jones, and Esther and Pete Wallace, who were generous hosts during research trips to London and Durham. As I revised the manuscript over the past few years, my colleagues at Erskine, Alessandra Brivio and David Grier, have offered wisdom and more than a little comic relief.

Yale University Press has been an ideal publisher for this book. My editor, Adina Berk, welcomed my pitch warmly and has always been enthusiastic about the project. She offered smart analysis on the manuscript and recruited two excellent anonymous reviewers whose comments strengthened the book. Susan Laity also offered sharp editorial assistance as the book neared completion. I have been guided through the final push to publication with just the right balance of urgency and understanding. I also want to acknowledge Meghan Cohorst, who produced several wonderful maps.

I would not have started or finished this book without the support of my incredible family. My parents, Ray and Ernest, have always encouraged me to pursue my love for history. Alongside my sister, Trish, and brother-in-law, Colin, they continue to show me what really matters in life, even from across the pond. My son, Dylan, who joined our family as I began writing up my research, has been another source of inspiration. My studies at Hopkins were a treat, but Dylan was Baltimore's greatest gift. In the later stages of revisions Jace brought a new dimension to our home, and along with Dylan, a glorious distraction. You are loved. Most of all, I thank my wonderful wife, Meg. She has supported me in more ways than I can explain. Thank you, Meg, for everything.

The Last Slave Ships

The Midcentury Moment

LUALE Kossola recalled that the Dahomeans approached at night. At daybreak, they broke down the main gate and terrorized the town. Kossola was still in bed but wakened with the commotion. He ran from gate to gate trying to escape to the bush but was grabbed by the raiders and tied by his wrists. He tried again to make a run for it but was captured once more. He watched as the assailants, men and women, decimated the population, capturing some, decapitating others. Taking the severed heads with them, the Dahomeans marched nineteen-year-old Kossola and the other captives to the coast. When they stopped along the way to smoke the rotting heads Kossola broke down. "All night I cry," he remembered as an old man. At Ouidah, a port on the Atlantic Ocean, Kossola and 109 other captives were sold to an American sea captain and forced aboard the ship *Clotilda*, bound for Mobile, Alabama.

It was 1860, and the *Clotilda* was the last slave ship to arrive in the United States.[1]

The voyage of the *Clotilda* violated national laws and international treaties throughout the Atlantic world. Some of the first anti-slave trade laws had gone into effect early in the 1800s after tumultuous wars of independence in the Americas fostered more expansive definitions of liberty and equality and gave increased urgency to abolition movements. In many cases the oppressed took up arms for freedom. In Saint-Domingue, in the Caribbean, slaves and free people of color secured independence from France, renamed their home Haiti, and banned the slave trade as well as slavery itself. In the wake of the American Revolution, the United States attempted to put the slave trade on the path to extinction, banning it completely in 1807, although slavery remained intact in many states. In the same year in London, Parliament outlawed Britain's slave trade, one of the largest at the time. By 1836 all nations that carried slaves across the Atlantic had banned the trade and African rulers were beginning to sign anti-slave trade treaties with the British.[2]

In spite of these laws and treaties, the slave trade remained remarkably robust during much of the nineteenth century because the financial incentives and anti-black racism that supported it remained in place. In the United States, Cuba, and Brazil, large tracts of fertile land remained uncultivated, and planters sought more slaves to expand their agricultural operations. These slaves grew sugar, coffee, and cotton, which were in great demand in the United States and Europe, increasing slave prices in the Americas and creating healthy profits for traffickers willing to defy the law. And while elites in Europe, Africa, and the Americas made commitments to abolish the trade, many of them were deeply connected to slave interests or the slave economy, and ignored or even abetted the trade for decades. Rulers such as King Gelele of Dahomey, who was behind the attack on Kossola's town, presided over a region that had been involved in the traffic for centuries and where traders had few commercial alternatives. The results of the illegal trade were staggering. Almost four million captives left African shores between the beginning of the century and the closure of the traffic in the 1860s, around a third of all captives who ever crossed the Atlantic Ocean.[3]

The United States was deeply involved in the illegal slave trade. Despite the 1807 ban (which went into effect in 1808), American slave traders continued to smuggle several thousand Africans to U.S. shores. When this flow largely dried up in the 1820s, Americans became deeply involved in the much larger trades to Brazil and Cuba, as shipowners and captains worked closely with traffickers in the major organization centers, Rio de Janeiro and Havana. Around two-thirds of all captives arriving in Brazil and Cuba in the 1830s and 1840s came aboard American-built vessels—over half a million men, women, and children in total.[4]

The United States played a crucial role in the slave trade after 1850, when Brazil effectively sealed its shores to the traffic. Forced to rethink their operations, a small number of slave traders from around the Atlantic world descended on the United States, incorporating American ports directly into their operations for the first time in a generation. New York and New Orleans now became key nodes in a new slaving nexus that stretched from Ouidah and Cabinda in Africa to Havana and Matanzas in Cuba. This was the slave trade's final triangle. Some captives, such as Kossola, ended up in

REGIONS INVOLVED
IN THE ILLEGAL
SLAVE TRADE AND ITS
SUPPRESSION IN THE
MID-NINETEENTH
CENTURY

London

EUROPE

Lisbon
Cádiz

AFRICA

Sierra
Leone

Bight of
Benin
Ouidah

West
Central
Africa

Cabinda
Ambriz
Luanda
Benguela

Southeast
Africa

ATLANTIC
OCEAN

St. Helena

the American South, but the vast majority emerged from the holds of filthy U.S. slavers in Spanish Cuba, the only remaining major market for trafficked Africans. The United States–Africa–Cuba nexus was powerful. Although the trade would never return to pre-1850s levels, an estimated 474 illegal voyages and 198,266 men, women, and children passed around this and other minor circuits by the time it was firmly established in 1853 until the end of the trade in 1867. Tens of thousands perished aboard illegal slavers, their bodies dumped overboard and into the deep.[5]

No American city was more closely tied to this trade than New York. A peninsular metropolis lying between the Hudson and East Rivers, New York was America's colossus. With a population soaring to over half a million and doubling every ten years, it was the largest city in the land. Trade was at the center of New York life. From Manhattan, dozens of wharves bearing small armies of dockworkers jutted out in all directions, servicing sailing ships that carried goods from around the world. Migrants also funneled into New York from across the United States and the globe, adding to the hubbub. The American publishing industry was based there, including the *New-York Times* and *New York Herald*, which vied for the attentions of an increasingly literate and information-hungry nation on a daily basis. New York was a city of extremes, home to the mega-rich and the abject poor, to the grand boulevard of Broadway and the sprawling slum of Five Points. Here the serene mixed with the chaotic. As construction on Central Park was getting under way, pigs and dogs still ran wild in the streets. In Gotham, order and disorder fought for supremacy, and it was never entirely clear which had the upper hand. A rising writer from Long Island, Walt Whitman, described

New York best: "City of the world! . . . mettlesome, mad, extravagant."[6]

Around a dozen illegal slave traders, collectively known as the Portuguese Company, entered this bustling scene in the early 1850s. Exiles from the collapsing slave trade to Brazil, they came determined to establish a new U.S. hub for the traffic to Cuba. The leading figure was Manoel Cunha Reis, who had left his native Portugal in his youth and became a slave trader in Rio de Janeiro and Portuguese Angola, Brazil's main slaving partner in Africa. His entire slaving career was conducted illegally. In Angola, Cunha Reis probably crossed paths with José da Silva Maia Ferreira, the man who would become his partner in New York. A proud Angolan of Portuguese heritage, Maia Ferreira worked temporarily for the joint British-Portuguese anti–slave trade court in Angola in the 1840s, learning the inner workings of the traffic, knowledge he would soon put to use as a slave trader in New York. Both Maia Ferreira and Cunha Reis were young men (mid-twenties and early thirties), had strong African ties, and were determined not to let the collapse of the Brazilian trade end their dreams of wealth and status. By the early 1850s, the pair had set up an office in Manhattan's merchant district and begun purchasing ships to send to Africa for slaves. Here they were assisted by a host of accomplices including ship captains, crews, and corrupt officials, and were rivaled by merchants with long-standing ties to Cuba who wanted a share of the slave trade for themselves. Soon Baltimore, Boston, New Orleans, and other American ports would become involved in their schemes.[7]

The slave trade would not have found a foothold in American ports without help from successive pro-slavery

Democratic administrations that failed to prioritize its suppression. While leading Democrats (and most Americans) did not support the trade, their preoccupation with expanding American slavery, particularly by incorporating Cuba into the United States, led them to neglect the trade itself at home and overseas. One of their key arguments for wresting Cuba from Spain was that the Iberian power had surrendered the legitimacy of its rule by permitting the slave trade to continue to Cuban shores. U.S. policymakers made a concerted effort to pin the blame for the traffic solely on Spain and largely turned a blind eye to growing American involvement.

America's increasing strength in the world also helped the slave traders. As the leading power in the hemisphere and a rising global force, the United States was in a position to defend itself against growing international criticism of its slave trade. The United States was the only major nation strong enough to prevent the British from summarily searching its merchant vessels for slaves by 1850—a huge boon to traffickers, such as Cunha Reis and Maia Ferreira, who came to New York largely to purchase American ships. Other powers directly involved in the trade, especially Spain and western African states, resisted British pressure not primarily on the basis of their own strength but because they were protected by geopolitical situations that made direct intervention by the British more difficult and less effective.

As the slave trade ramped up in the mid-1850s the prospects of full suppression seemed slim. The Portuguese Company and their native-born accomplices sent vessels from New York and other U.S. ports with little harassment, while on the African coast British Admiralty ships had no authority to seize them. An American squadron was also on patrol, but it was puny, frequently far away, and largely ineffective. Captive Africans did fight their enslavers, but had little success. The frustrated British responded creatively, hiring a slew of spies across the Atlantic world, including Emilio Sanchez, a Cuban-born merchant living in New York who reported to the British consul. Fearing for his life, but dedicated to ending the trade, Sanchez enmeshed himself in the slavers' world for more than three years, brushing up against men like Cunha Reis and Maia Ferreira. He wrote detailed reports several times a week, and his information would eventually wend its way across the Atlantic to the African coast, where the British fleet lay in wait and weighed whether to challenge American sovereignty by intercepting incoming slavers.[8]

As the British developed their international spy ring, American politicians began to attack U.S. involvement in the trade more vigorously. Not all Americans viewed Spain as solely culpable for the traffic or were willing to ignore America's increasingly obvious role in it. Opponents of slavery, including the newly founded Republican Party, saw growing American participation as further evidence that slave interests had taken over the federal government. Having already witnessed big victories for slavery in the United States, including the annexation of Texas as a slave state and the repeal of the Missouri Compromise, which had put geographic limits to the expansion of slavery, they viewed the growing slave trade, especially in northern cities, as a new sign that slavery was seeping inexorably throughout the republic. And although they were few, slaving voyages that ended up on southern shores of the United States, such as the *Clotilda*'s, suggested that the slave trade laws were being ignored entirely. It would take the election of a Republican president, Abraham Lincoln, and the onset of the Civil War before the United States would finally initiate robust action against the traffic and, subsequently, slavery itself.[9]

The American abolitionist Frederick Douglass had much to say about the raging battle between slavery and freedom in the United States and the Atlantic world. In 1852, he gave his most famous oration to an antislavery gathering in Rochester, New York, on the topic of what the Fourth of July meant to American slaves. In a sobering speech, he argued that to enslaved people Independence Day was not an occasion for celebration but a day that revealed "more than all other days in the year, the gross injustice and cruelty to which [the slave] is the constant victim." Although the United States had enshrined liberty and equality into its founding documents, Douglass knew these ideals had not been realized. He was particularly critical of the domestic, or "internal," slave trade that had been operating on a large scale between the upper and lower South for more than a generation. He noted that he himself had been exposed to this brutal, family-splitting traffic in Baltimore during the 1830s, when he had watched "slave ships in the Basin, anchored from the shore, with their cargoes of human flesh, waiting for favorable winds to waft them down the Chesapeake."[10]

But Douglass's speech also offered hope. He reminded his audience that the United States had banned the Atlantic slave trade, "denounced" it as piracy, and sent a suppression fleet to the African coast. "Everywhere, in this country," he argued, "it is safe to speak of this foreign slave-trade, as a most inhuman traffic, opposed alike to the laws of God and of man." Douglass was oversimplifying, using the Atlantic example to urge the United States to ban the domestic trade, but with the traffic to Brazil dead and the wider Atlantic trade at a historic low, it did appear that U.S. involvement in the slave trade had ended, and in truth, few Americans were tearful about that. Moving to a broader note, Douglass assured the crowd that "there are forces in operation which must inevitably work the downfall of slavery." These forces included what he described as the "obvious [antislavery] tendencies of the age," which would resurrect America's founding principles. The increasingly interconnected nature of the world meant that "intelligence" and "all-pervading light" was already spreading inexorably. "The arm of commerce has borne away the gates of the strong city," Douglass explained. "Oceans no longer divide, but link nations together." Under these influences, he looked ahead to the end of slavery in all its forms, exclaiming: "God speed the year of jubilee."[11]

Douglass's bright ending may have roused his antislavery audience, but he was too astute an observer to underestimate the struggles that lay ahead. As a formerly enslaved man who had run away to freedom, he knew better than most that antislavery faced serious headwinds in the United States and abroad. As he gave his speech, just a few hundred miles to the southeast a multinational group of slave traders was converging in Manhattan with the aim of thrusting U.S. ports back into the transatlantic slave trade. Their arrival would herald a new phase of American engagement with slavery and a new challenge for abolitionists across the country and beyond. Douglass was correct to note that the fight of the age was between slavery and freedom and that the international dimensions of that struggle would be key. His optimism turned out to be well placed, but antislavery activists would have many battles to wage, foreseen and unforeseen, before the year of jubilee would come.

CHAPTER ONE

The Final Triangle Takes Shape

I N the spring of 1854, John Crampton, the chief British diplomat in Washington, D.C., received a warning from the Foreign Office in London that an illegal slave trader, Joaquim Gaspar da Motta, had left Havana and was on his way to New York. According to information received by Joseph Crawford, the British consul general in Havana, Motta, an experienced Portuguese trafficker, was traveling to New York to purchase ships on behalf of the "Brazilian and Portuguese Slave Trade Association." This shadowy organization purportedly had tentacles in Europe, South America, and the Caribbean, and was deeply engaged in the illegal slave trade between Africa and Cuba. With Motta's departure, Crawford suspected that the Association was now aiming to bring the United States into its web of illicit dealings. Crampton had already warned the American authorities that slave traders might try to infiltrate the United States. Now he wrote to Anthony Barclay, the British consul in New York, who had a spy watch Motta's movements closely when he arrived in Lower Manhattan.[1]

By the time of Motta's arrival, every major slave trading nation had long since banned the trade. The British, especially, were attentive to the ongoing trade wherever it occurred and were most committed to quashing it. These prohibitions forced many slave traders to get out of the traffic and others to operate clandestinely. Many members of the Association were on the move precisely because they were under pressure from states seeking to suppress the trade. Motta traveled to New York because the governor of Cuba, Captain General Juan de la Pezuela, had kicked him out of the island under suspicion of trafficking. But although slave traders were feeling pressure from Pezuela and the British, the very existence of the Association indicated that some countries had not succeeded in suppressing the trade entirely. The trade to Brazil and Cuba, in particular, remained near record levels *after* it was formally abolished in the early nineteenth century. Behind this growth lay a rising demand for slave labor and strong attachments to the trade in Africa, not to mention a soaring demand for slave-produced commodities such as sugar and coffee on world markets. Many powers also had a strong interest in permitting the trade to continue, despite its illegality. In Cuba, Pezuela was one of the few governors before the 1860s to resist Cuban and Spanish pressure to turn a blind eye to it. Other nations, including the United States, were determined to suppress certain forms of American participation in the traffic but not all. Indeed, if any nation best summed up the contradictions and entanglements of the illegal slave trade, it was Cuba's northern neighbor.

The United States and the traffickers who would come to

operate from its ports were intimately connected to a much broader Atlantic story that would shape America's engagement in the trade in years to come. By midcentury the United States and other nations, as well as slave traders and enslaved people, had spent several decades navigating the myriad competing ideologies and interests of the age. For much of the 1830s and 1840s, traffickers and their allies seemed to be in the ascendant, forcing record numbers of captives illegally across the Atlantic Ocean. These enslaved men, women, and children came increasingly from West Central Africa to Brazil and Cuba, often aboard U.S.-built ships sailing under the American flag. Yet as midcentury approached, antislavery forces struck hard, limiting the options for the traders. In response, some, including Motta, would recast their networks, incorporating the United States more fully into their operations. As they did so, the final triangle took shape.

THE UNITED STATES AND THE
SLAVE TRADE BEFORE 1850

Most nations turned against the slave trade during the first half of the nineteenth century. Despite being the largest carrier of enslaved Africans during the eighteenth century, Britain struck one of the hardest blows. A popular abolitionist campaign led by religious and political reformers forced Parliament to ban the British traffic in 1807. The British were not the first to permanently end their trade—the Danes abolished theirs in 1803 and Haiti effectively did the same in 1804 by abolishing slavery—but British abolitionism had especially far-reaching implications. Fostering Britons' growing self-conception as liberators and eager to dominate "legitimate"

global commerce, successive British governments internationalized their abolitionist campaign dramatically. One important feature of this effort was a sustained attempt to convince other powers, including Portugal and Spain, to follow
suit. Britain was also the main force behind a network of
international slave trade courts known as Courts of Mixed
Commission, created to adjudicate violations of slave trading treaties that participating nations had signed with the
British. First established in 1819, these tribunals were dotted
around the Atlantic Basin from Freetown to Rio de Janeiro
by the 1830s. More cases would be heard before British Vice-
Admiralty Courts, which were also dispersed across the Atlantic and had become increasingly important by midcentury. In
addition, Britain created a slave trade suppression fleet known
as the West Africa Squadron to patrol the western coasts of
Africa for illegal slave ships. In 1833, Britain burnished its antislavery credentials further by becoming the first major power
to abolish slavery throughout its empire. By then, opposition
to the slave trade, and even to slavery itself, had become a core
element of British state policy and national identity.[2]

The United States was still a young republic when it also
took action at the turn of the nineteenth century. Although
North American participation in the trade had always been
limited compared to that of other regions, Rhode Island slave
ship owners and planters in South Carolina and Georgia had
been strongly tied to it during the eighteenth century. Yet
the trade came under increasing criticism, particularly in the
aftermath of the American Revolution. Although there was
no mass abolitionist movement as in Britain, a peculiar coalition gradually emerged in the United States. Some opponents,
mainly in the North, where slavery was already marginal,

objected to the traffic on religious and economic grounds. Others, especially in the South, were concerned about living alongside a growing and potentially dangerous enslaved African population. An important additional factor was that upper South planters believed they already had sufficient numbers of enslaved laborers; eyeing a potentially lucrative internal slave trade to the lower South, they sought to raise the value of their existing slaves by stemming the arrivals from Africa. In 1787 the U.S. Constitution attempted to reconcile the views of the traffic's proponents and detractors by permitting the importation of slaves for another twenty years, after which Congress would have the authority to end the traffic completely if it wished. Meanwhile, Congress outlawed American involvement in the trade to other countries in 1794 and through a more stringent act in 1800. Many U.S. states also banned the trade to their own shores. In 1807, Congress outlawed the traffic entirely. Even so, in the years immediately before the ban went into effect, the slave trade to the United States reached its historic peak in a final rush to import.[3]

American slave traders' defiance of the 1807 act and growing nationwide opposition to the illegal trade resulted in further legislative measures a decade later. Undeterred by the federal abolition law, Rhode Island slave traders brought thousands of slaves to the Spanish colony of Cuba, where the trade remained legal. Meanwhile, some slave traders smuggled captives into Louisiana, often intercepting Spanish slavers on their way to Cuba. The half-brothers Jean and Pierre Lafitte played a key role in this trade from their base on the Louisiana coast and later at Galveston, Texas. Playing the role of middlemen, the Lafittes bought captives in bulk on the coast and sold them quickly to Louisiana planters. Yet for many Americans, the continued slave trading of the Lafittes and others was at odds with their conception of the United States as the world's beacon of liberty. And to many policymakers, suppression of the slave trade, at least near U.S. shores, also offered a convenient pretext for pushing the Spanish out of Florida, a colony they sought to incorporate into the United States. Meanwhile, growing demand for slave labor in the Deep South was increasingly being satisfied by the slave trade from upper South plantations, reducing the importance of the transatlantic trade. Objections to the trade eventually found legislative expression in a series of new acts passed by Congress between 1818 and 1820 that increased fines for slave trading offences such as owning or serving aboard slave ships, offered cash payments to informants, and even sent a few vessels to African waters to patrol for illicit American slavers. The 1820 act also took the dramatic step of declaring the slave trade piracy, a crime punishable by death. This was a step not even the British would take until 1824.[4]

While the United States made progress on its suppression measures, other nations proved much less willing to take serious action. In France, Portugal, Spain, and Brazil, abolitionism remained tepid both in elite policy circles and in the public sphere until at least the 1830s, and in some cases much later. The weakness of abolitionist sentiment stemmed partly from these powers' intimate connections to the trade. Ships under their colors dominated the traffic in the early nineteenth century, especially after abolition in Britain and suppressive measures in the United States went into effect. Spain, France, and Portugal were also strongly tied to the trade through their Atlantic colonies. Portuguese Angola in West Central Africa had not only been the single most important slave exporting region on the continent for centuries, it was sending record numbers of captives to the Americas, especially Brazil, in the early nineteenth century. In French Guadeloupe, Martinique, and French Guiana, and in Spanish Cuba and Puerto Rico, planters sought new slave labor to boost sugar production, as Haitian sugar output remained low in the early nineteenth century, following the Haitian Revolution, when sugar production had plummeted. In Brazil, planters and merchants remained deeply committed to the trade after independence from Portugal in 1822, especially as the coffee frontier opened up in southern provinces.[5]

Despite the bad omens for the end of the slave trade, many of these powers formally abolished the traffic early in the nineteenth century. Under pressure from the powerful British, who had been strengthened by victories during the Napoleonic Wars, all the major slave trading nations condemned the traffic at the Congress of Vienna in 1815. Portugal agreed to abolish its trade north of the equator that same year in return for Britain's promise to pay the Portuguese government three hundred thousand pounds, and a further three hundred thousand to owners of the Portuguese ships they seized before June 1814. Soon thereafter, France committed to end the trade completely, and Spain promised to shutter its traffic in 1820 (receiving four hundred thousand pounds from Britain as an inducement). In the South Atlantic, Brazil, having gained independence from Portugal in 1822, promised to abolish its trade in 1830 in exchange for diplomatic recognition by Britain. With the trade to Brazil dipping sharply, the Brazilian legislature created its own law against the traffic in 1831. Five years later, Portugal became the final major carrier of slaves to abolish the trade completely. In addition to these measures, Spain, Portugal, and Brazil agreed to participate in the Courts of Mixed Commission, and Britain secured the right to stop Spanish slave ships and search them for slaves in 1817 (the agreement was updated in 1835), and a more limited right to seize suspected slavers under Portuguese and Brazilian flags. In Africa, in addition to Portuguese Angola, many slave exporting states signed abolition treaties with the British. By 1857 there would be forty-five such treaties, including agreements with Cabinda and Dahomey, key exporting polities in West Central Africa and the Bight of Benin.[6]

Although these powers formally abolished their trades, few made serious efforts to enforce their bans, at least initially. The Portuguese largely turned a blind eye both to the trade in Angola and to illegal slavers sailing under their flag for much of the 1830s and early 1840s. Angola's main slaving partner, Brazil, did likewise. Under the influence of the conservative Regresso movement, which was strongly tied to Brazilian planters, the Brazilian government rendered the 1831 law effectively toothless. (Some Brazilians had always considered it merely "uma lei para inglês ver," a law for English eyes.) The flagrant violations of these statutes and continued rejection of Britain's demands to concede a comprehensive right of search led the British foreign secretaries Lord Palmerston (in 1839) and Lord Aberdeen (in 1845) to authorize British cruisers to capture all Portuguese and Brazilian vessels suspected of slave trading, despite vigorous protests from Lisbon and Rio de Janeiro. Spain was especially duplicitous, making several agreements with the British while at the same time welcoming slave ships to Cuba and, less frequently, to Puerto Rico. Meanwhile, many coastal African states, which had been exporting slaves for centuries and saw little prospect in alternatives, failed to live up to their anti–slave trade commitments. One bright spot in this backsliding was France, which, although it failed to suppress the illegal slave trade after 1818 or the passing of a subsequent abolition law in 1826, did commit greater resources to suppression in the 1830s when a new reformist administration came to power. France even signed a right of search agreement with the British in 1831, though by that point the French slave trade was effectively over. In 1844 the French sent a squadron to the African coast to help the British prevent a revival.[7]

During these years, slave traders exposed the unwillingness of these powers to take definitive action against them, as the trade continued on a massive scale. In total, around 3.7 million captives were forced on board slave ships in Africa between 1800 and 1850, an average of more than seventy thousand per year. The trade actually increased between 1808, when the British and U.S. bans went into effect, and 1830. Perhaps most strikingly, over a million captives were transported on slavers *after* Portugal became the final carrier of slaves to outlaw the trade in 1836.[8]

The South Atlantic dominated this grim state of affairs. West Central Africa, comprising the Loango coast and the lower Congo River to the north and Portuguese Angola to the south, was an especially important source of captives. Although this region had always been a major exporter of slaves, its role increased relative to other regions starting in the 1830s. This was largely a result of Portugal's abolition of the slave trade north of the equator in 1815 and right of search agreement with Britain in 1817, as well as of the importance of Brazilian buyers, who had close ties to West Central Africa. Between 1837 and 1850, six of every ten captives departing

African shores came from this region. Elsewhere, the Bights of Benin and Biafra, southeastern Africa, and Sierra Leone remained important secondary export zones, especially after 1820. In the Americas, Brazil was by far the largest slave disembarkation zone, with Cuba a distant second. Between 1800 and 1850, Brazil accounted for 64 percent of new arrivals, compared to 17 percent in Cuba. By contrast, 2 percent of the total landed in the United States—and only a few hundred after 1820, when southern planters turned to the domestic slave trade and the more stringent American anti-slave trade legislation went into effect.[9]

The organization and financing of the trade mirrored its main routes. Rather than Europe, which had dominated slave ship outfitting during the eighteenth century, most voyages originated in the Americas, especially Brazil. The ships that set out to Africa from these regions were supported by tight connections between slave traders and their agents on the African coast. Many prominent traffickers, such as the Brazilian Francisco Antonio Flores, rose through the ranks, first operating in Rio de Janeiro and then, starting in the 1840s, in West Central Africa. Others, particularly in the Bight of Benin, such as Domingo Martins, had strong familial and business ties with Bahia. Slave traders in Cuba tended to have weaker links with the African coast in part due to Spain's historically limited presence in Africa, but some Havana traders, such as Pedro Martinez, had correspondents on the continent, especially along the Sherbro River in Sierra Leone. Although it is difficult to determine sources of capital with precision, most direct investors in voyages were located along these routes. In the trade to Brazil, investors were generally Brazilians and Portuguese, while most speculators in the Cuban trade were Spaniards or Cubans. These organizational and financial patterns became even more marked during the 1830s as the French got out of the trade. By that stage the traffic was centered in the South Atlantic with a smaller organizational node in Cuba.[10]

Despite the sharp decline in the trade to the American South in the first half of the nineteenth century, the United States played an important part in the traffic between other regions. One contribution was American-built vessels. Demand for U.S. vessels in major slaving ports such as Rio de Janeiro, Havana, and even on the African coast was small but growing in the 1820s, and it ballooned starting in the mid-1830s. Although U.S. vessels were also used by slave traders in Cuba, they were especially prominent in the traffic to Brazil. Between 1831 and 1850, 58 percent of voyages to Brazil took place in American-built ships, with the next largest builder, Brazil, far behind at 15 percent. Across the entire trade, around two-thirds of the captives arriving in the Americas during the 1830s and 1840s disembarked from an American-built vessel; exceeding half a million in total.[11]

One important factor underlying this shift was the growing supremacy of American shipbuilding in the early nineteenth century. Combining British and American shipping technologies and enjoying a plentiful supply of lumber from expansive forests, U.S. shipbuilders had a considerable competitive edge over the European nations that formerly dominated slave ship outfitting. Building on these advantages, the United States enjoyed a golden age in ship construction, as yards from Maryland to Maine produced record numbers of brigs, barques, and schooners. Many of these vessels, including the famed Baltimore Clipper, were especially fast, attractive to traffickers who sought to avoid the flotilla of cruisers off Africa and the smaller number policing Brazilian and Caribbean waters. Fast vessels also had the added benefit of shortening sailing times, which reduced slave mortality during the Middle Passage and costs such as food and sailors' wages.[12] In addition to the prevalence of U.S.-built vessels, the illegal slave trade was increasingly conducted under the American flag. In the southeast Brazilian market, slave ships flew the U.S. flag almost as regularly as they did Brazilian colors in the late 1840s. The American flag also appeared in the smaller trade to Cuba in the late 1830s and 1840s, as ships with Spanish and Portuguese flags came partly under the jurisdiction of the British. Traffickers based in Brazilian and Cuban slaving ports were careful to acquire the legal right to fly the U.S. flag, often by purchasing or chartering vessels through a resident American who acted as a straw buyer and retained legal ownership of the ship. This procedure permitted the vessel to fly American colors.[13]

One of the reasons why traffickers sought the U.S. flag was the protection it offered at sea. Most Americans jealously regarded the right of their merchant marine to sail without interference from foreign powers, especially Britain, whose interference with American vessels and sailors had helped spark the War of 1812. To many Americans, conceding the so-called right of search was a matter of principle; to do so would be, as Secretary of State John Quincy Adams put it in 1822, "making slaves of ourselves." Reflecting this thinking, U.S. administrations denied other nations' cruisers the right to stop and search American vessels, even in cases in which they were clearly carrying captives. When Congress did expand its suppression efforts, the sovereignty issue remained paramount. In 1842, the United States responded to increasing American participation in the slave trade by forging the Webster-Ashburton Treaty with Britain. This agreement required the U.S. Navy to send a permanent, although still relatively small, squadron to the African coast, but it did not grant the key concession, the right of search. Successfully resisting British pressure on this issue was a mark of growing U.S. strength on the world stage. Weaker nations, such as Portugal and Brazil, also denied Britain broad right of search powers, but Britain rendered their defiance meaningless by unilaterally declaring comprehensive right of search through the Palmerston and Aberdeen Acts of 1839 and 1845. Such a move could not be countenanced with the United States. By the mid-1840s, the United States was the only major maritime power able to keep Britain from routinely interfering with its vessels.[14]

More broadly, the value slave traders placed on U.S. vessels and the American flag was bolstered by the prioritization the United States placed on commerce over slave trade suppression. Although its navy did send a small number of vessels into African and Brazilian waters, as well as to the Caribbean, especially after the Webster-Ashburton Treaty, these cruisers had as their primary purpose supporting American commerce rather than suppressing the slave trade. Underscoring the point, U.S. cruisers in African waters spent most of their time north of the equator, where American trade was thickest, rather than in the main slaving grounds, which were increasingly located south of the equator near West Central Africa. Successive administrations refused to move the American supply depot from the Cape Verde Islands, near

Upper Guinea, to a more southerly point despite pleas from U.S. naval officers off the African coast. With these small deployments rarely in position to strike, slave traders had little fear of interception by American cruisers.[15]

Senior American diplomats held the same priorities as the navy. Although the Act of 1807 prohibited U.S. ownership of slavers, much depended on how far particular administrations would enforce the law. Most proved more interested in facilitating commerce than suppressing the slave trade. Secretaries of state were unprepared to interfere with the purchase or lease of American vessels in foreign ports, even when their consuls pointed out that local traffickers were snapping the ships up for the trade. During the 1840s, consuls in Rio de Janeiro wrote repeatedly to the State Department for assistance, but none came. As a result, Consul Gorham Parks wrote to Secretary of State John Clayton from Rio in 1849 that by following his orders from Washington, he had been obliged "to aid more in the Slave trade than perhaps any other Citizen of the United States."[16]

Although the use of the American flag and the sheer number and type of vessels were the main and most easily quantifiable ways of measuring American involvement in the slave trade, a final important factor was the indirect support provided by legal American commerce with slave trading regions. During the nineteenth century, the United States became the chief importer of Brazilian coffee and Cuban sugar, which encouraged planters to seek enslaved labor to increase production on their estates. Meanwhile, American capital and manufactured goods penetrated Brazil and Cuba at higher levels, underpinning both slavery and the slave trade. American vessels also delivered goods such as firearms to slaving zones in

Africa, where they were used to purchase captives for export to Brazil and Cuba. The United States was by no means alone in any of these contributions. The British probably supported the slave trade on an even greater scale by importing Cuban sugar, providing credit to slave traders in Brazil and Cuba, and sending manufactured goods and new technologies to the Caribbean and South Atlantic. Although the trade had been outlawed, international commerce brought almost every major power into the traffic in some way.[17]

American citizens on both sides of the Atlantic were most obviously responsible for U.S. participation in the trade. U.S. merchants living in slaving ports typically played important roles as middlemen, working in close association with local traffickers. James Birckhead and Maxwell, Wright & Company, two American coffee exporters in Rio, were the main suppliers of vessels to Manoel Pinto da Fonseca, the major slave trader in Brazil during the 1840s. Although they always remained a minority among crews, American ship captains and sailors sometimes took on the role of middlemen and occasionally sailed aboard slavers. Captains Joshua Clapp and Nathaniel Gordon were involved in several voyages between Angola and Brazil in the 1840s. (Gordon would repeat the offence from his new base in New York a decade later.) Even U.S. consuls became important conduits for the trade. Gorham Parks in Rio was a reluctant facilitator, but others, including Nicholas Trist, the U.S. consul in Havana during the 1830s, turned a blind eye and took kickbacks from traffickers. Each of these American roles—middleman, seaman, consul— would become a key element of the slave trade after 1850, when the traffic shifted to an axis that involved U.S. ports directly.[18]

THE MIDCENTURY ASSAULT

The promising, if inadequate, international assault on the slave trade of the early nineteenth century was followed by a newly reinvigorated campaign during the mid-1840s to early 1850s. Portugal dealt the first major blow in Angola. Successive Portuguese governments and colonial administrations had tolerated a large slave trade from Angola and under the Portuguese flag since abolition in 1836, but by the mid-1840s policymakers in Lisbon were beginning to take suppression seriously. This change was partly in response to external pressure. In 1845, Britain and France agreed to allow each other to make treaties with African polities, including those on the northern margins of Angola near the Congo River, and in some cases to occupy the coast. The agreement caused alarm in Portugal, where leading statesmen, including Prime Minister Sá da Bandeira, viewed African states in the lower Congo as under their sphere of influence. At the same time, an ideological shift was taking place in Portugal. Although the traditional approach of tolerating the slave trade remained powerful, policymakers were beginning to identify its suppression with national honor, largely because of Lisbon's growing isolation as a major violator of abolition laws. Portugal's action was therefore stirred less by concern about territorial encroachment per se than by the slight to national honor caused by the British doing what Portugal ought to be doing itself. The same principle applied to capturing Portuguese-flagged vessels, which the British had been intercepting throughout the Atlantic Basin since 1839. More active suppression efforts also afforded the Portuguese the opportunity to exert control over parts of Angola that enjoyed considerable independence from Luanda. The southern coastal town of Benguela was a particular concern. Several hundred miles distant from Luanda, the colony's second largest slaving port (after the capital) was heavily influenced by Brazilian traffickers, raising broader concerns in Portugal that Angola saw its political future with Rio de Janeiro rather than with Lisbon.[19]

Much of Portugal's improved suppression efforts focused on the African coast. Warships had already been stationed in Angolan waters since 1840, but between 1843 and 1850 their interception rate nearly doubled. Many of the resulting cases were adjudicated at a Portuguese prize court in Luanda established in 1844, and at Luanda's Court of Mixed Commission, created under joint British and Portuguese jurisdiction that same year. These activities went on despite the Brazilian government's complaints on behalf of Brazilian shipowners and slave trade investors. At the same time, the Portuguese and British jointly attacked the traffic in and around Benguela, damaging the trade in southern Angola and bringing the region under greater Luandan control. In the capital itself, officials brought a growing number of slave traders to trial for violations of the laws. And in 1847, Lisbon granted Britain the right to patrol much of coastal Portuguese Mozambique in southeast Africa, although it refused the same north of Angola.[20]

These efforts helped relocate rather than eliminate the slave trade in southern Africa. In West Central Africa, slave exportations declined markedly from Angola as Luanda and Benguela finally became minor ports, at least in terms of departures, which dropped tenfold after 1845 compared to the 1830s. Yet some traffickers simply moved their operations north, beyond Angola and Portuguese control. Some operated from coastal towns such as Ambriz and others along the lower Congo River and the Loango coast. In this region, a network of small decentralized states and many secluded creeks and thick brush, especially on the Congo, gave slave traders added protection from outside interference. In fact, the movement north had already been taking place since the 1830s, although it intensified with the added pressure during the late 1840s. Meanwhile, Luanda remained intimately connected to the trade. Traffickers in the capital continued to receive slaves from the interior, but instead of shipping them directly to the Americas, they sent them north for incoming ships. Rather than diminishing, then, the slave trade as a whole increased from West Central Africa and Mozambique during the late 1840s. Between 1845 and 1849, traffickers sent around fifty thousand captives from West Central Africa and Mozambique each year, a much higher figure than the twenty-nine thousand or so who embarked during the first half of the 1840s.[21]

A more consequential blow against the trade was struck in Brazil in 1850. Although there remains considerable debate among historians about the origins of Brazilian suppression measures, including the impact of a slave rebellion in the southern Paraíba Valley in 1848 and a yellow fever outbreak in 1849–50, both of which Brazilian legislators and writers linked to the slave trade, as well as the strength of anti–slave trade feeling in Brazil in general, British pressure was clearly an important factor. In 1846, Lord Palmerston became foreign minister for a second time and was determined to press Brazil even further than his predecessor the earl of Aberdeen, whose so-called Aberdeen Act had unilaterally given the British navy the right to intercept Brazilian slavers. Under Palmerston's direction and in association with James Hudson, the British minister in Brazil, and local consuls, the Foreign Office also began a series of covert operations that included bribing Brazilian politicians, funding the nascent Brazilian abolitionist press, and hiring spies to report on the movement of illegal slavers. The spies became especially useful when Palmerston strengthened the British naval presence off the Brazilian coast in 1849. Once the British fleet was reinforced, seaborne operations became much more aggressive and successful. In 1849 and early 1850, British cruisers entered Brazilian ports, opened fire on a coastal fort, and intercepted dozens of slavers. Much of this action took place just outside the main Brazilian slave trading hub, Rio de Janeiro.[22]

Britain's belligerence left Brazilian policymakers with little alternative but to crack down on the trade. Although Brazilian sovereignty had been flagrantly violated and some planters who relied heavily on the slave trade argued for war with Britain, few Brazilians backed armed conflict. Not only was the Brazilian navy no match for Britain's, but having become increasingly isolated as a slaving nation, Brazil could expect little support from other nations in the event of open hostilities. Even the United States, which had declared its opposition to European powers interfering in the affairs of the Americas since the Monroe Doctrine of 1824—and was itself deepening its commitment to slavery in the South and the West—was not prepared to come to the aid of a country so clearly committed to the slave trade. Lacking support from abroad, the Brazilian government opted to take action against the traffic, a move that it also hoped would preserve the empire's sovereignty, silence the British, and stabilize the Brazilian slave system. In the summer of 1850 the Brazilian Chamber of Deputies and the Senate passed a new law that included a raft of provisions targeting slave ships, their owners, and various accomplices. Meanwhile, the government strengthened its naval deployment off the coast and the police began searching estates for newly arrived slaves. Several more slavers would appear on Brazilian shores during the 1850s, but the decline was precipitous. By 1852, the largest branch of the illegal slave trade had ended.[23]

The government's new measures had a significant impact on slave traders in Brazil. Some withdrew from the trade, hoping the crackdown would be temporary and they could return to slaving in the future. Others faced punishment or expulsion. The Rio police arrested and charged several Brazilian traffickers with slave trading offences. Meanwhile, the government expelled several prominent Portuguese traders who had acquired considerable wealth through the traffic. Many of these exiles, including José Bernardino de Sa and Augusto Gomes Netto, returned to their homes in northern Portugal and Lisbon with large sums of money and purchased estates and titles through the Portuguese government (infuriating the British). In Brazil, American citizens who were formerly engaged in the trade also scattered. In the spring of 1852, Edward Kent, the U.S. consul in Rio, reported to the State Department that "the permanent and temporary residents in this city, natives of the United States, who were generally understood to have some connection directly or indirectly with this trade have failed in business, and nearly all of them have departed to 'places unknown.'" Kent, who was apparently glad to see them go, perhaps not least because U.S. policy itself had made his office complicit in their dealings, added, "I trust they will never return to disgrace this country and outrage humanity."[24]

The closure of the trade to Brazil reverberated powerfully in West Central Africa. In 1851, George Brand, the British vice consul in Luanda, reported with satisfaction that among the slaving merchants of Angola, "with the exception of two or three possessed of a little property and who have withdrawn from and are not now solely dependent on the traffic, there is scarcely one believed to be in a state of solvency." With the closure of the Brazilian trade, slave traders' credit was also drying up. According to Brand, one of the "largest" traffickers in the region had attempted to draw bills of exchange on a Rio source but they were rejected, "there being no funds belonging to him there" since "no slaves had been received." Because the slave trade formed such a major part of the economy in coastal West Central Africa, the effects of the collapse of the Brazilian trade went beyond traffickers. Brazilian gold, which was formerly abundant, especially in Luanda, was now scarce. Brand reported that the slave traders' inability to pay their debts meant that "the greatest distrust is felt in all transactions of a commercial character."[25]

Britain and the Portugal attempted to capitalize on these disruptions by stepping up their suppression efforts. Throughout the early 1850s, British cruisers heavily patrolled the coast of northern West Central Africa, especially around the key slaving town of Ambriz, just beyond Portuguese Angola. They also increased their attempts to make treaties with African polities in this region, resulting in accords with Francisco Franque, a powerful slave trader in Cabinda, which lay north of the Congo River (1853), and Cangala, the queen of Ambrizette, to the south (1855). Meanwhile, the Portuguese, concerned about British encroachment into Portugal's sphere of influence, bolstered their naval patrols and attacks on coastal slaving factors. These efforts would culminate in the occupation of Ambriz in 1855 and an 1856 decree expelling leading traffickers from Angola. For the Portuguese, suppression, imperial control, and expansion continued to be convenient bedfellows.[26]

The experience of Appleton Oaksmith shows how suppression efforts in the South Atlantic during this era combined with other factors to pressure slave traders. Oaksmith was a native of Maine who arrived in Rio de Janeiro in 1852 after a long and seemingly legal trading journey that had taken him to the Pacific Ocean and back. Even though American merchants and mariners were leaving the slave trade at this time, Oaksmith, who seems to have had no prior association with the traffic, agreed to carry freight for some Rio merchants aboard the *Mary Adeline* to West Central Africa. Such a move was the standard precursor to taking in captives, and although Oaksmith denied intending to enter the trade—a position he maintained throughout the ensuing ordeal—Brazilian officials were naturally suspicious. With Consul Kent's approval, they searched the brig for evidence of a slaving voyage. Oaksmith was furious with Kent for supporting the search, and as he recorded in his diary, he paced the deck trying to keep his "indignation from boiling over." Yet the search proved futile, and the *Mary Adeline* soon cleared Rio and began crossing the Atlantic. After a thirty-eight-day voyage the brig arrived on the Loango coast. Four days later, a launch arrived from the shore carrying the consignee for the freight, whom Oaksmith referred to as "Mr. G, a Portuguese"—probably Guilherme José da Silva Correa, a Portuguese trafficker who was well known to the British and maintained close connections with traffickers in Rio.[27]

The voyage had proceeded smoothly to this point, but now it began to unravel spectacularly. First the consignee ordered Oaksmith to sail to Shark's Point on the Congo River, a well-known slaving spot, to discharge his cargo and presumably take on captives. But Oaksmith, who had never been on the African coast before, was wary of entering the unfamiliar Congo, where he knew the currents were strong. His fears were well founded, and he duly spent the next two weeks struggling to navigate his way to the Point. Adding to his frustration, about a dozen Portuguese joined the vessel in the lower Congo and took up residence in his cabin, forcing him to retire to a "little room" in another part of the vessel. Worse was to come. After a week of failed attempts to round what he was now describing as "that infernal Point," the *Mary Adeline* ran aground on a sandbar. Around three thousand Africans armed with muskets and clubs were watching from the shore. During the next three days the Africans launched waves of attacks upon the vessel, aiming to claim the freight (or so Oaksmith surmised). It was a dangerous situation for the American. The brig's crew were only ten strong, several gravely ill, and the Portuguese, instead of defending the vessel, were apparently cowering below deck. In the end, they were able to hold off the assailants only thanks to the intervention of a British man-of-war that was, ironically, on an anti–slave trade patrol. The British did not generally assist suspected slave traders, but in this case the captain saw the opportunity to secure a salvage fee for recovering the vessel. (He eventually received ten thousand dollars.) Pointing the ship's guns at the shore, the

British fired grape shot indiscriminately into the crowd, probably killing scores of Africans. Meanwhile the *Mary Adeline* was lightened by the removal of freight, causing the sandbar to release its grip. A relieved Oaksmith promptly deposited the rest of his cargo, thanked the British profusely, and sailed back to the United States. He would go on to play important roles in a reconstituted slave trade during the next decade, but on the safer ground of Lower Manhattan.[28]

The slave trade from West Central Africa did not collapse in the wake of anti-slavery pressure and the *Mary Adeline*'s abandoned voyage. Ultimately, the Congo River region escaped the anti–slave trade pressure put on Rio. Several African polities made treaties with the British in the 1850s, though they were not wholly committed to ending the trade. Finding limited demand for alternative exports, their leaders were willing to play all sides: signing treaties with the British while accommodating the mostly Brazilian, Portuguese, and Luso-African traffickers on the coast. Moreover, Britain's wariness of Portugal's imperial ambitions meant there would be no Portuguese incursions on the coast north of Ambriz. In this context, slave traders like Correa proved adaptable. In one instance in the early 1850s, while the slave trade was at a low ebb traffickers in the lower Congo River forced captives to gather ground nuts and orchilla weed for export, planning to send the captives to the Americas when the slavers returned. The traffic in northern West Central Africa was therefore stalled rather than doomed.[29]

As efforts to eradicate the trade struggled on in West Central Africa, Britain stepped up attacks in other parts of the African coast. In 1849, the same year that British cruisers began aggressive action in Brazilian waters, the West Africa

SLAVE BARRACOON.

A barracoon at Gallinas, *Illustrated London News*,
April 14, 1849, 237.
(*Slavery Images: A Visual Record of the African Slave Trade and Slave
Life in the Early African Diaspora*, http://slaveryimages
.org/s/slaveryimages/item/1937)

Squadron launched a direct assault on slaving operations or
"factories" on the Gallinas River between the British colony
of Sierra Leone and Liberia. The river, which at its mouth
consisted of a series of shallow lagoons, was a haven for the
few Spanish slave trading agents, such as Pedro Blanco, on the
African coast, as well as a number of Portuguese and Brazilians who traded heavily with Bahia. Although this part of the
coast was a much smaller exporting zone than West Central
Africa, accounting for around 6 percent of slave exports in
the 1830s and 1840s, it was regionally significant. During the
1830s, the slave trader Théophilus (Theo) Conneau had described the Gallinas River as "the notorious slave mart of the
Northwest Coast of Africa." Noting the importance of the
river, the British navy had destroyed factories at Gallinas in
1840 during Palmerston's first stint as foreign secretary, and

then again in 1842 and 1845. In February 1849, the navy attacked once more, breaking up three factories and driving at least thirty-four slave traders—six Spanish, fourteen Brazilian, and fourteen Portuguese—from the river. Included in the destruction were ramshackle prisons known as barracoons, which held enslaved people awaiting incoming slave ships. This assault, in conjunction with the closure of trade to Brazil, was decisive in bringing the Gallinas slave trade to a close. After 1850, only one slaver brought captives from the river.[30]

Along the coast in the Bight of Benin, the British took further aggressive action. The Bight was second only to West Central Africa in terms of slave exports during midcentury, with Lagos an especially important hub, accounting for seventy-three thousand embarkations during the 1840s—around two-thirds of the regional total. The trade from Lagos was maintained chiefly by Brazilian and Portuguese slave traders such as Francisco da Souza, who operated in conjunction with King Kosoko, the ruler of Lagos from 1845 to 1851. In 1851 their operations were permanently disrupted when Royal Navy cruisers bombarded the port. After this successful attack from the sea, the British deposed Kosoko and replaced him with a new king, Akitoye, who signed an anti–slave trade treaty aboard a British cruiser and promised to work against the trade. Having effectively come under British control, Lagos would be annexed completely by the British in 1861. Meanwhile, in neighboring Dahomey, one of the key supply zones for slaves leaving the Bight, King Ghezo, having heard what had happened in Lagos, signed a treaty with the British in 1852 and promised to expel the Portuguese and Brazilian slave traders from his jurisdiction. Yet, unlike

Lagos, Dahomey and its main slaving port, Ouidah, were not at the mercy of the British. Dahomey was a large and powerful state, and Ouidah sat back from the Atlantic Ocean, rendering British cruisers much less threatening. With these advantages, some traffickers moved their operations to Ouidah after the Lagos attack and kept the trade open. (Ghezo would later renounce his treaty with the British.) As in West Central Africa, the embarkation zones in the Bight of Benin had narrowed but not closed entirely.[31]

As the slave trade came under renewed pressure in Brazil and on the African coast, the traffic to Cuba had almost dried up. After bringing large numbers of slaves to the island in the early 1840s, the trade declined sharply in 1845. This change was caused mainly by the Cuban planters' concerns about an uprising by slaves and free blacks. In late 1843 and early 1844 rumors had abounded that an insurrection was about to break out in the key slave importing zone of Matanzas and would then spread to other parts of the island. Although the rebellion never took place, the alleged conspiracy, which came to be known as *La Escalera*, had serious repercussions. In addition to torturing and executing scores of slaves and free blacks believed to be involved in the conspiracy, the colonial government, led by Captain General Leopoldo O'Donnell, took major steps to curb the illegal slave trade to the island. In 1845 a new penal law came into effect that stiffened punishments for crews aboard illegal slavers. These efforts were mainly a response to the demands of the planters. Illicit imports of slaves dropped dramatically, from around ten thousand in 1844 to five hundred in 1846. They would partially recover over the next few years, but major Cuban planters with strong ties to the slave trade began importing indentured laborers from China as an alternative.[32]

The Cuban government's assault on the slave trade did not, however, represent a fatal blow. As in other regions of the Atlantic world, after rebellion—or rumors of rebellion—planters' demands for enslaved Africans resurged. By the late 1830s, the island had become the world's largest producer of sugar, a crop that depended on an abundance of coerced workers. With the slave trade slowed substantially the labor problem became acute, especially since birthrates among Cuban slaves remained low and sizable imports from China and Yucatán failed to materialize until the mid-1850s. Some sugar planters were able to secure additional labor during the late 1840s by purchasing slaves from the island's coffee plantations, which were already in decline and were then devastated by a series of hurricanes that swept through the island in the mid-1840s, but this supply was unsustainable. Unlike the United States and Brazil, which had developed robust interregional slave trades by the mid-1850s, Cuba lacked a large internal supply of captive laborers.[33]

Another problem was that opposition to the slave trade was inherently weak. The 1845 penal law had been largely shaped by Cuban planters; it prevented the authorities from entering planters' estates to search for newly imported slaves. The colonial authorities had also used La Escalera to silence critics of Spanish policy in Cuba, including those who denounced the slave trade. In the aftermath of the conspiracy, O'Donnell had exiled dozens of island-born whites (Creoles) who attacked the authorities during the 1830s and early 1840s. One of the exiles' main arguments was that Spain encouraged the traffic to keep them from rebelling against colonial rule

because a rebellion could instigate a race war that would ultimately rebound on the Creoles themselves. In addition to its
concerns about the Cuban threat, the Spanish government
faced little pressure for suppression at home, where merchants
and industrialists, especially in Catalonia, were closely tied to
Cuban sugar interests. Indeed, many of Cuba's most important traffickers during the 1830s and 1840s had been born in
Spain and maintained strong ties to the Iberian Peninsula.[34]

The absence of strong abolitionist pressure within the
Spanish Empire limited the force that could be applied from
the outside. Unlike in Brazil and on parts of the African coast,
the British had to tread carefully in Cuba. One important factor was that Spain was a European nation, whose sovereignty
the British government felt more bound to respect than that
of Brazil or the African states. In addition, the Anglo-Spanish
Treaty of 1835 forbade any additional suppression measures
by the British upon the Cuban trade. Even more compelling
was the role of the increasingly powerful United States. After
the U.S. annexation of Texas in 1845, many American expansionists, including planters and leading policymakers, turned
their attention to Cuba. Spain resisted American pressure to
surrender the island, leaning heavily on the British, who also
opposed the growing U.S. aggression in the Caribbean. In
return for Spain's support against the United States, Britain sought robust Spanish action on the slave trade to Cuba.
Spain, however, would prove adept at playing off London's
fear of U.S. expansion against its opposition to the slave trade
during the 1850s. Although the midcentury assault on the slave
trade had produced some successes, especially in Brazil and
parts of Africa, intractable problems remained.[35]

THE SLAVE TRADE COMES TO U.S. PORTS

One consequence of the international suppression efforts was the dispersal of the trafficking community around the Atlantic world. As the trade to Brazil showed little sign of reopening, a small number of traffickers moved to Cuba, aiming to break into the inbound trade. One of these individuals was Antonio Augusto de Oliveira Botelho, a Portuguese trafficker living in Brazil. In 1851 he joined the small group of Portuguese and Brazilian slave traders in Cuba known to the British as the Brazilian and Portuguese Slave Trade Association. Although the members of this group received several slaving vessels at various parts of the island, most, if not all, were ousted in 1854 when Captain General Juan de la Pezuela, the governor of Cuba, began his purge. Pezuela found it easier to take action against the Brazilians and Portuguese than against local traffickers, who were often politically connected in Cuba and in Spain. In the spring of 1854 Pezuela's forces captured Botelho, who was hiding under an assumed identity, and expelled him from the island. The same year, they arraigned and deported two other foreign traffickers, Antonio Severino de Avellar and Gaspar de Motta.[36]

Having been thrown out of Cuba, these slave traders joined a small stream of others on their way to the United States. During the early to mid-1850s, around a dozen traffickers, mainly from Brazil, West Central Africa, and Portugal, converged on U.S. ports aiming to create a new node in the trade to Cuba. These men had deep experience in the slave trade, particularly in the South Atlantic. By the mid-1850s, they had established themselves in the merchant and shipping district of Lower Manhattan, where they became known as the Portuguese Company. Although New York would remain their base until the early 1860s, they would also dispatch vessels out of other U.S. ports, including New Orleans, Baltimore, and Boston, and move around the Atlantic Basin among the United States, Cuba, and various parts of Africa, as well as Brazil and Portugal, to organize voyages, supervise slaving trips in person, and, occasionally, escape pressure from U.S. authorities.[37]

The leading figure in New York, at least up to the late 1850s, was Manoel Basílio da Cunha Reis. Born in Portugal in 1822, he moved to Brazil as a young man, a common route for ambitious Portuguese who felt constrained by lack of opportunity at home. After establishing himself in Rio de Janeiro, in the 1840s he went to Angola as an agent for Brazilian slaving firms, imprisoning captives on the coast for incoming slave ships. By the early 1850s, he was based in Ambriz. At 5 feet 4 inches, with dark hair and eyes, and a straight nose, he was a man with few distinguishing features, but he was a powerful figure. In 1854, he was described by the British as a "notorious slave dealer" who kept captives in barracoons on the Congo River. The same year, the British and Portuguese targeted him, eventually running him out of Ambriz. He left Africa and, after stopping in Havana, arrived in New York in April 1855. He lived in Manhattan with his wife, Johana, who was eight years his junior, and with whom he would have two children, Manoel and Luiza.[38]

One of Cunha Reis's associates in New York, José da Silva Maia Ferreira, was an immigrant from West Central Africa. Born in Luanda in 1827 to a family with deep roots in the colony, he traveled to Brazil at the age of seven to be educated in Rio de Janeiro. In 1845, he returned to Angola and

José da Silva Maia Ferreira
(José da Silva Maia Ferreira Papers
Arquivo Nacional Torre do Tombo,
Lisbon [ANTT]., cx. 2, n. 16, doc. 8.
PT/TT/JSMF/0016/000008.
Image courtesy of ANTT.)

worked as a customs officer in the slaving cities of Benguela and Luanda and then as clerk to the new Anglo-Portuguese Court of Mixed Commission, where he gleaned information about the slave trade and Anglo-Portuguese suppression. It is unclear if Maia Ferreira was directly involved in the slave trade at this point, but in May 1851 he sailed to Ambriz, where he probably met and operated with Cunha Reis, who would act as his senior partner in New York. Maia Ferreira moved swiftly from Ambriz to New York, probably at Cunha Reis's

Margaret Maia Ferreira
(José da Silva Maia Ferreira Papers
Arquivo Nacional Torre do Tombo, Lisbon
[ANTT], cx. 1, pt. 14. PT/TT/JSMF/0014.
Image courtesy of ANTT.)

direction, and by 1852 was well established in Manhattan. In 1853 he married a wealthy New Yorker, Margaret Butler. Maia Ferreira and Cunha Reis were joined in New York by other migrants with experience in the South Atlantic slave trade, including Manoel José da Costa Lima Vianna (also referred to as José Lima Vianna), João José Vianna, José Lucas Henriques da Costa, Joaquim Miranda, José Pedro da Cunha, José Antunes Lopes Lemos, and Inocêncio Antonio de Abranches.[39]

New York was an attractive base for these slave traders. As their experience in Rio and elsewhere had shown, the best places to organize voyages were big ports with strong ties to slaving zones. In these respects, New York was an especially good fit. By midcentury it was not only America's largest port, it handled more trade than anywhere else in the Western Hemisphere. Positioned between the expanding American interior, to which it was connected by a growing network of canals and railroads, and the Atlantic Ocean, New York was a major global commercial and financial hub. While Britain remained America's main trading partner and chief source of credit, American ports were also connected to slave trading regions in the Caribbean and Africa. By 1840, the United States had become Cuba's largest trading partner, surpassing Britain and Spain. New York did more business with the island than any other port, its vessels carrying grain, lumber, and manufactured goods to Cuba and returning with sugar, rum, and molasses for American refineries and consumers. New Orleans was also tightly connected to Cuban markets and lay only a week away by sail and less by steam. Several U.S. ports, mainly in the North, also traded with slave exporting regions of Africa. A few firms even sent vessels to the lower Congo River basin, preferring to avoid paying tariffs to the Portuguese in Angola to the south.[40]

The physical geography of Manhattan and the tight clustering of its mercantile community helped the slave traders bond and operate efficiently. New York's merchants had been based at the tip of Manhattan since the arrival of the Dutch in the seventeenth century. It was a good location: the adjacent Hudson and the East Rivers were generously wide, deep, and sheltered, and the bay and the Atlantic Ocean beyond were easily accessible. By the mid-eighteenth century, these assets had helped the peninsula become one of the most important trade hubs in North America. By 1850, New York was second only to London in terms of global trade. The waters were filled with vessels that traded the world over, and wharves lined the shores. On land, commercial growth and massive influxes of European migrants were putting Lower Manhattan under unprecedented pressure. With space at a premium, shops, offices, and countinghouses were rising to several floors. The slave traders were within a few blocks of one another: One of the Portuguese, João Alberto Machado, was located at 165 Pearl, while another, Inocêncio Abranches, was a little farther along at 158 Pearl. Cunha Reis and Maia Ferreira worked out of an office at 40 Beaver Street. José Mora was only four hundred yards away at 54 Exchange Place. Juan M. Ceballos was nearby at 23 Broadway. The slave trade opponents were right next to them: the British consulate was at 17 Broadway, a few doors down from Ceballos, and Emilio Sanchez, the ship broker and commission merchant who would later spy on the slave traders for the British, had an office in the neighborhood at 187 Pearl. The major pro- and anti-slave trade agents in the United States were clustered face-to-face in Lower Manhattan.[41]

The newly arrived traffickers quickly created allies among the Portuguese overseas merchant community. One of their key associates was Machado, a native of the Azores who had immigrated to the United States in the late 1840s and was one of New York's main Africa traders. He traded, legally, at several places along the African coast, but he had previously resided in Sierra Leone, and the British believed he had formerly been "extensively engaged" in the traffic to Brazil. Other important allies included Portuguese merchant officials. When Cunha Reis arrived in New York, he and Maia

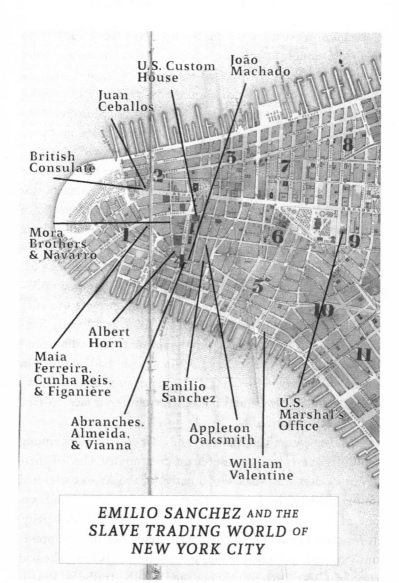

U.S. Custom House

João Machado

Juan Ceballos

British Consulate

Mora Brothers & Navarro

Albert Horn

Maia Ferreira, Cunha Reis, & Figanière

Emilio Sanchez

Abranches, Almeida, & Vianna

Appleton Oaksmith

U.S. Marshal's Office

William Valentine

EMILIO SANCHEZ *AND THE*
SLAVE TRADING WORLD *OF*
NEW YORK CITY

Ferreira attached themselves to Cesar Figanière, the Portuguese consul general, who ran a merchant house that imported wine from Portugal. In exchange for several thousand dollars, Cunha Reis became a partner in the firm, which subsequently changed its name to Figanière, Reis and Company. Meanwhile Maia Ferreira became the firm's secretary. In 1856 Cesar Figanière's father, Joaquim, Portugal's top diplomat in the United States, nominated Maia Ferreira to be Portuguese vice consul in New York, but to Maia Ferreira's enduring dismay Lisbon rejected the request. In Washington, D.C., Joaquim was assisted by another son, Frederico, who in 1849 had represented slave traders in Brazil and Angola when they brought a suit against U.S. officers for capturing an illegal slaver, the *Susan*, in African waters. The suit failed, but the Figanières' affiliations were clear. The newcomers made similar connections in other U.S. ports. Augusto Lopes Baptista, a Brazilian who operated both as a merchant and as the Portuguese vice consul in Baltimore, became an important ally for traffickers in the early 1850s.[42]

The New York Portuguese also forged alliances with merchants who had close connections with Cuba. These men came from diverse regions in the Spanish-speaking Atlantic, but all were residents of New York, New Orleans, and Charleston. Unlike the Portuguese they had little or no experience in the slave trade, but they did have strong trading interests with Cuba. One important figure, Antonio Maximo Mora, spent his formative years on the island before migrating in 1853 to New York, where he became one of the nation's largest importers of Cuban sugar. Another key ally, Albert Horn, was a New York merchant who had been born in Havana. In Charleston, the main figure was Ramón Salas, a Spaniard, who operated in the Cuba trade with his partner Charles Poujaud. In New Orleans, the key connection was with a Mexican named Salvador Prats. These individuals supported the Portuguese, but they also worked on behalf of traffickers in Cuba, especially later in the 1850s.[43]

The importance of mercantile connections was underlined in the development of a Masonic lodge in New York. Although many Americans viewed freemasonry with suspicion and even hostility during the nineteenth century, lodges proliferated in the United States and beyond. Described in an 1859 masonic manual as a "universal language" that promoted "kind and friendly offices" between brothers, freemasonry was an ideal institution for forging connections and engaging in clandestine activity. In New York, Cuban merchants founded lodge no. 387, La Fraternidad, in 1855. It soon became colonized by immigrant slave traders eager to exploit its secrecy, as well as its members' commercial connections with Cuba. Many of the Portuguese traffickers in New York became members, including Abranches, Francisco Diaz Perez de Almeida, and Manoel Fortunato de Oliveira Botelho (Antonio Augusto Botelho's brother). By 1857, these slave traders formed almost half the lodge's membership. They were joined by Justo de San Miguel, a sugar planter born in Santander, Spain, who was based in Cuba and implicated in illegal slaving voyages. Cunha Reis was the most senior member of the lodge. He had been a freemason since at least the 1840s in Rio de Janeiro and would become the most powerful slave trader in New York.[44]

When the New York Portuguese were not slave trading or forging new business connections, they spent time with one another and their families, often in opulent circumstances. Newlyweds José and Margaret Maia Ferreira entertained slave traders with dinner and champagne at their Manhattan home. They attended operas and balls and owned silver, diamonds, and expensive furs. José sent Margaret expensive purses and gloves when he was abroad arranging slaving voyages and settling accounts. Margaret was well aware that much of her lavish lifestyle was financed by the slave trade. Her husband was typically guarded in his letters to her, not wanting "to commit to paper" the details of his illegal work, but on one occasion he wrote gleefully from Havana that he had received "proposals to go to Africa as agent with 2 or 3 [slaving] vessels . . . to make a fortune in 6 or 8 months!" Their marriage was certainly turbulent. José spent long periods abroad and sent terse responses to Margaret's complaints from New York. Yet her frustrations appear to have concerned José's struggle to maintain their affluent lifestyle, rather than the work that funded it. The problem seems not to have been that he was a slave trader, but that he was not successful enough in his work.[45]

Portuguese traffickers developed important commercial and fraternal ties in U.S. ports, but they also benefited from broader national political priorities that were crystallizing at midcentury. America's concerns with sovereignty remained a serious obstacle to the abolition of the traffic. Despite continued British pressure on the United States to grant the right of search, this concession seemed less likely at midcentury than ever. Tensions were already high between the two powers after the United States annexed Texas over Britain's objections, and then went to war with Mexico, ultimately taking even more territory from its beleaguered neighbor. The Democratic Party, a major force behind these efforts, would maintain control over the government throughout the 1850s and was especially hostile to Britain. Making matters worse, the proximity of Cuba to the United States rendered British interference with U.S. vessels in the Gulf of Mexico untenable to policymakers of all stripes, as well as the vast majority of Americans. The U.S. position was captured by Andrew Hull Foote, who had commanded the USS *Perry* on the African coast in the 1840s. In his popular 1854 book, *Africa and the American Flag*, Foote noted that although he "sympathize[d] with the capture and deliverance of a wretched cargo of African slaves from the grasp of a slaver, irrespective of his nationality" it was "contrary to national honor and national interests that the right of capture should be entrusted to the hands of any foreign authority."[46]

While the sovereignty issue would continue to protect U.S. participation in the slave trade, additional cover was offered indirectly by American ambitions in Cuba. The island's dramatic economic growth in the early part of the nineteenth century caught the attention of many Americans, who were eager to incorporate the "Pearl of the Antilles" into the United States. For southern planters and prospective planters, Cuba held a special attraction as a new frontier for slavery. As a new state, the island would also send representatives to Congress and bolster legislative support for slavery, which was becoming a growing point of tension as Americans spilled into western U.S. territories from both slave states and free. Indeed, many northerners rejected the incorporation of Cuba into the Union precisely because it would strengthen the role of slavery in national affairs. At the same time, other northerners, especially in such states as New Hampshire and Maine that were already deeply involved in trade with Cuba, considered the economic benefits of adding the island to the

United States. While some Americans viewed the prospect unfavorably, the majority certainly agreed that in contrast to the energy of the United States, Old World, monarchical, and Catholic Spain was a corrupting and restraining force on Cuba.[47]

Expansionist impulses were shared and openly expressed in the highest political offices in the late 1840s. Leading American policymakers from Thomas Jefferson to John Quincy Adams had viewed the island as a natural appendage of the United States, but agitation over Cuba reached fever pitch during the mid-nineteenth century. Unlike the second major party, the Whigs, whose members were wary of slavery, most Democrats gave it their full-throated support and encouraged its westward and southward expansion. Following the annexation of Texas, prominent Democratic expansionists turned their attention to Cuba. Reflecting the increasingly forceful rhetoric, Jefferson Davis, a Democratic senator from Mississippi, stated his position bluntly on the Senate floor in 1848: "Cuba must be ours." In the same year, Democratic president James K. Polk authorized his minister in Madrid, Romulus Sanders, to offer the Spanish government $100 million for the island. The Spanish rejected the offer, but America's determination to wrest Cuba from Spain would grow, not wane, in the following decade.[48]

During this period of intense agitation over Cuba, some American expansionists used the issue of the illegal slave trade to support their case for acquiring the island. By 1850, Americans were well aware that the traffic to Cuba was ongoing, with newspapers' foreign correspondents and travelers reporting dramatic stories of the latest clandestine landings. Almost all these reports blamed Spain. The expansionist writer Cora

Montgomery wrote provocatively in her book about Cuba, *The Queen of Islands* (1850), "The supply [of slaves] is kept up by an energetic importation from Africa, under the patronage of Queen Christina [of Spain], who employs in the slave trade much of the $25,000 a month which she draws from the revenues of Cuba." According to this interpretation, Spain could easily suppress the trade. As the *New York Herald* explained: "It is possible, and even easy, for the government of Spain to stop the slave trade in Cuba, if it were so inclined." The *New-York Daily Times* correspondent in Cuba agreed, arguing that the slave trade "will be continued so long as the Spanish flag flies here." The implication was that the slave trade could be stopped only by U.S. possession of the island. This argument would be made forcefully later in the decade by many influential policymakers, including a sitting U.S. president. At that point, the idea that Spain was solely responsible for the trade still held sway and was powerfully shaping America's approaches to the traffic in its own ports.[49]

In some ways, Joseph Crawford's panicked message in 1854 that the Portuguese slave trader Motta was heading to New York ran counter to trends of the previous half-century. These were decades of remarkable anti–slave trade successes, when slave trading hubs were typically shutting down, not opening up. Although some nations had quit the trade reluctantly, slowly, and under considerable outside pressure, they had done so—after centuries of slaving. Major slaving ports such as Luanda and Rio de Janeiro, long the key hubs in Africa and the Americas, finally closed, and the pivotal axis between West Central Africa and Brazil disintegrated. While imperfect, the international apparatus of suppression—treaties, courts, and naval patrols—was impressive in scope and purpose. In terms of scale, the overall trade had dropped precipitously by midcentury. The days of slave traders forcing over seventy-five thousand captive Africans aboard ships each year were over. Traffickers themselves seemed to believe that the illegal slave trade's days were numbered. Most dropped out completely while others explored other forms of human trafficking from Mexico and China.

And yet the slave trade did not simply peter out. Cuban planters' demand for enslaved African laborers, backed by the global demand for sugar, had never completely disappeared. Several African polities remained on standby, their coasts dotted with barracoons and home to experienced slaving agents with strong ties to the Americas. The major force knitting these dark worlds together was exiles from the shattered South Atlantic trade who established a new hub in New York. Gotham was an ideal base, boasting a large port that lay within a nation determined to keep Britain at arm's length and increasingly committed to the idea that Spain alone was responsible for illicit slaving. As the commercial and geopolitical stars aligned, New York's new residents got down to their sordid work. The final triangle was taking shape.

CHAPTER TWO

Slave Traders at Work

N April 1857, the *New York Herald* described a special collection that had recently taken place at one of the city's uptown churches. The paper did not reveal the name or denomination of the church, but noted that it was "fashionable" and its congregation was well-heeled. Apparently, it was also generous. According to the *Herald*, the members had organized a collection to buy a "handsome present" for their minister. There were even rumors that they planned to send him to Europe if there were sufficient funds. This seemed to be a distinct possibility as the plate completed its early rounds. Already, it was carrying a "multitude" of notes. The warmth of this vignette diminished markedly, however, when it came to the moment the plate reached a "reverend looking" gentleman named Tom. As the plate approached, Tom reached into his pocket for a fifty-dollar bill, but when he pulled it out, he realized he was holding a hundred-dollar bill instead. Reluctant to part with this sum, he hesitated awkwardly. Thankfully, a friend leaned in with reassurance: "'Never mind, Tom, it's only two black birds, and you'll soon make it up.'" At this point, the *Herald* cut away from the collection and translated for its readers. "The two black birds," it explained, "signifies two negroes." To the *Herald*, the implication was clear: "the liberal and pious member of the church was deeply interested in the slave trade."[1]

By 1857, the traffic the *Herald* was referring to was running briskly between U.S. ports, Africa, and Cuba. The final triangle was approaching the midpoint of its lifespan and would eventually draw around two hundred thousand captives into its path. Despite its scale, the clandestine nature of this trade meant that most Americans knew little about who was running it and how it was run. Many newspapers attempted to fill the information gap. Some, including the *Herald*, created their own version of the truth. With its southern sympathies on full display, the *Herald* spun a yarn around domestic slavery politics, claiming that pious northerners who publicly distanced themselves from slavery in the South were privately bankrolling the transatlantic slave trade. It was a clever fiction, but that was all it was. Like most interested observers, the *Herald* was locked out of the slave traders' world. Only a few insiders understood how the trade operated and what the U.S. role entailed.[2]

Although traffickers sought to get rid of evidence of their crimes, often by destroying their papers and even their vessels after voyages had ended, important material has survived. British and Brazilian naval officers salvaged scraps of slave traders' correspondence and accounting documents from captured ships before they could toss them overboard, and Portuguese authorities unearthed similar documents in the home of a slave trader, João Soares, in Novo Redondo, Angola. Meanwhile, the British and American governments paid spies to inform on slave traders in New York and Lisbon, and Spanish diplomats in Washington, D.C., and Havana wrote revealing reports on the slave trade to their superiors in Madrid.³ These documents give access to a world that boasted New York as one of its main hubs. The *Herald* may have known little about the hidden workings of the slave trade, but it was correct in claiming that traffickers and their capital were operating right under the city's nose.⁴

U.S. SHIPPING AND THE SLAVE TRADE

In 1860, a few years after the *Herald*'s report on U.S. involvement in the slave trade, Gabriel García Tassara, the Spanish ambassador in Washington, D.C., compiled his own. Tassara was well aware that there had been a sharp uptick in smuggling to Cuba during the previous decade. In fact, more captives had arrived on the island during the previous year than in any other, with the exception of 1817. Knowing that the United States was playing a role in this growing traffic, Tassara's superiors in Madrid had demanded an account from the front lines. Several months later, after soliciting his own reports from Spanish vice consuls in U.S. ports, Tassara offered his conclusions. In his view, the U.S. role centered on shipping. His evidence clearly showed that American-built vessels were dominating the traffic. He also noted that the trade was being "done almost exclusively under the [U.S.] flag" and that U.S. ports had become major departure points for slavers. He identified one particular hotspot: "New York is generally the port where the ships leave for the trade."⁵

Tassara's claim that American vessels predominated in the slave trade was certainly true. After 1852, 91 percent of all 474 slaving voyages took place aboard vessels constructed in U.S. shipyards. Baltimore was by far the most prolific builder of ships that entered the traffic. Yards from Maine to New York lagged far behind, although collectively their production exceeded that of Baltimore. Despite their deep involvement in the domestic slave trade during this era, Norfolk, New Orleans, and Mobile produced only a few vessels that were employed in the transatlantic trade.[6]

Tassara's second claim, that the trade was carried out almost entirely under the American flag, was not quite accurate, although the U.S. flag was clearly preeminent. Between 1853 and 1866, 75 percent of all voyages sailed under U.S. colors. The Spanish flag accounted for 17 percent, and the Portuguese, Mexican, and a small number of other flags for a few percent each. The use of the American flag, and U.S. participation in general, decreased only after the Lyons-Seward Treaty in 1862, which permitted Britain to capture U.S.-flagged slavers. After 1862, only three vessels were American, and by this point the trade was in freefall, largely due to the treaty itself.[7]

Tassara was also correct that U.S. ports, especially New York City, were important departure points for slavers. Slavers headed to Africa from around the Atlantic Basin, but the majority left from U.S. and Cuban ports (40 and 42 percent, respectively). In the United States, slavers embarked from many points along the eastern seaboard as well as in the Gulf of Mexico, but New York accounted for two out of every three departures. In Cuba, slavers set sail from all over the island's long northern and southern coasts, but Havana was clearly dominant.[8]

Havana Bay, from Justo G. Cantero, *Los ingenios:*
colección de vistas de los principales ingenios de azúcar de la Isla
de Cuba (Havana: Litografía de L. Marquier 1857), 20.
(Image courtesy of University of Miami Libraries)

The Portuguese merchants in New York were largely responsible for harnessing U.S. shipping to the slave trade; they
had come with this aim in mind. From their new base in the
shipping district of Lower Manhattan, they purchased vessels,
often with input from their partners in West Central Africa.
In 1855, Guilherme José da Silva Correa on the Congo River
wrote to the João José Vianna in New York, instructing him
to "purchase a patacho or pilot-boat to carry 400 packages
[captives]." The ship "must be a fast vessel" and "come with
the American flag." Correa also suggested that Vianna consider purchasing the vessel in Baltimore, where he believed it
could be found more cheaply than in New York. The "Span-

ish" merchants, including Antonio Mora, who were deeply involved in the sugar trade with Cuba, also secured slaving vessels at this time. They purchased a few slavers for their Cuban associates at the beginning of the 1850s, and became major suppliers later in the decade.[9]

These merchants were stealthy both in their acquisition of American vessels and in securing the right to fly the U.S. flag. Their main problem was that only U.S. citizens were entitled to fly U.S. colors on their vessels. To overcome this difficulty, they paid American merchants, ship brokers, and ship captains to purchase vessels on their behalf. This strategy not only gave their vessels protection from British interference at sea, it also kept their names off the bill of sale and the ship's registry, making it harder to build a case against them in court. In large ports, such as New York, home to hundreds of merchants, ship brokers, and captains, straw buyers were not hard to find. In 1854 the Portuguese were doing some of the recruitment in New York indirectly through a ship chandler and outfitter named William Valentine, who reportedly paid American citizens a mere twenty-five dollars to register slavers under their names. According to Henry Wills, who served aboard the New York slaver *Julia Moulton*, Valentine claimed "he could go to the United States Hotel [in Manhattan] and any captain there with whom he was acquainted would do it for him with pleasure." By the late 1850s, some individuals were making numerous straw purchases for slave traders in New York. Captain Jonathan Dobson purchased the *Panchita* and *Isla de Cuba* for Cunha Reis in 1858. The following year, a New York merchant, Harrison S. Vining, bought the *Orion* for Joaquim Miranda. By the early 1860s, these maneuvers had prompted a former U.S. Africa Squadron officer, Robert Shufeldt, to claim that false ownership of U.S. vessels was giving "immunity . . . to the combined rascality of Christendom."[10]

Traffickers in New York and other U.S. ports were also adept at outwitting local authorities. The federal government tasked federal marshals and customshouses with policing the slave trade from their jurisdictions, but the traffickers' tactic of recruiting intermediaries to purchase slavers made their job more difficult. Since merchants and ship captains commonly bought and sold vessels, it was not necessarily clear when a vessel was being transferred into the slave trade. When it was time to clear the vessel from port, the traffickers simply had their intermediaries fill out the necessary paperwork at the customhouse. Slave traders were also careful in selecting their clearance destinations. Knowing that New York had a legal trade with several points on the African coast, they often had their intermediaries make clearances for these African ports. On other occasions, especially when the principals sensed increased scrutiny from officials, their operatives would give false destinations, throwing the customhouse clerks off the scent.[11]

While some officials were outfoxed by slave traders, at least a few were clearly corrupt. The unnamed American spy in Lisbon alleged, "Bribery is largely employed, and is relied upon as a sure and successful mode of getting the vessels off [from U.S. ports]." He pointed to the example of the slaver *Altivie*, which departed New York in 1856. Apparently, "an officer jumped aboard" the vessel just as it was about to head down the East River. Instead of arraigning the *Altivie* and arresting its crew, however, the marshal went below deck. There, "wine [was] produced, [and] five hundred dollars laid on the table in gold." Faced with lining his pockets or being carried away, the marshal allegedly "took the money." The case of the slaver *Storm King* proved such tales were not mere slander. In 1860, U.S. Commissioner Joseph Bridgham fired the New York deputy marshals Theodore Rynders and Henry Munn after learning they had boarded the suspicious *Storm King*, only to retire and let it slip out to sea. Bridgham made his decision after he discovered that the pair had received assurances from the men on board that they would receive fifteen hundred dollars the following day.[12]

After the slave ships cleared the U.S. ports, they would start on one of two main routes. The first ran directly, or almost directly, to Africa. Vessels on this path sailed from the United States in a northeasterly direction, following the North Atlantic's clockwise winds and currents, and then dropped down to the African coast using the Canaries and Guinea currents. One of these slavers, the *Mary E. Smith*, journeyed straight from Boston to the Congo River, where it received 520 captives. Others on the route might stop in the Iberian Peninsula, the Azores, the Cape Verde Islands, or São Tomé, for extra men, supplies, or repairs, or for information on shipments of captives and the locations of cruisers. The New York ship *Haidee*, for example, visited Cádiz to repair a yardarm before continuing its journey to the Loango coast in 1858. Another, the brig *North Hand*, left New York, paused at the Cape Verde Islands, and sailed on to Snake's Head, near the Congo River. Some vessels traveled all the way to southeast Africa. Depending on the stops, outbound voyages from the United States could take from three weeks to three months.[13]

Portuguese traffickers in New York dispatched most ves-

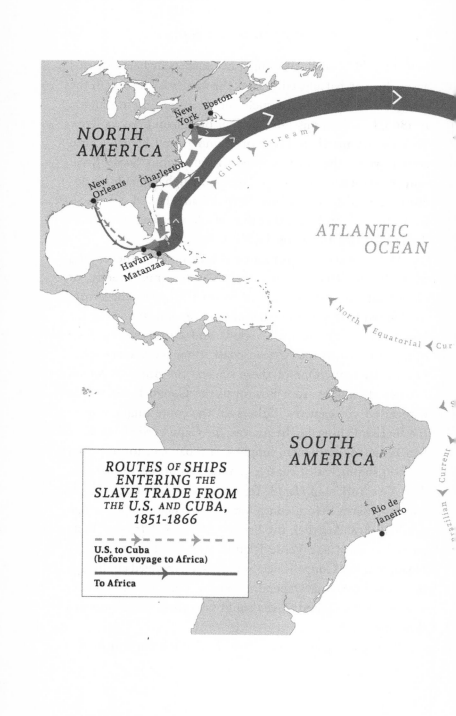

NORTH
AMERICA

New York
Boston

Charleston

New
Orleans

Havana
Matanzas

Gulf Stream

ATLANTIC
OCEAN

North Equatorial Cur

SOUTH
AMERICA

Brazilian Current

Rio de
Janeiro

ROUTES OF SHIPS
ENTERING THE
SLAVE TRADE FROM
THE U.S. AND CUBA,
1851–1866

– – ▶ – – ▶ – –
U.S. to Cuba
(before voyage to Africa)

——————▶
To Africa

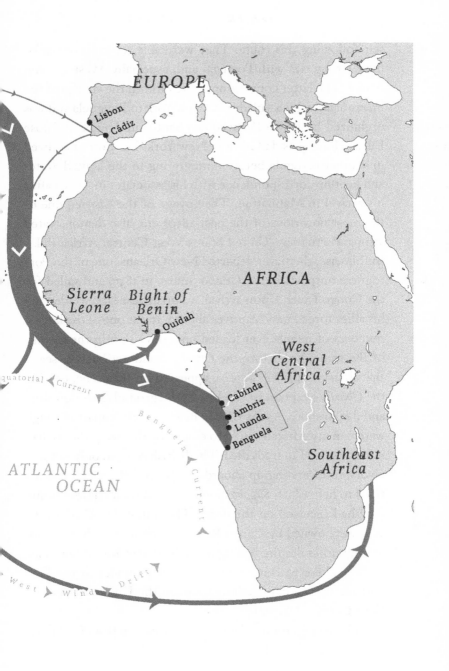

EUROPE

Lisbon
Cádiz

AFRICA

Sierra
Leone

Bight of
Benin
Ouidah

West
Central
Africa

Cabinda
Ambriz
Luanda
Benguela

Southeast
Africa

Equatorial Current

Benguela Current

ATLANTIC
OCEAN

West Wind Drift

sels following this route. They were able to do so owing to their strong ties with Portugal and, especially, West Central Africa. The latter connections were clear in the voyage of the *Pierre Soulé*, which sailed from New York to Benguela and was organized by Bento Pacheco dos Santos in Angola and José Lucas Henriques da Costa in New York. Da Costa had lived in southern Angola before immigrating to the United States and kept up correspondence with his associates in Africa after his arrival in Manhattan. The voyage of the *Charles*, one of the most notorious of the post-1850s era, also demonstrated strong Portuguese-United States-West Central Africa links. In this case, the slaver departed New Orleans, one of the Portuguese outposts in the United States, in 1857, and sailed for the Congo River. Upon arrival, a Portuguese slave trader and his allies forced 1,200 captives aboard. It was one of the largest numbers of people ever loaded on a slave ship in the history of the trade. Yet before the *Charles* could get back to sea, a British cruiser, HMS *Sappho*, appeared on the scene, causing the *Charles*'s captain to run his vessel aground, abandon ship, and flee to shore. As the *Charles* began to break apart in rough waters many Africans tried to escape by throwing themselves into the sea. Hundreds died. The British rescued only 358 survivors, most ending up aboard HMS *Vesuvius*, which had arrived to help HMS *Sappho*. Some bore on their chests a brand they had received on the coast. The initials "CR" indicated they were owned by Cunha Reis, who maintained barracoons in the region despite having moved to New York a few years earlier. These markings were a brutal reminder of the Portuguese slaving connections between the United States and West Central Africa.[14]

The second route taken by slavers leaving from U.S. ports

"Group out of 311 slaves on board HMS 'Vesuvius.'"
(ZBA2670, © National Maritime Museum, Greenwich, London)

also triangulated with Africa and Cuba, but the voyages began
with a short run south instead of a big swing to the east. Most
vessels following this path went to Havana. One of these was
the brig *Echo*, which arrived in Havana from New Orleans in
1858. Others went to Matanzas, Cárdenas, and other minor
ports such as San Juan de los Remedios, where the *Antelope* landed after clearing New York in 1859. Depending on
the ports involved, the journey to Cuba could take five days
or up to two weeks. When these vessels arrived, they were
manned, fitted out for transatlantic voyages, and dispatched
to Africa. This route was described by the assistant treasurer
of the United States, John J. Cisco, to the secretary of the interior, Caleb Smith, in 1861: "It is a well known fact that many
vessels are first sent [to Cuba] from our northern cities; and
then transferred to other parties, and dispatched to the [Afri-

can] coast; the preliminary arrangements being made here."
In fact, most voyages sailing from Cuba to Africa originated
in the United States.[15]

Spanish-speaking merchants in U.S. ports were central to
the United States–Cuba–Africa route. Their commercial and
familial ties with Cuba were crucial. The two Mora brothers,
Antonio and José, exemplified these connections. By the late
1850s, Antonio was running the Cuban end of their sugar
business in Havana while José looked after their affairs in New
York. In 1859, they arranged the delivery of three vessels, the
Panfilia, the *J.J. Cobb*, and the *City of Norfolk*, to the slave trading firm of Ximenes, Martínez, and Lafitte in Havana. This
prolific company was well known even on the West African
coast, where the British Admiralty described it as "wealthy"
and being "connected both with Paris and London." All three
of the Moras' vessels would make slaving voyages to Africa.
The prominent New York slave ship dealer Albert Horn had a
brother, William, resident in his native Cuba. In other cases,
perhaps where the Cuba-U.S. bond was not quite so strong,
Cuban slave traders traveled to American ports to ascertain a
vessel's suitability for the slave trade. Here too, commercial
ties were important. In 1859, the British spy Emilio Sanchez
reported that "parties from Havana" had arrived in New York
to inspect the *Antelope*. After approving the vessel, they called
upon Antonio Ros to facilitate the purchase. According to
Sanchez, Ros was "late a clerk with J[uan] M. Ceballos one
of the largest regents of Cuban [merchant] houses [in New
York]."[16]

By the late 1850s, the Portuguese and Spaniards in U.S.
ports no longer controlled their respective routes. The Portuguese in New York had gradually broken into the business

of supplying slavers to Cuba. In 1861, Robert Shufeldt noted that the Azorean João Alberto Machado was helping to send slavers to Havana from his new office at 75 Beaver Street in Manhattan. Around the same time, José Maia Ferreira was in Matanzas, arranging the sale and outfit of vessels for the slave trade. In 1859, Sanchez reported that Antonio Augusto Botelho was making frequent trips to Havana. In Baltimore, another Portuguese, Isaac Oliver, whom Solomon Beale, an American spy for the Department of the Interior, described as "smartly dressed, like lawyer or clergyman" and having a "reputation of being very sharp, shrewd, and keen," bought vessels for slave traders in Matanzas. Sanchez also noted that some of the voyages leaving New York were now doing so partly at the behest of Cuban traffickers.[17] These new ties did not displace the Cuban–U.S. Hispanic connection, but their emergence implies a merging of Cuban and New York Portuguese interests as the trade wore on, a development that would be mirrored in slave traders' financial arrangements.

FINANCING THE MIDCENTURY SLAVE TRADE

Investing in illegal slaving voyages was potentially lucrative, but it was also risky. On one hand, rising world sugar prices boosted slave prices in Cuba and created unprecedented profits for investors. Between 1856 and 1867, the average return on investment was 91 percent, far beyond the 10 percent common in the eighteenth-century trade. On the other hand, investors faced high risks. In addition to the traditional risks of shipboard revolt, shipwreck, and rampant disease, illegal voyages were in danger of capture by naval patrols. Interception was a serious concern. After 1850, around 40 percent of all transatlantic slavers were captured by international patrols in African and Cuban waters. Voyages that beat those odds faced further risks and costs once they reached their destination. Cuban officials typically demanded large bribes in exchange for safe disembarkations, and a few colonial administrations, such as Pezuela, were quite effective at "confiscating" newly arrived captives.[18]

The Portuguese in New York were willing to finance voyages despite these risks. Although they had come to the United States in part to exploit its shipping markets, their larger goal was to invest in voyages and make handsome returns. Their basic strategy was to purchase vessels in U.S. ports and send them to their correspondents in West Central Africa. They in turn would force the captives aboard and send the slaver off to Cuba. The advantage of this plan was that it combined assets: the New Yorkers' access to fast, U.S.-flagged ships, and the West Central Africans' expertise in supplying captives for incoming slavers. Failures like the *Charles*, they hoped, would be few.[19]

The strengths of the Portuguese New York–West Central Africa axis were counterbalanced by security problems in Cuba. In general, the Portuguese had weak ties with the island's planters, merchants, and officials who controlled the slave disembarkation zones. The tenuousness of their position had been demonstrated in the early 1850s when several of the New York–based traffickers had attempted to establish themselves in Cuba but were thrown out by Pezuela's administration. The problem persisted. In 1855, Pezuela's successor, José Concha, who was friendlier to the traffic, nonetheless issued further expulsion orders to his district governors and chiefs of police, resulting in the virtual disappearance of Portuguese traffickers in Cuba. Cunha Reis managed to buck the trend. Establishing himself on the island in 1858, he purchased land and slaves and traveled frequently between Havana and New York. Yet this move seems to have been eased by a masonic connection with Captain General Francisco Serrano, who was reportedly also a freemason and gave him permission to establish lodges on the island. José Maia Ferreira had a more typical experience. He followed Cunha Reis to Cuba in 1860, but although he hoped to stay, he ultimately failed to gain traction with the leading Cuban slave traders and returned to New York.[20]

The second major group of investors, Cuban planters, were long-term residents of the island and had few of the problems experienced by the Portuguese. These men, including Julián Zulueta, Salvador de Castro, and Mariano Borrell, exercised impressive local power. Many were wealthy planters and merchants who had profited from Cuba's nineteenth-century sugar boom and the illegal slave trade before 1850. One important asset was their large estates, which they used to house newly arrived captives temporarily and to conduct illicit slave sales. Another was their influence over the island's officials through bribes. These payments had been a feature of the Cuban slave trade for decades, but by the 1850s traffickers and officials had developed well-honed systems in many parts of the island. In the western jurisdiction of Pinar del Río, for example, investors and lieutenant governors established a formula that determined the size of bribes based on the number of incoming captives. At a more distant remove, but no less important, Cuban slave traders maintained strong business and political ties with Spain (as the New Yorkers did with Portugal), which gave them logistical and financial support for slaving operations, as well as a degree of protection from Cuban officials who were genuinely committed to suppression.[21]

The island's most powerful slave trader, Zulueta, enjoyed all these advantages. Born into a wealthy mercantile family in Álava in Spain's Basque region in 1814, he immigrated to Cuba in 1832. Zulueta was following in the footsteps of many Basques who moved to Cuba at the turn of the century, including some who became notorious slave traders, such as the Zangroniz family. By the mid-1830s, Zulueta had bought his first estate in the key sugar-producing province of Matanzas and secured more land along the expanding sugar frontier in Colón. By the 1860s, Zulueta owned four large, highly sophisticated estates, complete with triple-effect vacuum evaporators, centrifuges, and gas lighting for processing sugar cane. He named one of these Álava after his hometown. Over two thousand slaves labored upon his estates, many trafficked illegally from Africa. In one demonstration of his power, Zulueta's henchmen openly marched a group of captives overland from the coast. These *bozales* (newly imported slaves) were probably soon bearing false papers issued by Cuban authorities saying they had been born on the island. Bribes certainly helped make these actions possible, but so did familial connections. By the 1860s, Zulueta had married the niece of a powerful Spanish-born slave trader, Salvador Samá y Martí. (He was trumped by Mariano Borrell, who was uncle to Captain General Serrano's wife.) Although Zulueta was held by the Cuban authorities on slave trade charges in the 1850s, he was soon released. He was hardly considered a pariah. Later in life he became mayor of Havana, and the Spanish crown

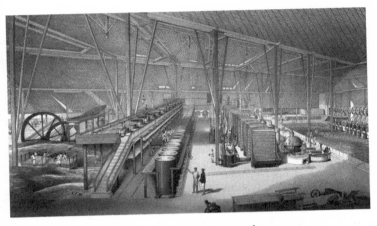

Julián Zulueta's sugar mill, Álava,
from Justo G. Cantero, *Los ingenios*, 37.
(Image courtesy of University of Miami Libraries)

awarded him the titles Marques of Álava and Viscount of
Casa-Blanca.[22]

While Zulueta exerted considerable local influence and
developed strong ties with ship suppliers in U.S. ports, he and
his fellow Cubans suffered from limited ties with traffickers
in Africa. This problem was mainly a legacy of Spain's narrow
interaction with the African coast during previous centuries.
Unlike the Portuguese, the Spanish did not develop a strong
foothold in the African regions that fed the slave trade. There
were no Spanish slaving forts like Elmina Castle on the Gold
Coast, which was variously under Portuguese and Dutch control for centuries, never mind a major African colony such as
Portuguese Angola. As other powers stepped up their slaving
in the eighteenth century, Spain continued to depend on them
to supply its imperium with captives. This pattern changed
after the expansion of the Cuban slave trade in the early nine-

teenth century, particularly after 1808, when Cuban slave traders took increasing control of the traffic from U.S. slave traders. The Cubans began developing stronger relationships with contacts on the African coast, sometimes sending agents and even family members to Africa to arrange shipments. Pedro Blanco of the Havana firm Blanco and Carvallo, for example, journeyed to Gallinas as early as the 1820s, while Juan José Zangroniz, of Zangroniz Brothers and Company was dispatched to Ouidah. The Cubans also worked with foreign agents such as the Italian Theodore Canot in Upper Guinea. Even still, there were limits to these links. Many of the leading figures had died or left the continent by midcentury, and the Spanish never established a strong foothold in West Central Africa, where the trade became increasingly based. By the 1850s most Cuban traffickers were still relying on Portuguese, Brazilian, and African merchants to organize shipments on their behalf.[23]

Portuguese and Cuban traffickers could find some ways of counteracting risk without fully embracing each other. Options included hedging their bets by spreading their investments over several voyages or opening their investments to small shareholders. The Cubans also invested in related fields, typically involving sugar and slaves. Zulueta was an example of an investor with large land- and slave holdings. Cunha Reis followed a similar pattern when he arrived in Cuba in 1858. The Portuguese trader secured land in the northern region of Sagua la Grande and in honor of his roots named his new estate Lusitania. Here he began growing the American staple, cotton, for which he hoped to develop a new market. He claimed that the labor could be done by poor farmers, but it was surely no coincidence that Lusitania was located right on the coast, convenient for landing captives illicitly from slave ships. We have no direct evidence that he did so, but others did elsewhere on the island. Cunha Reis and Zulueta also pursued other forms of human trafficking. The Portuguese was behind an ultimately failed 1860s effort to ship "free" Africans to Cuba via an allegedly voluntary emigration scheme, while Zulueta had been deeply involved in importing "voluntary" workers from China since the inception of this traffic in 1847. These operations, which contemporaries dubbed slave trading by other names, were all part of traffickers' portfolios in the mid-nineteenth century.[24]

Slave traders also cooperated with one another by changing the investment structure of their voyages. In most voyages speculators used an investment model called freighting. Under this system there were two ways to invest. The first was to buy shares in what traffickers called the ship. These shares funded the operating costs of the voyage such as the purchase or depreciation of the vessel, repairs, crew wages, and provisions. The second method was investment in the "cargo." The role of "cargo" investors was to purchase captives and force them aboard the slaver. After the vessel left the African coast, it would carry, or "freight," the captives to Cuba, with the "cargo" owners continuing to own them until their arrival in the Caribbean. When the voyage was completed, a consignee would receive all the captives and pay the voyage manager for the delivery, after deducting bribes and fees. As the consignee proceeded to sell the captives to Cuban planters, the manager would split the profits from the voyage, allocating one half to investors in the "ship" and the other half to investors in the "cargo." One variant of this model was for "cargo" owners to send their own captives to particular consignees in Cuba. In these instances, the various consignees acted for the "cargo" investors, selling the captives on their behalf, and paying fees to the "ship" investors who had funded the transatlantic crossing. Both scenarios, therefore, entailed investments in the ship and the cargo. Freighting, in other words, was the norm.[25]

The freighting model was not new to this era of the slave trade, but it was ideally suited to it. Unlike much of the British and French trades, especially from the mid-eighteenth century on, Portuguese, Brazilian, and Spanish traffickers had freighted captives extensively during the legal era. Whereas the British and French generally funded voyages in the metropole and entered into lengthy barters for captives on the African coast, the freighting model invited traffickers, typically in Africa, to purchase captives for the voyage themselves and hold them on the coast before forcing them aboard incoming slavers. On occasion, some captives were owned by American-based investors, such as Cunha Reis in the case of the *Charles*, but more often the captives were owned by African-based investors in the model the Portuguese slave trade had followed for generations. The main advantage of extending "cargo" investment in this way was that it resulted in good organization on the African side of the trade. This feature of freighting was particularly important with cruisers patrolling the coast. Because African traffickers' capital was also at stake, they were inclined to dispatch vessels as quickly and securely as possible. The bartering alternative was much slower and riskier.[26]

The case of the *Restaurador* indicates the importance of tying African suppliers to the outcome of a slaving venture, as well as the weak links between Cuban and African traffickers. This vessel journeyed from Cuba to the New Calabar River on the Bight of Biafra in early 1853. Upon his arrival, the Spanish captain, Juan Coll, declared that he would offer no freight but would exchange his cargo of *aguardiente* (sugarcane brandy) and Mexican gold for captives. Initially, Coll's plan seemed to be working. He struck deals with several African merchants, handing over the goods and specie in return for promises that the captives would be delivered after twenty days. But these arrangements, which left the merchants with the booty in hand and no stake in the voyage, quickly unraveled. Just a few days after the deal was made, one of the merchants, Ammacree of New Calabar, informed local white merchants about the slaver in the river. Soon, the news reached the British man-of-war HMS *Ferret*, which was cruising off the coast. Two weeks into Coll's wait for the slaves, the *Ferret* pounced, capturing him and the *Restaurador*. The expedition failed completely.[27]

Debacles of this kind encouraged investors in the shipping centers of Cuba and New York to draw on African support via the freighting model. In some cases, Cuban "ship" investors joined forces with "cargo" investors in the Bight of Benin. In these instances, vessels typically put in at Ouidah or Porto Novo, where Brazilian and African traffickers forced their captives aboard. In other cases, Spanish-registered vessels sailed for West Central Africa. One such slaver, *Dolores*, brought 595 captives to Cuba in 1855. The cargo of this vessel was owned almost completely by Portuguese-speaking residents of Ambriz and Luanda. In each of these ventures, the Africa-based investors made sure to dispatch the slavers swiftly, while ship investors in Cuba used their local influence to ensure the safe disembarkation and sale of the captives.[28]

The New York Portuguese also used the freighting model, typically drawing heavily on their strong ties with West Central Africa. The voyages of the *Braman* (1855), the *Pierre Soulé* (1856), and the *Mary E. Smith* (1856) all featured investment from both regions. In each of these examples, a handful of investors, sometimes as few as three, bought up "ship" shares and dispatched the vessel from the United States. When the vessels reached West Central Africa, "cargo" investors or their managers were waiting to put the captives aboard. Similar to the Cuba-Africa voyages, local accomplices watched the coast for cruisers, allowing all three ships to escape into the Atlantic Ocean with hundreds of captives crammed beneath their decks.[29]

Despite its benefits on the African side, freighting did not eliminate the insecurity of the Portuguese in Cuba. The case of the *Pierre Soulé* highlights their vulnerability. In this instance, several of the New Yorkers combined with thirty-five cargo investors in southern Angola to bring 467 captives to Cárdenas. When José Lucas Henriques da Costa, the voyage manager, arrived on the island, he applied for the delivery fee, but to his dismay the Cubans paid him far below market rates. With no recourse to the law or to powerful intermediaries on the island, he had to accept $85,000 for the captives. This sum, he wrote to one of the investors in Angola, caused "the whole business [to] suffer a loss of $48,000."[30]

The same difficulties seem to have been at work in 1855 when José Maia Ferreira was in Cuba trying to settle accounts. In this case, he complained to his wife, Margaret, he had only "succeeded with [settling] one & [was] yet to settle about three more & the most interested too." The problem, he said, was that "rascals" were "making a great farce to deliver the money that do not belong to them." One of those owing him money had recently gone to New Orleans, and

Maia Ferreira planned to follow him there to get it. These troubles appear to have been behind his conclusion that the "European Spaniards" who were the chief traffickers in Cuba, were "false as Judas."[31]

Although defrauding New York– and Africa-based slave traders was satisfying for the Cubans, such chicanery was ultimately counterproductive for the island's traffickers and its sugar economy. As the case of the *Dolores* had shown, Cuban investors needed West Central African support because a large portion of their trade was centered in the region. Cheating on the Cuban side would only harm their business prospects. Moreover, the island's planters relied on Portuguese-run voyages such as the *Pierre Soulé*'s to meet their growing demand for captives, especially as sugar prices soared in the late 1850s. Lacking both unfettered access to American ships and strong connections with Africa, Cuban traffickers could not satisfy the demand without outside help. New York– and Africa-based slave traders may even have underlined their importance to the island's sugar economy by briefly retreating from the Cuba trade after the *Pierre Soulé* affair. In the same year, 1856, they made one final, futile attempt to revive the traffic to Brazil with the voyage of the *Mary E. Smith*.[32]

In the late 1850s, historically high slave prices in Cuba and the promise of record returns on investment fostered a new spirit of cooperation among speculators in New York, Cuba, and West Central Africa. Other combinations may have persisted, but strikingly, each voyage made in 1858 and 1859 for which we have information was funded by investors in all three regions. Emilio Sanchez described investments in one of these voyages, that of the *Haidee*, which had set sail from New York in 1858. According to Sanchez, there had been six shareholders in the "ship." Four were Portuguese slave traders in New York and two were among Cuba's wealthiest planter-merchants. One of the Cubans was Zulueta. On the "cargo" side of the operation, he noted that some captives belonged to New York traffickers who maintained slave depots around the Congo River, while West Central African traffickers had sent the others "on freight." In other words, the voyage benefited from investment and logistical support on every leg. Underlining the brutal effectiveness of triple-region funding, Sanchez noted that the *Haidee* had brought 903 captives to Cuba, and its journey had been a complete success for all the investors.[33]

Although cooperation boosted all investors' chances of success, the various partners were not equals. The freighting system had always rewarded investors in the ship more generously than investors in the cargo. In the case of the *Pierre Soulé*, cargo investors received returns that were worth little more than the Angolan value of the captives, yet the ship investors made a profit of 100 percent. Cargo investors' dividends would have been much greater had the Cubans not taken advantage of Lucas, but the relative discrepancy between ship and cargo profits would have remained the same. There was logic in that discrepancy. Ship investors did much of the legwork in New York and Cuba, and many took on the personal risks of serving aboard the slave ship in managerial roles. It thus made sense that they would be generously rewarded. But when the Cuban speculators joined with the New Yorkers in triple-region voyages, they demanded the greatest spoils while taking the fewest personal risks. In the case of the *Haidee*, for instance, the Cubans bought up lucrative shares in the ship without ever setting foot on the vessel, much less sailing in it to Africa. Another example of Cuban dominance in the business, these arrangements demonstrate that the most powerful figures in the illegal slave trade were those who controlled the disembarkation zone.[34]

Growing cooperation, even close business ties, did not guarantee smooth financial transactions. In 1860 Maia Ferreira was again having trouble collecting money he was owed in Havana. The problem this time appears not to have been the Cubans but his old associate Cunha Reis, who was now living in a mansion outside Havana. Maia Ferreira had heard that Cunha Reis had recently "received more lots of money" and he had been unsuccessfully calling on Cunha Reis at his home to secure what he was owed. Now it was Cunha Reis to whom he referred as "that rascal." Maia Ferreira believed that if his claims "were of different nature, a court in a legal suit would decide it very quickly," although he knew this course was not open to him. Instead he intended to turn to the "influence of valuable friends, & the decision of private arbitrators." These were a Galician-born sugar planter and slave trader, José Plá, an individual named Calvo, and three other unnamed "parties" in Havana. After meeting them he wrote to Margaret, "Mr. Plá assures me I can collect my claim," adding gleefully, "I have found the way to twist [Cunha Reis]." Yet four months later Maia Ferreira confessed he had "got out of him only $340." Maia Ferreira was not nearly as significant a slave trader as Cunha Reis, who had stronger connections in Cuba and Africa, and the Cubans would only go so far in helping him.[35]

The world of slave trade investment was nonetheless fairly cooperative, especially by the late 1850s, though inherently risky and hierarchical. Pressure from slave trade suppression measures and the relative weakness of individual groups of investors necessitated some degree of collaboration. By the late 1850s, high prices for enslaved Africans in Cuba had encouraged speculators in all three zones to pool their strengths and resources. At the same time, some assets were clearly more valuable than others, and a hierarchy of investment emerged. Cuban investors such as Zulueta were at the top. They faced the unpredictable twists and turns of international pressures and the changing policies of Cuban officials, but these challenges were surmountable. Unlike the Portuguese, they did not endure the personal risks of serving aboard slavers, but they stood to make the largest profits. They also enjoyed substantial influence over payouts to investors, which were not guaranteed, especially to those outside the island. Next in the hierarchy came the Portuguese in New York, such as Botelho, who typically engaged in the risky business of managing voyages in person, but also stood to gain handsomely from shares in the "ship." At the bottom were speculators in Africa, who were generally relegated to "cargo" shareholding. They took few risks, but earned much smaller returns on their investments.

LAUNDERING AND CIRCULATING SLAVE TRADE CAPITAL

The illegal slave trade's disparate investment sources required speculators to discreetly move large amounts of capital over long distances. One major transfer occurred at the beginning of the voyage when investors pooled funds to cover its shipping expenses. These costs were substantial and heavily concentrated in the slaver's point of departure. In most cases, it took around thirty thousand dollars to get a vessel out of port. One of the largest expenses was the purchase of an appropriate vessel (it cost about ten thousand in New York, according to Sanchez). After further payments to intermediaries who purchased and registered the vessel, investors prepared it for an ostensibly legal voyage. These preparations involved sourcing the crew and hiring carpenters, caulkers, and others to perform repairs, and inconspicuously purchasing and loading all the stores and equipment necessary for a successful slaving voyage, including casks for water, provisions, and weapons such as cutlasses for the crew.[36]

According to the freighting model, it was the responsibility of "ship" investors to cover these expenses. Pooling ship capital in an outfitting port such as New York or Havana was sometimes a straightforward business because all the relevant investors resided there, but in many cases ship investors were located in two regions. Many traffickers retained credit with their distant partners, especially the Portuguese along the New York–West Central Africa axis, but they also sent investment capital on long-distance, border-crossing journeys so it could be put to use. Moving those funds was both technically challenging and risky. On the technical side, speculators had to ensure they issued funds in forms that were redeemable at their destination. Preferably, these funds would also be inexpensive to transport and retain their value during transit. The major hazard was that suppression authorities might seize investors' capital as it passed through their jurisdictions. With thousands of dollars on the move, steering capital into position was a complicated and high-stakes endeavor.

Sanchez appreciated these difficulties better than most observers did. In 1859 he wrote to his handler, the British consul in New York, Edward Archibald, describing the "ship" investments in the voyage of the *Haidee*. The 325-ton vessel had set out from New York the previous year and eventually disembarked nine hundred men, women, and children from West Central Africa at Cárdenas. According to Sanchez, there had been six "ship" investors in the voyage. Two of the speculators were planter-slave traders in Cuba, Julián Zulueta and José Plá. The other four were New York Portuguese. Among them, the six investors sank twenty-seven thousand dollars into the *Haidee*'s voyage. Individually, the sums ranged from Zulueta's eight-thousand-dollar stake to Antonio Augusto Botelho's twenty-five hundred.[37]

The international odyssey of the investors' capital began when Botelho made a trip from New York to Cuba. During his visit he collected a combined twelve thousand dollars from Zulueta and Plá. The merchant-planters issued the funds in two forms: a five-thousand-dollar bill of exchange and the rest in Spanish gold doubloons. Upon his return to New York, Botelho probably used the doubloons to help purchase the *Haidee*, which soon became the property of Inocêncio Abranches. He also presented the bill of exchange to Juan M. Ceballos, a merchant-banker of Cantabrian origin. According to Sanchez, Ceballos readily accepted the bill and used its value to buy a thousand barrels of flour on Botelho's behalf. The Portuguese then had the flour loaded onto the *Haidee*, which he cleared for Cádiz. When they arrived in Spain, Botelho sold the flour and had one of the *Haidee*'s yardarms repaired. Soon they set off again for the British crown colony of Gibraltar, where Botelho bought large amounts of rice and beans. After returning once more to Cádiz for bread, water, and further fittings, the *Haidee* finally set sail for the Loango coast.

Two months later, its crew was cramming eleven hundred captives beneath its decks.[38]

Through these twists and turns, the *Haidee* investors overcame the logistical challenges of the illegal slave trade, shifting capital from the Caribbean through North America and Europe to Africa with apparent ease. The gold doubloons issued by Zulueta and Plá at the beginning of the affair were both readily available to wealthy merchants in Havana and welcomed by traders in New York. Similarly, the bill of exchange was safe and convenient to transport, and, in the hands of the "respectable" Juan Ceballos, not at all suspicious. By turning the bill into flour in New York, Ceballos hid his slave trade capital in about as dull a commodity as New York could muster. In Cádiz, Botelho seems to have turned the flour into an innocent repair job on his ship. He had exposed the voyage to suspicion and the investors' capital to seizure when he bought large quantities of food, but his discretion (or possibly his bribes) was sufficient to get the *Haidee* out of Europe and on its way to Africa.[39]

The *Haidee*'s investors and their allies had planned every detail carefully, but they were also exploiting the opportunities offered by structural changes in the Atlantic world economy during the nineteenth century. The most significant of those changes, the liberalization of trade, had effectively opened up the laundering routes. Freer trade between Spanish jurisdictions and the United States was especially germane. When Zulueta and Plá sent their bill and gold to Ceballos, they were relying on a relationship built upon the booming Havana–New York sugar trade. This trade had grown steadily since Spain opened Cuba to foreign commerce in the late eighteenth and early nineteenth centuries. By 1858, when the

Haidee's voyage took place, the United States had surpassed the Iberian power to become Cuba's largest trading partner. Several of the individuals who laundered the *Haidee* investments—Zulueta, Plá, and Ceballos—were among the biggest operators plying the Havana–New York route. In fact, according to Sanchez, Ceballos was one of the most important merchants in the Cuban sugar trade. Moreover, he was "an intimate friend" of Zulueta and Plá. With such credentials, Ceballos was an ideal slave trading accomplice.[40]

The New York–Cádiz connection was another important axis in this affair. When the *Haidee* made its journey with the barrels of flour, it was following a relatively new but increasingly popular commercial route. The disintegration of Spain's Atlantic empire in the early nineteenth century had helped diminish Cádiz's commercial preeminence, but it also encouraged an expansion of the port's trade with foreign nations. The United States was one of its new trading partners. When the *Haidee* reached Cádiz in 1858, it joined a stream of vessels from every major port east of the Mississippi River. New York merchants, including Sanchez, sent goods to Cádiz, and during his long career as an overseas trader Ceballos probably did likewise. As a merchant of Spanish origin, he would certainly have known that Cádiz was a major gateway to the Iberian Peninsula and that Botelho would find a good market for American flour there. As his work in New York demonstrates, he had no scruples about assisting traffickers.[41]

These capital transfers took place at the early stages of a voyage, but the ones that probably interested speculators most took place at the end. These were the all-important remittances of dividends. As the case of the *Pierre Soulé* shows, investors, merchants, and bankers in the United States, as well as their partners abroad, all had crucial roles to play. In this case, investors had run the voyage along traditional freighting lines. The "ship" shareholders appear to have been the Portuguese in New York, since it was one of their number, José Lucas Henriques da Costa, managed the voyage's affairs in the Americas. On the "cargo" side were thirty-five residents of southern Angola, where the slaver had departed the African coast late in 1855. This pattern meant that returns would have to be distributed to individuals in Cuba, the United States, and Angola before each investor would receive his share. Da Costa initiated the laundering process in Havana shortly after the *Pierre Soulé* arrived with its captives at Cárdenas. First he contacted Justo Mazorra, a wealthy merchant in Havana, who eventually agreed to pay him eighty-five thousand dollars in drafts and specie. The records from this case do not explain how Mazorra made the payment, but they do disclose that he called on two Havana merchant-bankers, Martín Riera and Nicolás Martínez Valdivieso, for help with the transaction. Both Riera and Martínez Valdivieso were influential figures in the Banco Español, which had been established under Royal Charter in Havana the previous year. Riera was the bank's subdirector, the second-most senior position, while Martínez Valdivieso was a *consejero*, or board member. According to the bank's charter, two of its main roles were dealing in bills of exchange and issuing specie. Although it is unclear whether Riera and Martínez Valdivieso used their influence in Banco Español to help issue Mazorra's payment, the bank was uniquely equipped to do so. The island's most senior official, Governor Domingo Dulce, certainly believed that there was a connection between the bank and the slave trade. In 1863, he identified several Portuguese traffickers who had recently taken up residence in Cuba and specifically mentioned their shareholdings in the bank as a point of suspicion.[42]

The specie and gold that da Costa carried back to New York were part of a broader current of slave trade remittances moving north from Cuba. Several traces of this flow emerge from merchants' papers, spy reports, and newspaper columns. The correspondence of the New York sugar importer Moses Taylor shows that in 1854 Drake Brothers, an Anglo-Cuban merchant house in Havana, issued two bills of exchange worth a total of $12,000 in favor of José Lima Vianna, a Portuguese trafficker with no business in Cuba except the slave trade. Vianna brought the bills to Henry Coit, a sugar merchant in New York, who endorsed them and released the funds. According to Emilio Sanchez, Cunha Reis traveled the same route in the winter of 1858, carrying a massive $60,000 in drafts from the voyage of the *Panchita*. It was also common for traffickers to step off the Havana steamer lugging boxes of specie. In 1860, the *New York Herald* noted that Vianna had recently brought home a box of specie worth $7,650 from a recent trip to Havana. Incriminatingly, this list appeared right above an article from the paper's Cuba correspondent wherein he claimed he was in possession of "proof strong as holy Writ" that from six to eight thousand Africans had arrived on the island within the previous ten days. On other occasions, investors received remittances in commodities. In the case of the *Mary E. Smith*, whose voyage marked the final, unsuccessful attempt to bring captives to Brazil in 1856, Cunha Reis wrote to shipboard manager João José Vianna, explaining, "I want to have my share [of the profits] here [in New York], for which purpose the barque *Isla de Cuba* is to go there [Rio de Janeiro] and come loaded with coffee." Other remittances may have been received by Appleton Oaksmith, who set up a merchant firm in New York after his failed voyage to the Congo in 1852 and kept an account for José Lima Vianna.[43]

Havana to New York was only one leg on the journey of slave trade remittances. Slave trade capital flowed into New York, but it also flowed outward to investors in Africa. These speculators also expected their dividends. In the case of the *Pierre Soulé*, da Costa sent the funds through João Alberto Machado, the Africa trader in New York. In the summer of 1856, Machado sent the schooner *Flying Eagle* from New York to southern Angola with a legal trading cargo worth $30,000 and 432 gold doubloons. Machado had consigned most of the goods to João Soares of Novo Redondo, who had sent forty-eight captives aboard the *Pierre Soulé*. Two months later, the vessel arrived safely in Benguela. Soares was about to take his portion and distribute the rest to the others when the Portuguese authorities launched a surprise raid on his home. After searching his residence and discovering his incriminating correspondence with da Costa, they seized the *Flying Eagle*'s cargo and gold.[44]

Traces of similar capital movements can be seen in José Maia Ferreira's correspondence. Himself an inveterate mover—he shuttled among New York, Havana, Rio de Janeiro, Portugal, and probably Africa in the 1850s and 1860s—Maia Ferreira wrote to a wide array of slave traders around the Atlantic world. Among his correspondents were his partner Cunha Reis (who was likewise always on the move), Severino de Avellar in Rio, José Plá in Havana, and João Soares and Luis Antonio Ferreira Reis in Angola. In his letters to Soares and Ferreira Reis in 1855 Maia Ferreira included a list of legal trading goods he was sending aboard the New York barque

Isla de Cuba. Although he made no explicit references to the slave trade (no doubt deliberately), he was probably sending the proceeds from a previous voyage that had recently completed the United States–West Central Africa–Cuba circuit. A few years later, they would employ the barque outright as a slave ship.[45]

Remittances that Maia Ferreira and others sent from the United States were part of a larger flow of capital from the United States and Europe that supported the slave trade in Africa. Merchants on the African coast received legal trading goods such as guns and cloth from these regions and sent them inland to be exchanged for slaves, who ended up on the coast and ultimately aboard slaving vessels. Some of these goods came to Africa from the Portuguese in New York, but others came from Africa traders in Manhattan and Massachusetts who sent legal cargos of trade goods to Africa and sought palm oil and other products in return. Merchants involved in this trade included Robert Brookhouse of Salem, Massachusetts, who had an agent in West Central Africa. Britain, which was increasingly involved in the legal Africa trade, made even greater indirect contributions to the slave trade. The Angolan governor Sebastião Lopes de Calheiros e Meneses made the problem clear to the British government in 1862 when he complained that British powder, arms, and other goods "contribute, at present, more than any other . . . to attract the negroes from the interior, who bring down and sell slaves at the points where these goods can be obtained." Palmerston rejected the claim, but privately instructed his Foreign Office to write to "the British shareholders of the packets [delivering slave trading goods to Africa] and . . . point out to them that whether legally guilty or not they are morally guilty of slave trade." For as long as the slave trade existed the British were unable to resolve the conflict between support for free trade in legal goods and opposition to the slave trade.[46]

The entangled nature of slave trade remittances and other forms of commerce that supported it was a major boon for traffickers and a major problem for suppressionists. The case of the *Pierre Soulé* notwithstanding, the forces of suppression rarely intercepted remittances in transit. Slave traders and their allies typically moved these funds around the Atlantic Basin with impunity. The African side of the trade seemed to be as secure as it was anywhere else. In 1857, John Willis, the U.S. consul in Luanda, informed Secretary of State William Marcy in Washington that the trade was flourishing in West Central Africa. American gold was supporting this traffic, he said, and was "quite plenty" on the lower Congo River, "having been brought in those vessels which clear from New York." Traffickers would continue to circulate funds in this way until the trade was finally suppressed in the 1860s.[47]

In 1863, Edward Archibald reflected on the way his adopted city had come to play such a key role in the illegal slave trade. Writing to the Foreign Office, Archibald summed up his surroundings: "A large and populous maritime city, within a few days sail of, and in constant communication with, Havana, here have congregated the Spanish and Portuguese projectors of slaving voyages; and here have they been enabled, by a liberal expenditure of money, to command all the requisite means for carrying into execution their nefarious purposes."[48]

It was awkward prose, but it caught the essence of what had made New York a successful slaving port. Crucial factors were beyond the slave traders' control, including the city's proximity to Havana and its immense mercantile facilities, not to mention the long-standing American position on the sovereignty of the U.S. flag and the liberalization of world trade. At the same time, slave trading merchants had exploited the opportunities they had been given. With their strong ties to distant slaving ports, their slave trading experience, and their deep pockets, they had turned U.S. ports into headquarters for the illegal traffic. Committed to their illicit business, Cunha Reis and his ilk were adept at moving, adapting, and exploiting. Their purview was always global and never reckoned with the human costs.

These traffickers extended and created new forms of U.S. participation in the illegal slave trade. American ships, the Stars and Stripes, and capital originating in the United States were hallmarks of the traffic at midcentury, and all were closely connected with U.S. ports. At the center was New York, which had developed from a peripheral slave trading port in the first half of the century to one of the trade's last Atlantic hubs. The *New York Herald*'s shocking exposé may have had some of the details wrong, but in pointing to the central role of American ships, at least some American financing, and the prominence of Manhattan, its essence was correct.

CHAPTER THREE

Aboard an Illegal American Slaver

I N the summer of 1856, the fledgling poet Walt Whitman visited an impounded slave ship named the *Braman* at the Brooklyn Navy Yard. With *Leaves of Grass* debuting to a tepid early reception, Whitman had accepted a commission from *Life Illustrated* to describe the vessel, one of the few illegal slavers intercepted by U.S. authorities before it sailed for Africa. It was a rare sight, and Whitman took his readers through the vessel step by step. Beginning on the main deck, he took a "peep into the little dark forecastle, and another into the cabin at the other end." Then he crawled into the hold. Faced with a dark, empty hole, Whitman conjured a scene from the Middle Passage. Explaining that the hold was the place where the slaves were "laid together spoon-fashion," he entreated his readers to imagine "the miserable chattels . . . wondering to each other whither their white conquerors are carrying them. Perhaps, in desperation, they attempt to rise upon the crew [but] are quieted either by promiscuous musket volleys fired down the hatchway, or by a few pounds of tacks plentifully dispersed among them, so that the motion of a limb in the dense crowd inflicts smarting, punctured wounds." Having completed his portrayal of what he acknowledged was a "horrid vision," Whitman retreated from the *Braman* and ended his exclusive tour of the would-be slaver.[1]

Whitman's vision of the journey was intriguing and dramatic, but how accurate was it? What were midcentury slaving voyages actually like? How closely did they resemble voyages from earlier periods? What made them distinctive? The realities of a slaving voyage were well known within the secretive world of the illicit slave trade, but outsiders like Whitman had to rely on their imagination.

A more accurate picture is offered by the voyage of the brig *Julia Moulton*. This 1854 voyage was broadly typical of the midcentury traffic in the route it followed, the profile of its captives and crew, and its successful arrival in Cuba. The voyage is unusually well documented because of a high profile court case after the voyage and a remarkable interview given by the captain, James Smith, to the *New York Evangelist* newspaper. By piecing this evidence together, we can reconstruct the brig's journey and some of the experiences of the people, enslaved and free, who were connected to it. If we examine the voyage of the *Julia Moulton* in light of other voyages, we can also determine the key features of the midcentury trade and the factors that shaped them. As with most post-1850 American slaving voyages, the story begins in downtown New York and moves out into the wider Atlantic world.[2]

OUTFITTING THE *JULIA MOULTON*

The voyage of the *Julia Moulton* was jointly organized by traffickers in the United States, West Central Africa, and Cuba. As for many slaving expeditions after 1850, the Portuguese connection between New York and West Central Africa was imperative. In Manhattan, where the voyage began, the chief planner was José Antunes Lopes Lemos, an experienced and highly mobile trafficker who had operated in Brazil before the shuttering of its illegal trade in 1850. He subsequently moved to New York and, with the help of fellow Portuguese and Brazilian immigrants, helped incorporate the United States into the triangular slaving route that became predominant after 1850. Manoel Cunha Reis was the second key player in the voyage. He was the main slave dealer near Ambrizette in West Central Africa, where the *Julia Moulton* arrived for its captives in the early summer of 1854. Cunha Reis had not yet moved to New York, but he had strong ties with the Portuguese slave traders there and would establish himself in Manhattan the following year. His associate, José Maia Ferreira, who had arrived in New York two years earlier, wrote to him about the *Julia Moulton*'s voyage as he made his way to Manhattan in 1855.[3]

The Cuban side of the voyage was planned by a father and son, Salvador de Castro, Sr., and Salvador de Castro, Jr. Following a well-worn path from Spain, the elder Castro hailed from Galicia and had risen to become a major trafficker in Cuba. He was based in Trinidad de Cuba, an old port town on the island's southern coast, part of a larger jurisdiction bearing the same name. His son Castro Jr. was a native Cuban. He shuttled frequently between the island and the United States

to organize slaving voyages in conjunction with the Portuguese.[4] The Castros were a major force in the Cuban slave
trade during the early 1850s. Together they helped raise slave
imports to Trinidad from 1,465 to 2,690 between 1853 and
1854. These numbers represented a small but growing share
of total arrivals to the island: 8 percent and 18 percent, respectively.[5]

In the fall of 1853, Castro Jr. met with Lemos in New York
to plan the latest voyage to Trinidad. One of the first matters
at hand was purchasing a vessel. Slave traders had particular preferences, some of which had not changed significantly
since the trade became illegal in the 1830s. Traffickers continued to favor U.S. ships, the superior craft of the Americas. Fast models with barque, brig, brigantine, and schooner
rigging still appealed because they quickened crossings and
could potentially outrun patrols. Yet the tightening noose
of international suppression measures after 1850 encouraged
traffickers to cut costs and use older vessels. In the 1830s and
1840s, slave traders, especially in Cuba, had ordered new vessels, often from Baltimore shipyards, that were designed specifically for the trade. After 1850, they shifted to well-worn,
cheaper vessels sourced from the open market in U.S. ports.
Another change was scale. In general, traffickers used much
larger slavers after 1850 than before. During the 1840s, the
average slaver weighed 151 tons, but after 1850 the average tonnage increased to 234. This trend seems to have been mainly
a response to the rising profitability of illegal slaving. Traffickers in big ports such as New York had access to vessels of
all sizes but chose large ones because they could carry more
captives and earn larger returns on investment.[6]

Castro and Lemos followed these principles in their selection of the *Julia Moulton*. Built by shipbuilders Tengue and Hall in Newcastle, Maine, in 1846, the brig spent seven years sailing mid-length journeys from its base in Boston. The vessel's main trade route ran along the eastern seaboard and then around Florida to New Orleans, although the brig sometimes journeyed to the Caribbean for sugar and molasses. In fact, Castro, who spent much of his time in Havana, may have identified the vessel as a potential slaver during its final sugar run to the colonial capital in December 1853, just before it entered the slave trade. Castro would have noted its qualities. As a brig, the *Julia Moulton* offered considerable sailing speed and good maneuverability, especially in light winds. At 200 tons, it was also big enough to carry a large number of captives and, potentially, bring handsome returns to its investors.[7]

Having located a vessel, Castro and Lemos sought a crew. There were many roles to fill. The typical midcentury slaver carried a captain, one to three mates, a supercargo, carpenter, cook, and boatswain, and around a dozen ordinary hands. Overall, these roles were not markedly different from their counterparts in the legal U.S. slave trade of the early nineteenth century. The major difference was the inclusion of a supercargo, who managed the business of the voyage, especially on the African coast. This role had been common in the South Atlantic trade to Brazil, but rare in the British and North American trades, in which the captain typically transacted business. In most midcentury voyages the supercargo was Portuguese or Brazilian and had experience on the African coast, was a confidant of the principals, and was an investor in the voyage. Maia Ferreira and José Lucas Henriques da Costa possessed all these traits, as did Antonio Augusto Botelho, who was probably the most sought-after supercargo working out of New York.[8]

Slave ship crews were large, but they began to get smaller after 1850. Slavers had always required heavy manpower compared to vessels in other commerce, mainly due to concerns about slave revolt. After the voyage of the *Julia Moulton*, Captain James Smith noted that his vessel could have been "manned by four men" if it had been in legal trade. Slaving crews had grown larger over time, especially at the turn of the nineteenth century, as the ships and their captive cargos increased in size. By the early 1800s, tiny vessels such as the *Hare*, which left Rhode Island with nine men in 1755, were a thing of the past. In fact, between 1808 and 1849 crews aboard slavers consisted of an average of twenty-three men, well above numbers from previous eras. But this figure fell to eighteen after 1850, when slavers carried a higher proportion of children, who were not perceived to be a serious threat. This trend allowed investors to recruit fewer crewmembers and to minimize their costs.[9]

The single most striking feature of midcentury crews compared to those of other eras was not their size but their cosmopolitanism. The slave trade from North American ports had traditionally been composed of local men. Before the United States outlawed it, 95 percent of sailors boarding slavers in Newport, for example, were Rhode Islanders.[10] The illegal slave trade, and its final phase in particular, was much more varied. Naval officers frequently commented on the mix of nationalities they discovered when they captured slavers. One British officer, reporting the capture of the *Abbot*

Devereux near Ouidah in 1857, described a "crew of Spaniards, Americans, Portuguese, and Brazilians." The particular blend of slavers' crews depended partly on their port of origin. Vessels departing the booming metropolis and immigrant hub of New York typically included Americans and Europeans, with at least some Portuguese. By contrast, crews on Havana vessels often contained a few Portuguese and Americans, but more Spaniards and Cubans. Ultimately, the diversity of the crews reflected both the broader ranks of the local marine community and the outsized influence of the Portuguese over slave trade shipping.[11]

The *Julia Moulton* boasted a typically mixed crew. Captain Smith was born in Hannover, Germany, and was originally named Julius Smidt. After attending navigation school in Hamburg, he immigrated to New York in the 1840s, serving as first mate aboard the ship that carried him to the United States. He was twenty-four years old when he captained the *Julia Moulton* and spoke English and Portuguese in addition to his native German. The first mate was James Willis, a native of Amsterdam, who had migrated to the United States in 1847. Willis spoke Dutch, German, and a little French, and he picked up some Portuguese aboard the *Julia Moulton*. The supercargo was a Portuguese named Vilela. Little else is known about him, except that he was in his twenties and spoke some English. The rest of the crew are similarly obscure. They included a second mate named Young, common seamen George Cooke, William Robinson, Thomas McDermot, John McDonald, two unnamed Portuguese, and Henry Fling, who was the nineteen-year-old cook and a native of New London, Connecticut. As a whole, this variegated mix of Europeans and Americans mirrored the wider patterns of illegal slaving crews, particularly those embarking from New York.[12]

Lemos and Castro recruited the *Julia Moulton*'s crew through intermediaries. Indirect hiring was a common practice in the maritime industry in big ports such as New York, where principals hired shipping masters to man their vessels. In the case of the *Julia Moulton*, Lemos and Castro hired the ship chandler and outfitter William Valentine, who was a favored middleman for the Portuguese in New York. Smith was Valentine's first recruit. Having already captained an illegal slave ship, *Republic*, in 1853, Smith was well known to the slave trading community and an obvious target for recruitment. Once Valentine had engaged his captain, the pair worked together to hire the rest of the crew. First they approached Willis outside Valentine's store in Lower Manhattan. He had never been on a slaving voyage before, but he readily accepted the position of first mate. Valentine and Smith then sought out the seamen, including Fling, Cooke, and Robinson. The records do not indicate who recruited Vilela and the Portuguese sailors, but it was probably done directly through their fellow Portuguese, Lemos.[13]

Many, if not all the crew, were hired on the understanding they were going on an illegal slaving voyage. The senior officers and Vilela certainly knew what they were doing; Smith and Willis made no attempt to deny the fact later in court. Yet the purpose of the voyage was probably not explained directly to all the seamen. After the voyage, Fling testified that Smith had given him the impression they were heading to the Caribbean. Cooke stated that Smith had told him and another seaman, Robinson, that they were heading to the Cape of Good Hope. These claims are difficult to verify, although it was common for sailors to argue they had been duped into serving aboard slavers, especially in court. The sailors must at least have questioned the size of the crew. Altogether, Smith and his friends recruited fifteen men for the voyage. As Smith later confessed, it was an "almighty crew" for an ostensibly legal voyage.[14]

The main aim of these men was to make money. Their wages varied: they were somewhat negotiable and were clearly stratified by rank. But even the lower wages vastly exceeded what crews made in previous generations, when the traffic was both legal and much less profitable. Slaving captains were always paid the largest amount. We do not know what Smith received, but captains of slave ships were usually paid about five thousand dollars. Captain J. W. Delano accepted that figure to captain the *Braman*, the vessel visited by Whitman in 1855. Other captains bought shares in voyages, a lucrative option given the potential returns. The much-traveled New York captain Jonathan Dobson invested around three thousand dollars in shares in the voyage of the *Isla de Cuba* in 1858. These large sums reflected the risks that captains were taking. In addition to sailing the vessel, which exposed them to capture at sea and prosecution, as well as to the dangers attending any sailing voyage, many captains further exposed themselves by purchasing the slaver on behalf of the principals. In the case of the *Julia Moulton*, Smith went to Boston, where the brig was based, bought it, sailed it back to New York, and registered it at the customhouse under his own name. In such transactions, the captain took nearly all the risk; the principals were invisible.[15]

After the captain, the first mate was next on the pay scale.

After haggling with Smith, Willis signed up for $40 a month for the outbound voyage and a flat $2,000 for the return voyage to Cuba. This extraordinary differential took account of the risk; being caught with captives was much more incriminating, and therefore more dangerous, than being caught without them. The higher return pay also encouraged Willis to stay the course. Smith made the point when Willis requested the $2,000 upfront. Smith's reply, paraphrased by Willis, was, "It was not customary to do so, as I might change my mind when I got to the Coast of Africa." The same principle applied to the other crew. Smith, having agreed to pay the cook, Henry Fling, $13 a month for the fictional legal voyage to West Indies, gave him $340 in gold pieces on the African coast, just before they set sail for Cuba. He also promised to pay the crews' passages back to the United States after the voyage had been completed.[16]

With the vessel and crew secured, Lemos and Castro outfitted the *Julia Moulton* for its transatlantic voyage. The fittings were strongly shaped by the need to outwit the suppression agents. Unlike legal slaving voyages, midcentury slavers could not afford to carry obvious slaving equipment such as shackles or chains. In most cases, they also dispensed with trading cargos since the suppression measures necessitated short stays on the African coast and quick loading rather than protracted bargaining. Fast turnarounds also meant there was little time to purchase or load provisions for the Middle Passage. As a result, illegal slavers often brought large stores of food and water from their port of departure. A final distinction was the vast quantities of lumber they carried. Since it was too risky to build a slave deck before leaving port, traffickers brought long planks and wooden supports known as scantling so the crew could construct the deck on the outward passage.

Lemos and Castro drew on New York's vast resources to equip the *Julia Moulton* along these lines. They bought seventy-two casks and had them filled with water and placed in the brig's hold. They also sent four barrels of wine and rum, seventy of beans, thirty of flour, eight of pork, two of beef, and ten of rice, as well as fourteen barrels of pails from which captives would eat using wooden spoons. In addition, they supplied the vessel with scantlings and planks for the construction of a slave deck, as well as three medicine chests to be used for sick captives and crew. The brig also shipped at least some firearms, as well as the standard equipment of maps and charts and a chronometer. Finally, the vessel probably carried large boilers to cook the large quantities of food needed for captives and crew. In the words of Assistant District Attorney Philip Joachimsen, who was part of the team that prosecuted Smith after the voyage, the brig "had on board everything necessary to fit her at sea for the transportation of slaves." The vessel would have looked much like the slaver *Isla de Cuba*, which was owned by Cunha Reis and intercepted and sketched by a British naval officer in 1859.[17]

The final step before embarkation was clearing the *Julia Moulton* from port. Smith, who was not only the captain of the vessel but also ostensibly its owner, went to the New York Custom House to clear the vessel himself. He handed over the ship's manifest, which listed only the food and included an oblique reference to woodenware. He also took oaths that he was an American citizen and the true owner of the vessel, thereby earning the vessel the right to fly the U.S. flag and a guarantee of protection against British interference. Smith

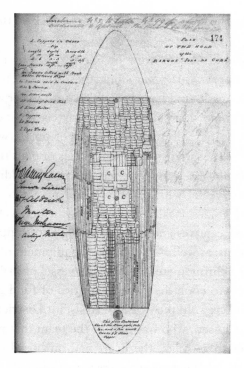

"Plan of the Hold of the Barque
'Isla de Cuba,'" 1859.
(FO84/1100, f. 174, The National
Archives, London)

further claimed he was going on a legal voyage to Cape Town, a less conspicuous choice than the true destination, West Central Africa. All these falsehoods proved satisfactory to the clearance clerk, who approved the *Julia Moulton*'s departure, seemingly without reservation. Wasting little time, the crew piled aboard the brig. The next morning, Lemos and Castro gathered at a Manhattan wharf to watch the *Julia Moulton* sail down the East River toward the open ocean.[18]

THE *JULIA MOULTON*'S CAPTIVES

The *Julia Moulton* spent the next sixty-five days journeying to Africa. Tracking prevailing winds and ocean currents, the brig followed a clockwise arc around the North Atlantic before dipping down to the Cape Verde Islands and the continental mainland. Meanwhile the crew were busy refitting the vessel. Forty days into the voyage, they began laying lumber over the casks in the hold, making a crude slave deck for the "cargo" they would take back to the Americas. Up on the main deck, they fixed gratings over the hatchways, creating a prison for captives below. They also hung an awning between the mainmast and the galley door to shield the deck and its occupants from the equatorial sun. The *Julia Moulton* was ready to receive it captives.[19]

By the time these preparations were complete, the slaver was nearing its destination. The traffic had come under attack in this region by the Portuguese and British in the late 1840s and early 1850s but remained robust due to imperial tensions between the two powers in the lower Congo and the Loango coast, as well as the various African societies' continued attachment to the trade and accommodation of coastal traffickers. By the 1850s, many of these slave traders had developed thriving slaving enclaves at Ambriz and Ambrizette, which lay to the south of the Congo River, at Cabeça de Cobra, near its mouth, and at Cabinda on the Loango coast. Some captives were forced aboard incoming slavers at remote beaches or even in the river itself.[20]

The traffic from these and other minor points in West Central Africa dominated the midcentury slave trade on African shores. Around 156,000 captives boarded slave ships on the coasts of West Central Africa between 1851 and 1866. This figure accounted for almost 70 percent of all captives, up from 46 percent during the entire history of the trade. The other main exportation regions after 1850—the Bight of Benin, and southeast Africa—fell far behind, accounting for 15 and 13 percent, respectively.[21]

Slave traders in the West Central African interior forced these captives to the shore. Most captives embarking from this region between 1831 and 1855 came from locations less than 250 miles inland. Almost all captives came from the south side of the Congo River and the west side of the Kwango River. Captives from northern West Central Africa, where the main slaving ports were located at midcentury, largely belonged to the Kikongo linguistic group, which dominated the immediate interior. Although their ethnicities were diverse, a large majority were Nsundi and were connected to the Kingdom of Kongo, which lay close to the south bank of the river.[22]

Many midcentury captives entered the traffic as a result of conflict within Kikongo-speaking communities, rather than through large-scale warfare between competing states, a source of captives that had been standard earlier in the trade. Kidnappings were common at midcentury, but legal systems in the key provenance zone of the Kingdom of Kongo were also increasingly corrupted in the nineteenth century to accommodate the slave trade. Gradually, lineage heads began selling groups of people who were previously considered ineligible for export, including free men and slaves who had already been assimilated into their lineages. Similar patterns can be seen among West Central Africans purchased by the French in the 1850s. This short-lived scheme, which was ostensibly designed to supply French colonies in the Caribbean with "free" laborers but really functioned much like the slave trade, drew on the same interior sources as the slave trade. Many captives caught up in this traffic were originally sold for what were previously considered minor crimes in their societies, such as theft or sexual misconduct. In many cases, they were expelled by kin without having committed a crime at all.[23]

Another, more violent, picture of enslavement, this time in the Bight of Benin, is offered by two survivors of the slave ship *Clotilda*, which arrived in Alabama in 1860. In separate interviews conducted in the American South during the twentieth century, Oluale Kossola (also known as Cudjo Lewis) and Sally "Redoshi" Smith recalled being captured by Dahomean raiders in their town, Bantè, before being sent to the coast and forced aboard the *Clotilda*. The Dahomean king, Gelele, had sent the raiders to Bantè, using its ruler's failure to pay tribute as a pretext to attack the town. His purpose was to secure captives for ceremonial sacrifice back home, although he was open to selling others. As Kossola recalled, the raid was exceedingly bloody.[24]

Most of these traumatized captives were young and male, and by midcentury around half the captives were children. At the extreme end of the scale were infants born aboard slave ships, as happened aboard the *Grey Eagle* and the *Thomas Watson*. (In the latter case, a woman gave birth to twins, one of whom soon died.) The proportion of males was also rising. By midcentury four-fifths of the captives shipped out of northern West Central Africa were male. Kossola and Redoshi from the Bight of Benin were both fairly young and representative of broader age patterns, although at nineteen, Kossola was older than most midcentury captives. He had already gone through the customary initiation rights of his community that preceded a boy's recognition as a man.[25]

These demographic changes can partly be explained by regional factors. More male slaves were available for sale because the societies supplying increasing proportions of captives were matrilineal. In these communities, retaining female rather than male slaves was an important way of holding and increasing wealth and status. Women were also highly valued because they took a leading role in labor, especially in relation to food production. John Monteiro, a Portuguese traveler who visited Boma, a key slave market on the lower Congo River about fifty miles from the coast, noted the gendered labor distinctions. A male slave, he wrote, "cannot be made by his master to cultivate the ground, which is women's work, and the mistress and her slaves till the ground together." Male slaves, especially adults with fighting experience, were also potentially dangerous and therefore eligible for sale. The rising proportion of children, on the other hand, can perhaps be explained by changing norms governing eligibility for exportation in states such as Kongo. Children, who had low status within the kinship groups, may have been particularly vulnerable to sale.[26]

Slave trade suppression was a second and perhaps more important factor in the changed makeup of the slavers' "cargo." In each exportation region, from Senegambia to southeast Africa, the number of child captives doubled between the early and mid-nineteenth century. In West Central Africa, around half of all captives had been children since the 1830s. Although local and regional African factors probably shaped the exact demographics of captives shipped from each zone, the uniform increase across each of these culturally distinct regions suggests the broader influence of suppression initiatives. One of these influences was an overall decline in slave exports, which may have overloaded internal African slave markets and left children, who were the least productive and least valuable to their societies, at the greatest risk. Suppression efforts also created practical inducements for slave traders to acquire children. Enslaved African children were more easily coerced than adults, an important factor in an era of coastal patrols, when traffickers needed to move captives quickly along the coast and onto ships. Children also did not require shackling, so the ship could dispense with tell-tale slaving equipment and have fewer crew members.[27]

Information on the origins and demographic profiles of the *Julia Moulton* captives is limited, but they appear to have fit these broader patterns. No records identify exactly where they came from, but their coastal embarkation point, Ambrizette, offers a basic guide. Located between Ambriz and the Congo River, Ambrizette was closely tied to the supply zones of northern West Central Africa. It is therefore likely that many of the captives came from the Kingdom of Kongo, the chief source of captives during this period. Many were probably Nsundi. Almost all would have been members of the Kikongo linguistic group and could therefore have communicated with one another to some extent during their ordeal.

The demographics of the captives are more certain. Six hundred and sixty-four captives were taken on board the *Julia Moulton* in April 1854. After the voyage, Henry Fling recalled that among this number were "40 women, the rest were men and boys." Fling did not mention girls, perhaps counting them among the "40 women." If so, females formed only 6 percent of captives who boarded the *Julia Moulton* at Ambrizette. Although, as noted above, females typically formed a minority of captives in the nineteenth century, this proportion was particularly low. One possible explanation is seasonality. In Kikongo-speaking territories, January to April marked the beginning and end of an agricultural cycle. Since the *Julia Moulton* arrived on the coast in April, inland slave traders may have preferred to retain women to gather the harvest rather than sell them abroad.[28]

The proportion of children who ended up aboard the *Julia Moulton* is not revealed in the sources, but the distribution of captives around the brig suggests it was within the common 30 to 50 percent range. According to Smith, he and the crew put the "boys and women" above deck and forced the "men" below.[29] If the majority of captives had been children, the boys would probably have been sent below with the men to free up space on deck. Equally, the limited space in the hold suggests many children on board the vessel. If there had been a small number of children, the slave deck would have struggled to accommodate the remaining five hundred or so adult males.

These largely male and young captives probably journeyed from the interior on foot and by water. Having been sold to external markets, they would have come under the authority of *pombeiros*, itinerant traders who brought goods to the interior and sold slaves to the coast. Using the natural aid of the Congo River, pombeiros brought many of the region's captives to the coast in dugout canoes. Heading downstream, slaves arrived at Boma, where powerful rulers levied fees on slave sales and captives passing through their jurisdiction. After passing through the town, perhaps having been separated from kin, the captives moved toward the mouth of the Congo. Here the path split in several directions. Some captives would have been transported by boat out into the Atlantic and around the coast to embarkation points at Ambrizette, Ambriz, or the Loango coast, while others would have traveled to these places by land or via the lower Congo's dense network of creeks. The *Julia Moulton* captives may have taken one or more of these routes.[30]

When captives neared the coast they were shut into barracoons while they awaited an incoming slaver. Barracoons were deadly prisons. Andrew Wilson, an American sailor who deserted the slave ship *Mary E. Smith* in 1855, spent time among captives at a barracoon near Cape Padron at mouth of the Congo. The enslaved, he observed, were "kept chained in gangs of from eight to twelve" and branded on the chest, arm, back or thighs a few days after they arrived. Wilson also said the superintendent at his barracoon, "went heavily armed, and . . . shot one negro dead for disobedience of his orders." Slave traders described similarly violent episodes in their private correspondence. After the voyage of the *Pierre Soulé* in 1856, the trafficker João Soares wrote to a "cargo" investor, Bento Pacheco dos Santos, informing him that one of his slaves "came off from the shore dead from blows given by [another trafficker,] Luiz, on the eve of embarking, so that on board he was never able to rise." Soares was presumably able to identify the unnamed captive as belonging to Pacheco dos Santos because of the brand the traffickers had seared into his flesh.[31]

Captives fought for survival in this lethal environment, frequently for long periods. The illegality of the trade probably meant increased time in captivity. Kossola described spending weeks incarcerated on the coast in the Bight of Benin. Wilson spent two and a half months at his barracoon near Cape Padron. In 1857, William McBlair, the captain of an American cruiser USS *Dale*, noted that some slaves on the Loango coast had "been detained from shipment for eight months." Unlike in previous eras, when many captives spent time on the ship waiting for it to be filled with more captives, in this era slavers stayed out to sea, dodging cruisers until the coast was clear and captives could be brought aboard all at once. Sudden departures produced further heartache for captives. Kossola's barracoon held many people from his nation, and when slavers forced some of them out to the *Clotilda* he recalled, "We cry, we sad 'cause we doan want to leave the rest of our people in de barracoon. We all lonesome for our home. We doan know whut goin' become of us."[32]

When the coast was clear of cruisers a fast loading process began. The threat of capture encouraged slave traders to embark captives as quickly as possible, often within a few hours. This was much faster than the many months spent at multiple locations in previous eras, particularly in the slave trades run by northern Europeans. The transfer of captives from the shore was typically conducted by local boatmen. Hired by coastal agents, they were knowledgeable about the local surf and could transfer captives quickly. In the case of the *Julia Moulton*, boatmen from Ambrizette delivered the captives to the brig, a mile offshore, by dugout canoe and lighter. When the captives reached the vessel, Smith and Willis hauled them up ladders and aboard. Crews typically stripped captives of all their clothing. Kossola reflected on this painful humiliation years later: "I so shame!"[33]

Captive Africans were not the only people to board illegal slavers on the coast. Jurisdictional disputes and confusion between suppression powers occasionally led to the capture

"Shipping Slaves Through the Surf," *Church Missionary Intelligencer: A Monthly Journal of Missionary Information* 7 (1856): facing p. 241. (*Slavery Images: A Visual Record of the African Slave Trade and Slave Life in the Early African Diaspora*, http://slavery images.org/s/slaveryimages/item/2059)

and release of slave trade crews, as in the case of the New York schooner *Glamorgan*, which was captured near Ambriz by the American cruiser USS *Perry* in 1853. In this instance, the captain of the *Perry*, Lieutenant Richard Page, sent the *Glamorgan*'s American captain to the United States for trial, but uncertain about American jurisdiction over the foreigners among the crew, he had released five Portuguese sailors onshore. The Portuguese subsequently took refuge there, perhaps with Cunha Reis. The stranded sailors eventually found a ride home when the *Julia Moulton* appeared at Ambrizette a few months later. In exchange for the journey back to the Americas, they agreed to serve aboard the brig, thereby bolstering its crew to twenty-one.[34]

With the arrival of the Portuguese sailors, the *Julia Moulton* was ready to depart. The crew set sail for Cuba.

THE MIDDLE PASSAGE

After the captives boarded the illegal slavers, the crew would force them into position around the ship. Many captives spent most of their time below deck. On the slaver *Echo* in 1858 all the captives were confined below the deck, the men imprisoned in one hold and the women and children in another. But on other vessels, captives were located both above and below the deck. Henry Fling later recalled that on the *Julia Moulton*, "the women and boys were put on deck, and the men were passed below." Similarly, on the *Thomas Acorn*, in 1860, the men were confined to the hold, while the women were held above on the poop deck. In 1854, the crew of the *Grey Eagle* put the children in the vessel's long boat, which sat on the deck hatch. Captives could therefore often be found both above and below the deck; the only rule was that men were positioned below most of the time and brought above each day to eat, wash, or take forced exercise, or for punishment.[35]

Slave traders' longstanding concerns about security and space restrictions determined these allotments. The placement of men below deck was a security measure, both before and after abolition. Captain Smith described the rationale: "The boys and women we kept on the upper deck. But all those strong men—those giant Africans that might make us trouble—we put below on the slave deck." Underscoring his concerns, Smith also had the *Julia Moulton*'s crew secure the hatches on the main deck so that "a man could not crawl up through the open places." At the same time, the distribution of captives on any slaver was influenced by the availability of space. Slave ships came in various shapes and sizes, and so did captives, who varied by age and sex. Although men were held below, the precise location of women and children was determined based on these variables. Holds, cabins, and long boats were all possibilities.[36]

These distribution decisions largely mirrored those of the legal slave trade, but illegality did alter the occupation of space *during* the voyage. Many illegal slave traders opted to keep all captives below deck and out of sight while they were near the African coast and in the Caribbean, where cruisers were active. By contrast, when the vessel was in open water, they would bring captives above. In the early twentieth century, Kossola and Sally "Redoshi" Smith recalled that slaves aboard the *Clotilda* were kept below for thirteen days after leaving the Bight of Benin, but thereafter spent much time on deck during the day. At the same time, crews also moved captives down below decks to avoid detection, often at short notice. After his voyage aboard the *Grey Eagle*, the seventeen-year-old sailor Joseph Town recalled that during a chase, the crew took the women and children from the deck "so they might not be seen." According to Smith, his own approach in such a scenario was to "put them all below deck, and nail down our hatches."[37]

Traffickers packed captives into horribly tight spaces aboard illegal slavers, especially beneath the deck. Henry Fling and Captain Smith explained the "spoon" formation aboard the *Julia Moulton*. "In the day time we had them sitting on each other's legs," Fling recalled. According to Smith, at night, "they lie down upon the deck, on their sides, body to body." This pattern was common on midcentury slavers. Edward Manning, who had been a sailor aboard the *Thomas Acorn*, described the same formation: "Commencing forward, we made the first man lie down, head to the windward, facing toward the bow, the knees slightly drawn toward the chin. Another one was placed alongside with his breast touching the back of the first and his knees bent at a similar angle. In this manner we stowed them, in tiers, the length and width of the hold."[38]

On the *Julia Moulton* men were terribly confined beneath the deck. At its largest extent, the vessel measured ninety-two feet, ten inches, in length and twenty-four feet in breadth. The number of captives occupying this space was probably close to four hundred, resulting in five square feet of horizontal space for each man under the deck. The height, or headroom, in the hold is more difficult to estimate. The *Julia Moulton*'s hold measured ten feet from top to bottom. Casks holding provisions lay at its base, with the slave deck positioned somewhere above. The traffickers would have wanted adequate room to gain access to the provisions, so the slave deck was probably located close to the main deck. The observations of a British officer who seized the *Abbot Devereux* off Ouidah in 1857 depicted a similar layout. In this case, the slave deck was three feet, six inches, in height, "just room enough, to clear the top of [the slaves'] heads when they are in a sitting position."[39]

Did captives face more cramped conditions aboard illegal slavers compared to those on legal ones? Captives aboard Liverpudlian slave ships at the turn of the nineteenth cen-

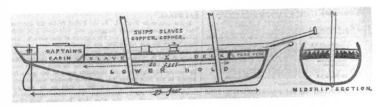

"Section of the Slaver 'Abbot Devereux,'"
Illustrated London News, September 19, 1857, 284.
(Image courtesy of University of Missouri Libraries)

tury occupied an average floorspace of between five and nine square feet. Moreover, the Liverpudlian vessels offered head room of between four feet, seven inches, and five feet, four inches, which exceeded the space observed by the captor of the *Abbot Devereux*. One possible mitigating factor may have been the higher number of children aboard illegal slavers and thus the smaller sizes of captives. Yet, as we have seen, not all traffickers put children under the deck. In addition, the absence of shackles on illegal slavers, especially after 1850, suggests extreme packing. In the legal British slave trade, men were afforded more space than women because they were shackled. When Smith was asked by an interviewer after his voyage whether they had chained or handcuffed the men, he replied: "No, never; they would die." The implication was that the absence of shackles in illegal slave ships allowed tighter packing beneath the deck. While the disruption to the slave trade caused by naval suppression meant that some vessels escaped with fewer captives than slave traders had sought, easing the crowding somewhat, when they succeeded in filling the ship, as in the case of the *Julia Moulton*, the space was appallingly tight. The grim reality was that the most common relief from these extreme conditions came from the death of fellow captives, whom crews removed from the hold and tossed overboard.[40]

The extremely cramped conditions were ultimately driven by the slave traders' greed, but ironically, abolition and suppression offered some encouragement for the practice. "Tight packing" had been a focal point of the British abolitionist campaign, captured in the famous depiction of the hold of the slave ship *Brookes*, in which captives were laid out in rows like sardines. Parliament had responded with Dolben's Act (1788), which required slave ships to increase the ratio of tons to captives, thereby modestly enlarging the space available to each slave. However, as slave trading nations, including Britain, abolished the trade, they surrendered control over these issues. Now, instead of observing laws such as the Dolben's Act, illegal slave traders packed as many captives onto a slaver as they could. Furthermore, as abolitionism and suppression gradually took hold in many parts of the Atlantic world, the prices for captives fell in Africa. Slave traders always responded to low prices by cramming more captives onto their vessels. In midcentury, traffickers carried more captives than ever. The average midcentury slaver contained 604 captives, almost double the average for the trade during its entire lifespan (309). In some ways, therefore, suppression gave impetus to the traffic and made conditions for captives even more extreme.[41]

These conditions often led to sickness and death. In many ways, the harrowing sketch of the branded Africans on the *Vesuvius* in the previous chapter speaks for itself, although many observers offered other, equally gruesome written accounts. In June 1860, an American reporter describing another intercepted slaver, *Wildfire*, noted that of the 510 Africans still alive, "about a hundred . . . showed decided evidences of suffering from inanition, exhaustion, and disease." "Dysentery" he added, "was the principal disease." Another described the arrival of two intercepted slavers in Monrovia, Liberia, noting, "Most of [the Africans] are nothing but skeletons, and so weak that at present they are unable to stand." On the *Thomas Watson* captives died during the first night at sea. According to Edward Manning, when the crew discovered the dead the following morning, they were "hoisted to the deck and consigned to the deep. There was no pretence of any religious ceremony. Just as they were, naked and forlorn, they were tossed overboard, and for a long time we could see the bodies floating in the wake of the ship."42

The *Julia Moulton*'s captives endured similar hardships. After the voyage, Smith acknowledged in a disturbingly off-hand manner: "I lost a good many the last cruise—more than ever before." In fact, 150 of the original 664 captives—23 percent—died during the Middle Passage. Smith did not describe the symptoms of the dead, but these probably included gastrointestinal diseases, which were among the most common ailments. He did locate the disease center: under the deck, among the men. When his crew came across sick captives, above or below, they laid them on the deck, presumably for better air, more space, and possibly some form of treatment. Supercargoes were typically charged with taking care of the sick. On the *Julia Moulton*, however, Vilela had also fallen ill, and he died about a week after leaving the coast. Another Portuguese, José Cayetano, who had joined the vessel in Africa, took his place. An experienced slave trader, Cayetano had been the supercargo of the *Glamorgan*, and according to Willis, now became "Doctor" to the *Julia Moulton* captives. Caetano's strategies to heal the sick are not mentioned in the sources, but with a death rate of three per day, they were clearly inadequate.[43]

Death was more present aboard the *Julia Moulton* than on most voyages after 1850. The brig's 23 percent mortality rate exceeded the average 17 percent rate along the West Central Africa–Cuba route after 1850. In fact, mortality rates were higher after 1850 than previously (they had been 12 percent between 1810 and 1850). The rising mortality rate is puzzling for a few reasons. First, the duration of the voyage, which historians have correlated with mortality, was becoming shorter. The average voyage along the West Central Africa–Cuba route decreased from sixty-six days to forty-seven days during the years mentioned above (the *Julia Moulton* made the crossing in forty-five days). In addition, historians have not found that mortality rates increased with more cramped conditions, although these became worse as the nineteenth century wore on. And finally, the proportion of deaths among children, who may have been more susceptible to diseases found aboard illegal slavers, was certainly high after 1850, but it had been high since the 1830s.[44]

It is likely that the rising mortality rate was related to growing suppression activity on the African coast. The epidemiological conditions for the captives before they boarded slavers were the main determinant of shipboard mortality rates. The disease environment may have worsened during midcentury as suppression tightened because the traffickers moved to more remote parts of the coast and erected barracoons to imprison the captives before setting sail. The conditions in the barracoons were probably worse than those in the slave pens of Luanda and Benguela of earlier generations.

In some cases, barracoons were far from food and water. The American sailor Andrew Wilson remarked that "the nearest water was three miles off" from his barracoon, and "it was no small labor to bring the water necessary for drink." The British naval officer Charles Wise suggested that "insufficient diet" contributed to "fatal diseases" such as dysentery in barracoons. And the captives spent a long time in these barracoons. William McBlair, who had noted that captives were enduring eight months on the coast, also remarked that they had "subsisted upon only one plantain a day each for that time." In 1860, the captain of an American cruiser, USS *Saratoga*, made a direct connection between time spent at barracoons and mortality rates. He had recently intercepted the slaver *Nightingale* near the Congo River and had witnessed the subsequent deaths of 150 Africans under his own jurisdiction. In his view, the captives' "long confinement in the barracoons, was of itself sufficient to account for the many deaths."[45]

A final distinctive feature of midcentury voyages was provisioning. During the legal slave trade of the early nineteenth century, and later, when the illegal traffic was only weakly policed, slavers typically brought some food from their outfitting port, but picked up most of their provisions on the African coast. For some African societies, provisioning slavers was an important offshoot of the traffic itself. But the presence of cruisers made provisioning on the African coast more difficult, especially as patrolling became more focused in the 1840s. Captain Smith deeply appreciated the perils of provisioning on the African coast. On a previous voyage, he had been captured by a British cruiser after nearing the coast in search of water and only escaped by running the ship into shore. He later made off with the help of allies on the coast.[46]

Such close shaves encouraged traffickers to shift their provisioning away from Africa to the main outfitting ports in the Americas and Europe. The *Julia Moulton* was one of many vessels to load with rice, beans, and pork in New York. In another case in 1855, the West Central African trafficker Guilherme Correa wrote to João José Vianna in New York instructing him to "fit [the next vessel] out complete, except beef." Slavers sometimes stopped in Europe for provisions. In 1858, the *Haidee* sailed from New York to Alicante, Spain, picked up rice and beans, and journeyed on to the Loango coast in 1858. Some vessels continued to take in food and water on the coast, especially fish and water from the Congo River, but by midcentury, provisioning had largely shifted away from Africa.[47]

The slave traders' changing provisioning strategies had several implications for their captives. Unlike earlier periods of the traffic, captives were exposed to a largely new diet during the Middle Passage. Illegal slavers carried mainly carbohydrates and proteins—usually rice and beans—to Africa. Rice, in particular, was not widely grown in West Central Africa, the main provenance of captives. The biscuit and beef aboard the *Julia Moulton* would likewise have been foreign to them (Correa ultimately used local fish instead of beef in 1855). These new foods presumably contributed to the gastrointestinal problems that were common on illegal slavers. More significant factors were captives' vulnerability to the slave traders' greed and the inaccuracy of their calculations. Traffickers regularly squeezed more captives aboard than they had provisions for. Lack of water was a particularly serious problem, especially since stopping for fresh supplies was out of the question. Kossola remembered not having much to eat, but he recalled his thirst even more vividly. He complained that the crew of the *Clotilda* gave him "a little bit of water twice a day," and that the water was sour, possibly due to the addition of vinegar, which was believed to prevent scurvy. Some traffickers made the connection between the lack of water and the death of the captives. The sailor John McCarthy of the *Huntress*, which sailed from West Central Africa to Cuba in 1863 and had 250 captives perish on board, recalled that the "voyage was full of hardships and suffering, and there was a great scarcity of water."[48]

As they had been for centuries, slave ships were very violent places. In addition to the emotional trauma of separation from home and kin seen in Kossola's earlier remarks, captives endured the brutality of their captors. Edward Manning catalogued a series of violent incidents on the *Thomas Watson*. Early in the voyage, most of the traumatized and nauseous captives did not want to eat. According to Manning, one of the crew "seized a rope's end and raised their appetites by showering blows on their bare shoulders." He also noted the crew patrolled the ship with knives and swords and beat the hatchway on the deck at night, threatening the slaves below. One of the captives who refused to stay clear of the hatch was brought on deck, laid "full length, face downward, and tied to the ring-bolts" and lashed by one of the crew until he tired. Then another took over. The captive was beaten almost to death before the captain ordered him released. The captors also attacked women. One woman attempted to throw herself overboard in an apparent suicide, but was caught by a member of the crew, who beat her and tied her up. According to Manning, the captain frequently entered the poop deck, where the women were located, "whip in hand . . . and fiercely cut out right and left." Manning did not specifically mention sexual violence on this voyage, but its frequency aboard slavers throughout the history of the trade, the placement of the women on the deck, and the frequency of the captain's visits, suggest it occurred on the *Thomas Watson* as well.[49]

Africans responded to the conditions of midcentury passages much as they had done in previous eras. Some resisted by attempting suicide, including the woman who tried to end her suffering on the *Thomas Watson*. Others fought their captors. In 1853, an unnamed slaver arrived in Cuba after a voyage from southeast Africa. According to the *New-York Daily Times* a large number of the captives had been maimed during a violent, but ultimately failed, uprising. In an even more striking case in 1859, a slaver reached Cuba after having lost almost its entire complement of over a thousand captives from insurrection and disease. Yet large-scale rebellions were rare. There are only three known cases of insurrection after 1850; less than 1 percent of the total number of voyages. This percentage is far below the 10 percent average for the entire history of the trade. One factor to account for the decrease may have been the concentration of captives coming from West Central Africa, a region whose captives had always had a disproportionately low number of shipboard rebellions. Other issues may have been the faster voyages and large number of children. Whatever the cause, the historically low ratio of crew to captives during this period was rarely a major problem for slave traders.[50]

Instead of attempting to overcome their enslavers physically, most captives tried to forge bonds with shipmates. In the case of the *Clotilda*, one of the few mid-nineteenth-century slavers to arrive at U.S. shores, the captives formed a connection based on shared experience, and they even appear to have welcomed a Dahomean, whose nation had enslaved them, into their shipboard community; they mourned their separation in the Americas. In West Central Africa, the concentration of Kikongo speakers aboard illegal slavers would have enabled captives to form bonds during the Middle Passage. Some of these speakers might have been part of the group of Africans who were seen by observers singing and dancing in Saint Helena after their liberation from a slave ship. By shoehorning the slave trade into relatively tight supply zones, suppression measures might therefore have indirectly provided at least some relief for captives.[51]

THE END OF THE JOURNEY

Captives who survived the horrific Middle Passage might land in any of an unusual array of possible destinations. Slave trading routes had narrowed substantially compared to previous eras due to suppression measures. When Brazil closed the traffic to its shores in 1850, Cuba became the only major importer of enslaved Africans. About twenty slavers did make port in Brazil in the early 1850s, and two vessels brought captives to the United States in 1859 and 1860, but these numbers were dwarfed by the Cuban figures. Between 1851 and 1866, around three hundred slavers arrived on the island's shores, bringing about 164,000 captives. It was partly for this reason that many observers dubbed the slave trade the "Cuban" slave trade after 1850.[52]

Despite limiting the smuggling routes, the suppression measures in some ways diversified the range of destinations for Africans. Naval patrols intercepted around two thousand

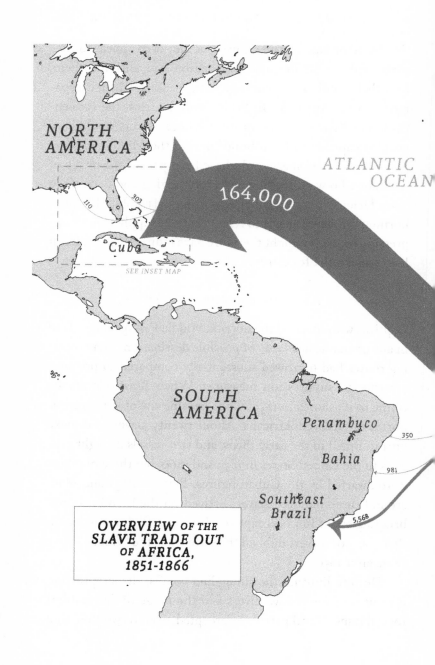

NORTH
AMERICA

ATLANTIC
OCEAN

164,000

110   303

Cuba

SEE INSET MAP

SOUTH
AMERICA

Penambuco

350

Bahia

981

Southeast
Brazil

5,568

**OVERVIEW OF THE
SLAVE TRADE OUT
OF AFRICA,
1851-1866**

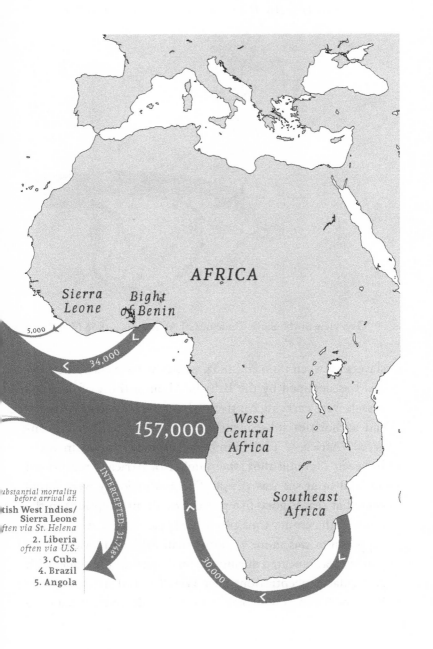

AFRICA

Sierra
Leone

Bight
of Benin

West
Central
Africa

Southeast
Africa

5,000

34,000

157,000

30,000

INTERCEPTED: 31,748*

*substantial mortality
before arrival at:

tish West Indies/
Sierra Leone
ften via St. Helena

2. Liberia
often via U.S.

3. Cuba

4. Brazil

5. Angola

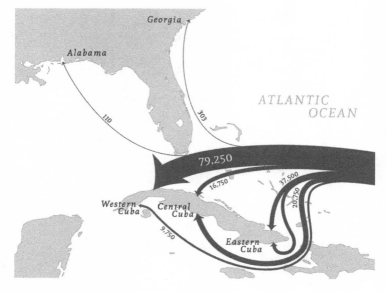

Overview of the Slave Trade out of Africa, 1851–1866 (detail)

slavers between 1800 and 1863, when the last vessel, the *Haydee*, was detained by the British. About a third of detained vessels were carrying captives, whom the British and American authorities subsequently called "liberated" or "recaptured" Africans. They numbered around 181,000 in total. Between 1851 and 1863, the number of Africans recaptured on land or at sea was 31,748. The vast majority were intercepted at sea. Eighty-five percent of all interceptions in the nineteenth century took place in African waters, where naval suppression was more vigorous than in the Americas. This pattern was repeated during the final phase of the trade, with particular concentrations near West Central Africa and the Bight of Benin. The remaining captives detained at sea were on ships intercepted in the Americas, especially in the Gulf of Mexico.[53]

The final destination for these Africans depended on the nation that intercepted them. Britain recaptured 16,608 captives after 1850, about half of those who were intercepted overall. In most cases, British cruisers escorted the slavers and their Africans (if any) to the nearest British Vice-Admiralty Court (VAC). Such courts were widely dispersed across the Atlantic and Indian Oceans. In the majority of these cases, whether slaves had been found aboard or not, the VAC judge condemned the ship. If Africans were involved, he typically placed them under the jurisdiction of the Colonial Office.[54]

The subsequent fate of Africans "liberated" by British patrols was strongly influenced by the growing demands of West Indian planters. Until the late 1830s, Britain had sent most Africans to its West African colony, Sierra Leone, to serve as unpaid apprentices for fixed terms. This pattern shifted after the expiration of post-slavery apprenticeships in the Caribbean in 1838. Complaining bitterly of labor shortages, Caribbean planters urged the Colonial Office to send them recaptured Africans to replace the apprentices. The Colonial Office acquiesced, and by the mid-1840s the transshipment of Africans to the West Indies became routine. By the 1850s, two-thirds of Africans from intercepted ships were passing through the VAC at Saint Helena on their way to the British Caribbean, mainly British Guiana, Trinidad, and Jamaica. Upon their arrival they would begin their indentures, sometimes lasting up to six years, after which they became legally unbound and eligible for paid work.[55]

Captives on ships intercepted by American cruisers had a

Africans from intercepted slave ships at Saint Helena.
(S0010841, Royal Geographical Society)

different experience. In total, the U.S. Navy recaptured 6,452
Africans after 1850. In a new policy devised during midcentury,
the government sent these Africans to Liberia in West Africa,
often after a temporary stay on U.S. soil. This policy emerged
from the maelstrom of racial politics in the United States and
the historical connection between the country and Liberia.
As the status of free blacks roiled American politics in the
early nineteenth century, an emigration movement headed
by the American Colonization Society encouraged free African Americans to resettle in the newly founded Republic of
Liberia. Although deeply unpopular among black Americans
and largely unsuccessful, the colonization movement offered

Congress an opening for dealing with Africans from intercepted ships in the 1850s and early 1860s. As the permanent settlement of Africans on American soil was considered out of the question (at least by most whites), the Liberian option proved a convenient solution to the "problem" of these Africans. Sensing the opportunity, Congress authorized and paid the American Colonization Society to oversee the transport and settlement of the Africans in Liberia. Upon their arrival, they became apprentices, mainly to African American emigrants, for seven to fourteen years.[56]

The Spanish were the final major contributor to the interception figures. Although the Spanish navy failed to interdict any ships with captives in Cuban waters after 1850, the colonial authorities did recapture five thousand newly arrived Africans on land. Under the terms of treaties made with the British government in 1817 and 1835, these captives were declared *emancipados* (emancipated slaves) and hired out, often to planters. Some well-connected slave traders also secured emancipados, including Cunha Reis, who moved to the island in 1858. He was surely behind an 1861 missive sent from the Spanish government to the Cuban governor directing him to supply Cunha Reis "with enough emancipated negroes of those who are in deposit." The letter went on to explain that "they are necessary for the advancement of [Cunha Reis's] cotton plantation [Lusitania]." According to the treaties, emancipados were expected to serve as apprentices for five to seven years and then become free, but during their indentures most planters employed them like slaves, forcing them to work in the cane fields and treating them in the same fashion. The Cuban authorities often permitted planters to continue the apprenticeships well after five years, and many Africans endured decades of apprenticeship and never became free, working effectively as slaves for the rest of their lives, or until large-scale Cuban emancipation, which began in the 1870s. In fact, the situation was in some respects worse for emancipados; as already "liberated" persons they were denied the traditional right of Cuban slaves to *coartación*—the purchase of their own freedom.[57]

The *Julia Moulton* captives were among the comparatively small number intercepted en route to Cuban sugar estates. After a relatively speedy Atlantic crossing, the brig approached Trinidad de Cuba in mid-June 1854. Following detailed instructions that were probably given to him by Correa in New York, Captain Smith sailed to a specific latitude and longitude between Cayo Blanco and Cayo Zarzo, just east of Trinidad. As the vessel slowed, the crew made a signal to the shore using a white-and-red flag. Receiving this cue, Cuban traffickers immediately came off the coast in three launches. After some discussion, they ferried the captives ashore. When everyone had reached land, the Cubans forced the Africans to walk a few miles to a farm. Those who were too sick to walk were carried by other captives. Meanwhile, back on the water, one of the Cubans ran the *Julia Moulton* into shore and burned it. Filthy, worth little, and offering plain evidence of a shocking crime, the brig followed the fate of most midcentury slavers after its work was done.[58]

Up to this point, the voyage had gone to plan, but now things began to unravel. The winds of suppression had temporarily shifted in the Spanish Empire. As we have seen, in 1853, the Spanish government in Madrid was particularly concerned about the growing threat of Cuban annexation by the United States. To stave off the Americans, Spain needed British support, and the price for that was tougher action against the slave trade. The metropolitan government dispatched the aggressive Pezuela to Cuba as the new captain general, and he got to work immediately. In early 1854 he removed several corrupt officials throughout the island, and in May he gave Cuban authorities permission to enter estates to search for bozales, newly imported slaves, a right they had been denied since 1845.[59]

The *Julia Moulton* captives were intercepted in the midst of this crackdown. In June 1854, Pezuela sent a trusted deputy, Brigadier Juan Rodriguez de la Torre, to lead an assault on the slave trade in Trinidad and Sancti Spíritus in southern Cuba. Within a few weeks, the lieutenant governors of both jurisdictions, Juan Martín and Santiago Gurrea, had been suspended from office, and the regions' leading traffickers, Salvador de Castro, Sr., Pedro Choperano, and Mariano Borrell, had been arrested and imprisoned in Havana. More than 800 bozales had been intercepted in Trinidad and Sancti Spíritus by September. According to John Backhouse, the British commissioner at the Court of Mixed Commission in Havana, 490 of this number had "landed from Julia [Moulton] at a place called San Carlos at a sugar estate not far from Trinidad." This estate, in Trinidad's valley of *ingenios* (sugar mills), was the second-biggest sugar-producing plantation in the jurisdiction and lay a dozen miles from the coast.[60]

After the Cuban authorities intercepted the *Julia Moulton*'s Africans at San Carlos, they transferred them to the *deposito de emancipados* in Havana. In July 1854, the Cuban government made an announcement in the official paper, *Gaceta*, inviting a list of "persons favored" to come to the deposito. The listed parties, who included men and women, Cuban officials, and the government itself, had applied for a specific number of apprentices well before the landings in Trinidad and Sancti Spíritus had occurred. Now they had their chance to select their labor. In a process that closely resembled a slave auction, the Africans were paraded and the buyers decided whom to take on. Prices were set by age and sex, and buyers made their choices carefully. One man, who had signed up for five emancipados, selected two boys for a combined price of eighty-four dollars, a twenty-two-year-old woman for forty-eight dollars, and a seventeen-year-old girl for thirty-eight dollars, but discarded his fifth option because he did not like the price.[61]

The distribution and subsequent fate of the *Julia Moulton* Africans is unclear, but apprenticeship offered little to emancipados. The money paid by the buyers was meant to be given to Africans for their first four months of labor, but in many cases emancipados never received it—or any other payment. Similarly, although the apprenticeships were to last five years, with emancipados retaining the right to seek reassignment each year, these terms were often broken by buyers, breaches that were ignored by the Cuban government. And while the *Gaceta* announcement reminded consignees that they should "fulfill the duties which religion, morality, and the existing regulations impose upon them," this meant little in practice. By the fall of 1854, the threat of American annexation had subsided, and the Spanish government recalled Pezuela. A new governor, José de la Concha, took his place. He was more closely connected to Cuban slave traders and gave little regard to emancipados. Soon, the "Cuban" slave trade picked up again.[62]

As Pezuela's crackdown fizzled out, Captain Smith went on trial in New York. Many of the *Julia Moulton*'s crew had returned unhindered to the United States after the voyage, but trouble was brewing. First mate James Willis was angry that Smith had not paid him his full wages and threatened to go to New York district attorney John McKeon with evidence of Smith's crimes if Smith did not give him the $440 he was owed. McKeon, Willis surmised, might offer him immunity in return for turning state's evidence against a slave ship captain. When Smith still refused to pay, Willis followed through on his threat. McKeon was receptive, and Willis began talking. Smith was arrested and indicted under the Act of 1820, the law that rendered slave trading a capital offence.

Smith's subsequent trial was a dramatic affair, featuring a packed courtroom, stunning testimony from Willis and other turncoat crewmembers, Smith's eventual conviction, and a threatened filing for a mistrial, finally resulting in Smith's guilty plea on a lesser charge under the Act of 1800. In the end, Smith was sentenced to two years in jail and a thousand-dollar fine. Justice had hardly been served. Smith had escaped the death penalty, and the rest of the crew and the principals were never indicted. The *New-York Daily Times*, which had reported on the trial extensively, acknowledged the strange circumstances of the case: "We believe this is the first time in which a conviction of being engaged in the African Slave-trade has ever been had in this City—and this is due entirely to a disagreement between the captain and his mate about the payment of a trifling sum of money."[63]

Those who had followed the case would have learned something about the essential features of the still flourishing slave trade in the 1850s. New York was a crucial node in a thriving triangular slaving route and home to traffickers who sent large, fast vessels with multinational crews to West Central Africa and Cuba, where their holds would be packed tight with enslaved men, women, and, increasingly, children. That Willis's anger at being shortchanged had led to a criminal trial underlined another aspect of the illicit trade: the rampant greed of the participants. For traffickers, profit had always been king, and although the *Julia Moulton* voyage ended in failure, in most midcentury voyages they made it at record levels.

The saga of the *Julia Moulton* also showed the way the trade became indelibly marked by efforts to stop it. Suppression measures determined the routes the voyages followed and to a large degree the experiences of captives and crews. Yet what suppression efforts did not do, at least by the time the brig arrived on Cuban shores, was end the trade. That failure vexed abolitionists across the Atlantic world. Chief among them were leading officials in the British government.

CHAPTER FOUR

Ring of Spies

I N March 1860, the British prime minister, Lord Palmerston, wrote to his foreign secretary, John Russell, suggesting a plan for suppressing the illegal slave trade to Cuba. The island was the only major remaining market for enslaved Africans, and the previous year around twenty-six thousand captives had disembarked on its shores, the highest annual figure in over four decades. Noting that traffickers were paying handsome bribes to Cuban officials to ignore or even abet these arrivals, Palmerston mused whether "it would be but fair to fight the slave traders with their own weapons." What he meant was that the Foreign Office should hire local spies to report on the traffic. Palmerston envisaged these informants reporting on all kinds of industry secrets, including the complicity of officials, but what he really valued was intelligence on the movements of slave ships. This information, he believed, could be crucial in helping Britain's navy interdict slavers at sea. It might even help bring the trade to an end.

Paying spies, he wrote, was a way "to kill [the] trade with 'silver lances.'"[1]

Palmerston's suggestion was hardly far-fetched. Suppression powers were well aware that slave trading zones, especially ports, were marketplaces for information. Britain had hired slave trade spies since the 1830s in Brazil. When other nations became serious about suppression they did likewise. After shutting its trade in 1850, the Brazilian government hired a former British informant, Joaquim Alcoforado, a steamship captain who plied the waters around Rio de Janeiro. A few years later, in Cuba, Pezuela was taking soundings from unofficial sources. The United States actually enshrined spying into federal legislation. The slave trade Act of 1819 invited "any citizen, or other person" to report illegal disembarkations on American soil and promised fifty dollars in return for every intercepted captive. Federal outlays for intelligence tailed off in the United States as slave arrivals declined, but they increased in 1862, when the government finally clamped down on slave ship outfitting in American ports. By that point, the British, the spymasters par excellence, had constructed an extraordinary network of spies that ringed the Atlantic world from Africa to the Americas, creating a dozen hidden fronts in the battle over the slave trade.[2]

In the late 1850s and early 1860s in New York, the British hired Emilio Sanchez, a Cuban-born immigrant with an ax to grind. He would turn out to be the most important informant in slave trade history. As Sanchez and the British navigated their sometimes fractious relationship, a broader question emerged: What difference were spies making? Britain was fighting a global suppression war in foreign ports, but it was doing so precisely because suppression had not yet become globalized. Palmerston was serious about ending the slave trade, but the question remained: Would it be possible to stop the traffic without support from the U.S. government?

THE RISE OF SPYING IN BRITAIN'S CAMPAIGN AGAINST THE SLAVE TRADE

Britain's use of spies was rooted in frustration with its ineffective suppression efforts. By the 1830s, London was pursuing a wide-ranging campaign, spearheaded by a large deployment of naval vessels off the African coast and in Brazilian waters, and supported by a network of anti-slave trade treaties with states on both sides of the Atlantic Ocean. In terms of direct costs, British governments devoted between 0.2 and 1.3 percent of total annual spending to slave trade suppression from 1815 to 1865. Nevertheless, the traffic continued on a very large scale, especially in the South Atlantic, though also in West Africa and the Caribbean. Since Britain was wary of openly violating the sovereignty of some of the nations in these regions, most notably Portuguese Angola, Brazil, and Cuba, the government chose to pursue a subtler approach.[3]

The new plan was fostered in the Foreign Office during the 1830s. Palmerston, who was foreign secretary (1830–34, 1835–41, 1846–51) and later prime minister (1855–58, 1859–65), dominated British slave trade policy for a generation. An anti-slavery zealot, he authorized the attack on Lagos in 1851 that deposed King Kosoko, and he was determined to act forcefully against the trade, despite the geopolitical complications. His views were largely supported by the Foreign Office's two senior staff, the permanent and parliamentary undersecretaries. The parliamentary undersecretary—John Wodehouse for much the 1850s—was largely responsible for slave trade matters, although the instinctively Palmerstonian Edmund Hammond was always part of slave trade deliberations in his capacity as permanent undersecretary (1854–73). Another important figure was William Henry Wylde, the senior clerk of the Slave Trade Department, a branch of the Foreign Office that had been established in the 1820s to administer legal and diplomatic aspects of British suppression measures. The department worked closely with British consuls in regions where the trade was active. Wylde was typically the strongest advocate of the spy system during high-level discussions at the Foreign Office.[4]

These officials needed to operate free of outside scrutiny. Confidentiality was essential, not only to prevent the international disputes that could stem from covert operations that were later exposed but also because Parliament and the press were already casting a more critical eye on British suppression policies in the 1840s. The naval campaign in particular was under fire for being costly and seemingly ineffective. It was ironic, then, that Parliament unwittingly sponsored the Foreign Office's new tactics through its annual provision of the Secret Service Fund (SSF). Established by Parliament in the 1820s, the fund was intended to allow the Foreign Office to carry out secret operations free of parliamentary oversight and public knowledge. The annual allowance ranged from twenty-five thousand pounds to more than fifty thousand and was administered by the Foreign Office's permanent undersecretary. Undersecretary Hammond destroyed many SSF documents during his tenure, but the surviving records show that the Foreign Office supported a wide cast of informants and agents across the globe, although some were hired for

Edward Archibald
(84.XM.479.34, J. Paul Getty Museum)

clearly political purposes. In 1858, for example, the office recruited a spy through Edward Archibald, the British consul in
New York. The Foreign Office charged the agent, who is unnamed in the sources, with infiltrating local "Irish clubs." His
job was to report on what the Foreign Office called the "dis-
affected Irish" who were joining the Fenian Brotherhood, a
newly founded Irish independence organization in New York.
Although it is unclear how this infiltrator performed, it was
the SSF that had given the Foreign Office the resources and
confidentiality it needed to make the hire.[5]

The adoption of new suppression methods was also aided by the growth of British official representation across the Atlantic Basin. As the Fenian Brotherhood case in New York indicated, the Foreign Office required help from its overseas representatives to handle its distant agents. These officials, including ministers and the more junior consuls and unpaid vice consuls, answered directly to the Foreign Office. Charged mainly with facilitating trade and migration, their ranks had swollen over the course of the nineteenth century as British commerce penetrated global markets. By midcentury, British representatives were distributed across the Atlantic world and in all the major slaving zones. There were ministers or consuls in each of the key departure ports: Rio, New York, Havana, and Cádiz. Other British officials were located in several key slaving ports in the Bight of Benin and at Luanda, although not in northern West Central Africa, where the traffic was based. Britain also had seven consuls or vice consuls in Cuban ports.[6]

By the midcentury, these officials were more tightly connected to the Foreign Office than ever. Widening and thickening patterns of global trade and migration ensured that as goods and people moved across the Atlantic Basin in increasing scale, ships would need to carry dispatches to and from the Foreign Office with greater frequency. In 1852, for example, a new monthly mail service opened between Liverpool and Fernando Po (today's Bioko), an island in the Bight of Biafra, in response to Britain's growing palm oil trade with West Africa. The Foreign Office used this steamer to correspond with its African consuls. Revolutions in transportation and communication technologies also helped. Steamships were replacing sail, doubling the speed of transatlantic crossings.

These innovations drew disparate consulates closer to London. Meanwhile, within Britain, Foreign Office mails traveled on the nation's rail network, the most developed in the world. By the 1860s, the Slave Trade Department was even receiving and transmitting messages almost instantaneously via telegram. In short, the Foreign Office could draw on a vast and increasingly connected network of antislavery agents to help execute its new strategies.[7]

During the 1830s, the Foreign Office began drawing on its far-flung diplomats and the Secret Service Fund to encourage prominent Brazilians to take anti–slave trade positions. One early recipient of secret British funds was the Brazilian foreign minister, Caetano Mario Lopez Gama, who was in charge of slave trade treaty negotiations with Britain in the 1830s. Another was Leopoldo de Câmara, the port captain of Rio de Janeiro, who was in the pay of British government in 1849. Under Palmerston's instructions, the Foreign Office also funded anti–slave trade newspapers in Brazil, including the Brazilian anti–slave trade society's paper *O Philantropo*, and the Rio daily *Correio Mercantil*. As Palmerston explained to James Hudson, the British minister in Rio, these payments were designed to secure "the promotion of anti Slave Trade and anti Slavery principles in Brazil." Like Consul Archibald in New York, Hudson made the payments to the papers and ensured that they printed what they promised.[8]

The British government supplemented its attack on the Brazilian trade by hiring slave trade spies. The Foreign Office paid informants in Rio and Pernambuco in the 1830s, but the first spy to produce big results was Joaquim Alcoforado in Rio in the 1840s. As captain of a coasting steamer, Alcoforado claimed to know when slavers were due to leave port and when they would return from Africa. He was well aware that Britain would value this information, having previously reported occasionally to the British navy patrolling the Brazilian coast in return for small payments. After several years out of the business, he signed on with the Foreign Office on a more formal basis in 1849. This time, Hudson played the middleman, passing Alcoforado's intelligence to the navy. In return, the Foreign Office promised him fixed rates for captures based on his information: £5. 10s. per ton of the slaver if it was not carrying captives or £5 per ton plus £1. 10s. per captive if it was. These rates amounted to 10 percent of the total bounties the British government paid its seamen for captured slavers.[9]

Although his notes to Hudson have not survived, Alcoforado was clearly an impressive informant. Commander Grey Skipwith regularly received his intelligence while patrolling the Brazilian coast. In 1850, Skipwith reported to the Admiralty, "[Alcoforado] knows almost to a day when a full vessel is expected on the coast of Brazils [*sic*] and where she will land her cargo, also when and where from, any vessel fitted for slave trading will leave for the Coast of Africa." In total, the Foreign Office attributed 18 British captures to his information and paid him a total of £2,659 (about $13,000) in bounties. Palmerston would later recount to Foreign Minister Russell that Alcoforado had "brought the Slave Trade [to Brazil] to an end." Since more than 140 slavers successfully left Rio de Janeiro between 1849 and 1851, this was not actually true, but by raising the slave traders' risk and leaving a light diplomatic footprint, Alcoforado had shown that spying could be an effective and sensitive tool of suppression.[10]

Buoyed by Alcoforado's success, the Foreign Office considered applying the spy strategy to the highly robust slave trade to Cuba. One of the biggest problems Britain faced in this traffic was the slave traders' use of the American flag. Intercepting slavers off the Brazilian coast had been a relatively straightforward business because most of the vessels sailed under Brazilian or Portuguese colors, which Britain openly policed after the Palmerston and Aberdeen Acts. By contrast, the majority of voyages to Cuba took place in vessels under the American flag, which Britain was not permitted to detain. To Wylde at the Slave Trade Department, spies offered a way around the problem. Recognizing that the real owners of the slavers were typically not U.S. citizens but Cubans or Portuguese, he argued that American law did not entitle them to the U.S. flag. In his view, these vessels were pirates and as such were subject to seizure by any nation. Thus, he wrote to his colleagues, "If we can ascertain on good authority that a vessel although sailing under American colours and furnished with American papers has been actually sold to the Cuban [or other non-U.S.] Slave Traders, our own cruisers can deal with her." Predicting objections from the American government to such seizures, Wylde also suggested the West Africa Squadron pass the spies' intelligence to the U.S. Navy, which could intercept the slavers itself. In these ways, he believed, "the money paid for the information would be well spent." In fact, he estimated, "A few thousand pounds spent [on spies] would not amount to a third of the annual cost of one cruiser, and would be more effective than half a dozen."[11]

The success of Wylde's ambitious plan depended on the ability of the Foreign Office to hire good informants such as Alcoforado. Although the job was never advertised, Britain's well-known stance against the slave trade seems to have been sufficient to attract applicants. One of the prospective hires was James Groth, an Englishman by birth who had moved to New York and was the former owner of a secondhand furniture store in Manhattan. In 1858, he presented himself to Archibald alleging that several slavers were about to set sail from New York and that he was in a prime position to expose them. To bolster his case, Groth claimed to have supplied a slaver with a medicine chest a few years previously. Archibald was not impressed. Surmising that Groth's "intelligence" was "founded in a great measure on very insufficient information, if not on mere suspicion," he advised the Foreign Office against the hire. The British-born Charles Edwards, who was legal counsel to the British consulate in New York, suggested that Groth's hire would present another problem: Groth was currently unemployed and lived "in the neighborhood of the lowest class of Catholic Irish." Edwards's comment implies that British officials screened candidates, at least in part, on the basis of their ethnicity, religion, and social status. His assessment of Groth would probably have been endorsed in London, where underlying assumptions about the unreliability of the poor ran deep. According to an 1850 Treasury Committee report, the Foreign Office specifically excluded lower classes from clerkships because of their perceived propensity to share state secrets.[12]

The issue of trust was made even more thorny by the fact that many prospective informants were closely tied to the slave trade. Alcoforado was one of these. Both before and during his tenure as a spy, Brazilian traffickers hired him to transport newly arrived captives along the coast near Rio. José Barreto, a Portuguese informant to Consul Benjamin Campbell in Ouidah, also worked for local traffickers. Francisco Rovirosa, a Spaniard living in Cuba, was one of the island's principal slave traders when he offered intelligence to Consul Joseph Crawford in Havana in the 1860s. The continued involvement of many spies in the slave trade, even as they worked for the British, created uneasiness, and even disgust, among British officials. Antislavery ideology was partly behind these feelings, but their continued slaving also called into question these spies' basic allegiances. This may have been why Hudson noted to Wylde in 1859, "Informers, as we all know, are an abominable race." Yet the Foreign Office also recognized that these individuals were effective precisely because they were immersed in the trade. Even Hudson, who never trusted spies, believed that the slave trade could not be crushed "save thro efficient informers." In many cases, the Foreign Office simply held its nose and took the intelligence.[13]

After the Foreign Office screened candidates, it made financial offers to successful applicants. Britain offered formal contracts that linked pay to performance. Sanchez (New York), Alcoforado (Rio), and Rovirosa (Havana) all secured these contracts. They amounted to 10 percent of the total net bounty the Treasury would pay to West Africa Squadron captors on an intercepted slaver, although the capture would have to be completed on the spy's information. To make up for the uncertainty—a cruiser might not be able to capture the vessel in question—the Foreign Office also offered an annual retaining fee of £400. This sum would serve as a minimum salary. These contracts were renewed annually; the Foreign Office could terminate them if the trade subsided, although it did retain Alcoforado and a second Rio spy named Brito on a combined annual salary of £600–£700 throughout the 1850s, in case the Brazilian trade made a resurgence after the mid-century slump. Aside from these formal contracts, the Foreign Office offered large sums for good information about particular voyages. Before Palmerston instructed Crawford to offer the 10 percent rate to Rovirosa, Crawford gave him $799 for specific information about a recent voyage. The Foreign Office also gave smaller cash payments to informants in locations where the trade was less intense. In Santander, Spain, the British vice consul Lieutenant Leopold March paid informants out of an annual £100 spy budget.[14]

As the Foreign Office extended these offers, its spy network gradually expanded to include every slaving region in the Atlantic Basin. In the main disembarkation zone, Cuba, Britain had at least three spies after 1850. They included Rovirosa in Havana, Laureano Thomes, a schoolteacher in Bahía Honda, and an unnamed informant in Pinar del Río, in the far west of the island. Britain also had spies in the trade's shipping hub, New York. In the early 1850s, when the first Portuguese slave traders started arriving in Manhattan, Consul Anthony Barclay wasted no time in hiring a spy to tail them. In 1859, his successor, Archibald, hired Sanchez, the most prolific of all the British spies. Coverage was also impressive in Africa. In West Central Africa, the Portuguese believed that George Jackson, a British commissioner on the Luanda Court of Mixed Commission in the late 1840s and 1850s, had a network of local spies. Another British commissioner in Luanda, Edmund Gabriel, also took soundings from informants. Meanwhile, in the Bight of Benin, the embarkation zone for 13 percent of captives after 1850, Consul Campbell occasionally received intelligence from Barreto and another Portuguese, Carvalho, a decade later. In Iberia, the Foreign Office paid spies in the Basque country and Cádiz when their ports became major outfitting centers in the late 1850s and early 1860s. In Brazil,

Alcoforado and Brito remained on standby. Spying had become a major tool of British suppression.[15]

EMILIO SANCHEZ, MASTER SPY

Britain's most effective spy, Emilio Sanchez, was born in Havana in 1821. His family had deep Cuban roots. In the sixteenth century, his forebear Mateo Sanchez immigrated to Havana from Yucatán, where he had been governor. By the late seventeenth century, the core of the family had relocated three hundred miles east of Havana to the small regional city of Puerto Príncipe. Although it had been one of the first places settled by Europeans and Africans, this part of Cuba remained relatively underpopulated and isolated in the eighteenth century compared to the Havana region. The Sanchezes were nevertheless one of its more prominent families. Two of Emilio's ancestors were mayors of Puerto Príncipe. His grandfather Pedro Sanchez y Boza was postmaster. His father, Bernabé, was a second lieutenant in the Royal Guards and was decorated for his service in the Peninsular War in Spain (1808–14). In 1813, Bernabé was considered worthy of marrying Joaquina Dolz, the well-heeled daughter of an elite Havana family.[16]

As Joaquina and Bernabé welcomed Emilio into the world, sugar production was transforming Cuba's economy and society. Up to the mid-eighteenth century, the island's economy depended on tobacco cultivation, ranching, and subsistence farming. Its population was predominantly of European descent, although it also consisted of large minorities of African and Afro-Cuban slaves and free people of color. These patterns began to change in the late eighteenth century as Cuban

planters, merchants, and the colonial administration capitalized on the island's abundance of fertile land and the collapse
of sugar production in Saint-Domingue by slowly turning the
island over to slave-grown sugar. To support these endeavors,
slave ships brought thousands of African captives to the cane
fields each year. The influx continued unabated after Spain's
formal abolition of the trade in 1820, and it was largely owing
to this traffic that Cuba became the world's leading sugar
producer later that decade. By then, sugar production was already deeply entrenched in much of western Cuba, and by
midcentury it had encroached on the eastern portion of the
island. Puerto Príncipe and its neighbor, Nuevitas, were the
jurisdictions touched least by the sugar boom, but they were
still affected in important ways. Many new ingenios (sugar
mills) appeared in both jurisdictions and previously small
slave populations grew substantially. Meanwhile, railroad
building and maritime commerce expanded, helping connect
the region's sugar, molasses, and rum to markets at home and
abroad.[17]

Although the sugar boom never fully took hold in their
home region, the Sanchezes grasped the opportunities it
offered. In the 1840s, the eldest of Emilio's three brothers,
Pedro, became a major stockholder in a railroad line that connected the towns of Puerto Príncipe and Nuevitas, the jurisdiction's main port. He was also one of the region's major
landholders and enslavers, owning two hundred slaves by
1869. Many of these enslaved people labored on his sugar
estate, Desengaños, in Nuevitas. Pedro was also a merchant
who focused on foreign markets. Reflecting the growing trading links between Cuba and the United States, his brig, the
Pedro Sanchez Dolz, carried staples, lumber, and manufactured

goods between Nuevitas and New York. A second brother, José, also capitalized on the growing Cuba-America trade. In 1843, he briefly secured the U.S. consular post at Nuevitas and oversaw American commerce on behalf of the State Department. A third brother, Adolfo, was also strongly tied to the United States. He too was a merchant. He lived in Philadelphia in the 1840s and became a U.S. citizen in New York in 1854. By the late nineteenth century, he had been appointed U.S. deputy consul in Havana.[18]

Emilio Sanchez equaled his brothers in mobility, enterprise, and business acumen. He immigrated to the United States as a boy, and in 1843, at the age of twenty-two, he was naturalized as an American citizen in New Orleans. He began his career as an overseas merchant there in the 1840s before moving to New York in 1850. Operating from an office in the shipping district of Lower Manhattan, he was a shipbroker and a commission merchant focusing on the Hispanic markets of Cuba, Mexico, and Spain. The latter task entailed linking distant buyers and sellers and earning a small percentage on their transactions. These labors yielded a moderate income. By 1859, Sanchez was earning three thousand dollars a year, more than most New Yorkers, but far less than Manhattan's big Cuba traders like Moses Taylor who owned and operated their own vessels. Sanchez's home reflected his income and status. He lived with his Massachusetts-born wife, Susan, and their two young daughters in a brick house in New York's twentieth ward, three miles north of the tip of Manhattan on the West Side near the Hudson River. Their neighbors were lawyers, grocers, shoemakers, and physicians. Like Emilio, many were immigrants trying to make their way in the largest, busiest, and most ethnically diverse city in the United States.[19]

When Sanchez approached Archibald in the early spring of 1859, he brought many qualities that marked him as a useful spy. He first made contact through an intermediary whom Archibald described only as an "estimable English gentleman." Sanchez probably used an intermediary in part to hide his identity from local slave traders—something he guarded fiercely throughout his tenure as a spy—but his choice of go-between may have carried some weight with Archibald. That Sanchez held a steady and respectable job was also in his favor, given the prejudices of the Foreign Office. His best assets, however, were his knowledge of New York's merchant community and his ties with Cuba. He displayed them during his initial meetings with Archibald. In March 1859, the consul reported glowingly to the Foreign Office: "Through his connections and correspondents in Cuba as well as from his acquaintance with parties engaged in the trade with Spain and Cuba, [Sanchez] possesses peculiar facilities for obtaining information [about] the slave trade."[20]

Sanchez and his fellow spies were constantly preoccupied with security. Speaking on his behalf to the Foreign Office, Archibald explained that Sanchez would incur "no little hazard should his proceedings be discovered" by slave traders. It was a common concern for spies. In 1854, Barreto, the informant in the Bight of Benin, reported to Consul Campbell that he was being "looked upon at Whydah [Ouidah] as a spy." Sensing that his life was now in "peril" he fled the town. Consul Dunlop in Cádiz was more explicit about the perceived threats. In 1865, he complained that spies were unwilling to come forward because they were "all afraid of being stabbed." In some regions, the connections between the slave traders and government officials were such that it was hard to tell who was the greater threat to British informants. In Bahía Honda, the schoolteacher, Laureano Thomes, had the misfortune of having his spy letters intercepted by the colonial government. According to Consul Crawford, he was then thrown in prison for seven months "upon a false charge of some offense against the government." When he emerged from jail, he "begg[ed]" Crawford to get him to Mexico, "where he said he had some relatives, as his prospects had been ruined." Crawford paid his ticket to Veracruz and gave him twenty dollars to help him on his way.[21]

Archibald and Sanchez devised many strategies to keep his work confidential. One ploy was for Sanchez to write to Archibald anonymously and mainly in cipher. This strategy meant that his notes could be understood only by staff at the New York consulate. To prevent any obvious association with the British, Sanchez would send these missives through trusted intermediaries. For his part, Archibald committed to not mentioning Sanchez's name in his correspondence with the Foreign Office. He did so only once, when he recommended Sanchez for hire. He also promised Sanchez that his intelligence would never be used in evidence against slave traders. As an added precaution, he kept Sanchez's correspondence at his home, rather than at his office in the consulate.[22]

In his extensive correspondence with Archibald, Sanchez never explained why he took on such a risky job, but three reasons are particularly compelling. The most immediate motive was revenge for the tumultuous 1857 *Haidee* affair, in which Sanchez had been approached by Juan Ceballos, the wealthy and respected New York sugar importer, with a proposal to purchase the *Haidee* from the Portuguese merchant Inocêncio Abranches and then accept a request from another

Portuguese, Antonio Botelho, to charter it. Sanchez understood that Botelho would take the *Haidee* to Spain and sell its cargo, along with vessel. Sanchez, who was in line to receive a commission on the cargo and a profit from the sale of his ship, had agreed to the proposal, but when Botelho reached Spain he refitted the *Haidee* and proceeded on a slaving voyage, heading first to the Loango coast and then to Cuba. A few months later, news of the voyage reached District Attorney John McKeon in New York, and Sanchez was indicted by a grand jury for violating the anti–slave trade Act of 1820. No American had ever been executed on this charge, but a conviction technically carried the death penalty. Fortunately for Sanchez, the jury acquitted him, although it was no thanks to Botelho, who was long gone from New York, or to Ceballos, who refused to help Sanchez during the trial. Ceballos even told the beleaguered Sanchez he had "rejoiced" at the good fortune of the *Haidee* investors. Sanchez made his own views clear to Archibald, branding Botelho and his friends "scoundrels" for attaching "disgrace" to his name and causing him "great distress of mind."[23]

Although Sanchez presented himself as an innocent, duped merchant, this portrayal is questionable. Sanchez may well have known what he was getting himself into when he chartered the vessel to Botelho. Several Portuguese merchants, including the notorious Cunha Reis, had recently been charged with slave trade offenses in New York, and although the charges were always dropped, or the defendant was found not guilty, the association between the traffic and New York's small Portuguese merchant community was clear. Sanchez, an active merchant in Lower Manhattan, would probably have made the connection. He certainly would not have been the first U.S. citizen in New York to knowingly dabble in the trade. The shipbroker J. B. Gagner and the Cuban-born Mora brothers, merchants, also chartered their vessels to slave traders, and probably received large fees for their services. At the same time, New York was an extremely large port by midcentury and Sanchez could not have known everyone, especially recent arrivals such as Botelho, and Ceballos, a respected merchant, had vouched for him. Furthermore, there was nothing intrinsically peculiar about the transaction. Trading vessels internationally was commonplace in the Atlantic Basin, and as a shipbroker, Sanchez did it on a regular basis. Certainly, Archibald seemed to accept Sanchez's innocence. After grilling him about the incident, he reported to the Foreign Office, "[Sanchez] has impressed me very favourably as to his character." [24]

Whether Sanchez had knowingly participated in the slave trade or not, many prospective agents shared his desire to get even for entanglements arising from it. In June 1859, a Rhode Island slave ship captain named Edward Townsend approached Archibald with a startling offer. His plan was to take command of a slaver in New York, sail it to the African coast, and give it up to a British cruiser. Townsend's apparent change of heart was linked to the voyage of the slaver *Echo*, which he had captained the previous year. Near the end of this voyage, the U.S. Navy had intercepted the vessel and put Townsend on trial in Key West. Although he was acquitted of all charges, he was angry at the voyage investors. According to Archibald, Townsend's new plan was driven not by "shame but from a sense of injury done by the principals who had abandoned him during [his] trial." Another slave trader, Rovirosa, was also out for revenge. In 1864, John Crawford, the acting British consul in Havana, explained to the Foreign Office that Rovirosa was "actuated by motives of private vengeance," and that "philanthropy is all out of the question." Although the Foreign Office rejected Townsend's plan on the grounds that it was unworkable, it did accept Rovirosa as a spy.[25]

Sanchez's second motive was plainly financial. Although most, if not all, informants expected to be paid, Sanchez's pecuniary requirements were especially pressing. The *Haidee* affair had jeopardized his financial standing. He had purchased the ship for twenty thousand dollars in 1857, and his scheme to make a profit by selling it in Spain had fallen apart when the slave traders had forgone the sale. They had even sunk the *Haidee* near Montauk, New York, after the voyage, leaving Sanchez with no chance of reclaiming it. For a while, Sanchez hoped he would be informally indemnified by the *Haidee* investors, who had enjoyed impressive returns from the voyage. Julián Zulueta and José Plá, the main investors in Cuba, did make promises to that effect, but in the end they gave him nothing. As he explained to Archibald, the whole ordeal had left him "circumscribed in his pecuniary affairs."[26]

Spying for the Foreign Office promised to improve Sanchez's position markedly. After Archibald's warm recommendation in the spring of 1859, the foreign secretary, Lord Malmesbury, presented Sanchez with a contract based on the Alcoforado scale. In return for his information, the Foreign Office offered him a guaranteed minimum annual income of £400 (about $2,000, significantly increasing his existing income of $3,000). This figure could rise substantially if his information led to voyages being broken up. The Foreign Office, which envisaged passing some of Sanchez's information to U.S. authorities, offered him £50 for every voyage disrupted in U.S. ports or captured by the U.S. Navy. For vessels intercepted by the British West Africa Squadron, he stood to make much more. The Foreign Office even drew up a typical scenario to show Sanchez how much he could make. For a British-captured slaver of two hundred tons carrying five hundred slaves, he would net £280 ($1,400). This sum represented almost half his regular annual salary. Given the dozens of vessels leaving U.S. ports in 1859, the job promised to pay extremely well.[27]

Sanchez probably had a third, political, reason for becoming a spy. His Cuban roots were the key. Although the island's sugar boom had benefited many Creole families, including the Sanchezes, some feared that the large number of Africans arriving through the slave trade increased the probability of a bloody, Haitian-style slave rebellion. At the least, the new arrivals threatened the "white" character of the island. These Creoles blamed the slave traders (many of whom hailed from Spain) for the influx of Africans, but they also criticized the Spanish government for turning a blind eye to the traffic. Exacerbating the Creoles' frustrations, Spain had instituted more direct control over the island in the 1830s, hoping to shore up what remained of its American empire after the shattering revolutionary era. In doing so, it had eroded the traditional autonomy that Creoles had enjoyed over Cuban affairs.

The most prominent critic of the Spanish government was José Antonio Saco. An elite Creole from Bayamo in eastern Cuba, he was a prolific writer and had been expelled from the island for undermining Spanish rule in 1834. In his writings, Saco depicted Spain as a corrupt overlord that encouraged the slave trade in order to force Creoles into submission. In his view, Madrid calculated that Creoles would cling to

Spain because they feared a race war against a rising population of Africans and Afro-Cubans. Saco could appreciate the logic underlying this calculation. He believed that a slave rebellion was a real threat, and he opposed the abolition of slavery ostensibly because it could unleash such a conflict. To Saco, the best way out of the bind was to push Spain to suppress the slave traffic. Once the trade had been abolished, the slave population would gradually "whiten" over time, and Creoles would secure greater autonomy within the Spanish Empire. In Saco's mind, therefore, opposition to the slave trade, support for slavery, and a commitment to Creole rights all went hand in hand.[28]

Although the Sanchezes never openly identified with Saco's position, their associational and occupational history suggest they broadly shared his views. Emilio's father, Bernabé, is an important figure in this regard. Although not much is known about him with certainty, in the 1820s he appears to have lived in Philadelphia and led an active group of Creole reformers who originated in Puerto Príncipe and other eastern jurisdictions. Among them was a young José Antonio Saco. Bernabé's views were apparently inherited by his son Pedro. Although a large slaveowner, he was fervently opposed to the slave trade. In 1856 he became the unpaid British vice consul at Nuevitas and reported on local slaving to Consul Crawford in Havana. Given Britain's open and persistent criticism of the Spanish government's role in the traffic, Pedro's acceptance of this post was a very public statement against the slave trade and the government's role in it. The Spanish government certainly did not consider him the most loyal of subjects. During the Cuban War for Independence (1868–78),

Spanish officials suspected him of siding with Creole patriots and briefly threw him into prison.[29]

A strong strain of Creole-reformist sentiment clearly ran through other British spies in Cuba. In 1869, John Crawford, now the consul general in Havana, made the point to the Foreign Office. Although the final slaving voyage had probably arrived on the island in 1867, rumors of slave landings were still circulating. The conscientious Crawford wrote to the Foreign Office to say he had sent out his "Creole friends" to learn if the rumors were true. The informants, he added, "are all opposed to the slave trade both for political reasons as well as from personal motives."[30]

Sanchez's motives appear, therefore, to have been many and largely distinct from those of the British government. Although the Foreign Office and Sanchez shared a commitment to suppressing the slave trade, they came to this position from different angles. Britain's agenda was rooted in ideology, markets, and world status. The spy program was a natural extension of Britain's existing campaign, given the robust nature of the post-1850 trade and tools that were now at hand. Sanchez, by contrast, had immediate, firsthand concerns. He had debts to pay, both to his creditors and to his foes. He did not appear to have ethical problems with the trade. Yet like the British government, he also thought in broad terms, specifically about Creole liberty in his native Cuba. His motives were therefore personal and distinctively Creole, while his employer's were distinctively British and governmental. But their differences did not prevent an alliance. The critical point was that both parties opposed slave traders and were willing to work diligently against them.

Sanchez began his new career with zeal. Seven months into his contract, Archibald summarized his early labors to Lord Lyons, the senior British diplomat in Washington. According to Archibald, Sanchez was sending a steady stream of intelligence. "I have, since March last," he wrote, "been in almost daily communication with my special informant." Many of these missives were in cipher, and Archibald's clerks had been busy decoding them. The consulate had already sent thirty dispatches to London containing Sanchez's "voluminous" reports. Archibald had also sent slivers of his information to U.S. officials in New York, but they apparently did nothing with them. In fact, their sensitivity to "foreign interposition," Archibald noted, made his interventions "worse than useless," and he had given up. The Americans' inaction was particularly frustrating to Archibald because as far as he could tell, Sanchez's information was remarkably full and accurate. As he explained to Lyons, Sanchez's notes included "the names and descriptions with, in most cases, detailed information of the movements of no fewer than fifty vessels." All but a half dozen, he judged, were "beyond question engaged in the African Slave Trade."[31]

Sanchez had gathered this intelligence with little guidance from Archibald or the Foreign Office. Throughout his tenure as a spy the British government never attempted to prescribe methods for information gathering. Other informants in Cuba, Spain, and Africa were similarly left to their own devices. The Foreign Office may have adopted this approach because no one there felt equipped to offer advice. Each spy and local context differed from the others, and the informants, after all, were supposed to be the experts. The Foreign Office may also have wished to be in a position to distance itself from spies and their labor, or simply deemed it impossible to control them. In any case, Britain's approach was one of noninterference, and consequently spies had considerable autonomy.

Sanchez used his independence to devise three main methods of intelligence gathering. The first was spying on slave traders. Sanchez lived cheek by jowl with the slave traders in Lower Manhattan, which enabled him to watch his neighbors closely. Beginning with the *Haidee* offenders, he put the traffickers, in Archibald's words, "under surveillance." Taking advantage of both his role as a merchant and Manhattan's busy streets and wharves, Sanchez followed the traders, keeping careful notes of their whereabouts. His job would become harder when they laid low, which usually occurred immediately after a voyage, when the U.S. authorities tended to be more alert. In 1859, Sanchez noted that a slave trader named Almeida, probably Francisco Almeida, had returned to New York from Havana after a recent voyage and been "concealed here for some time." On other occasions, however, he saw that same Almeida "boldly about" the streets and docks. Sometimes he monitored the offices of slave trading firms. In the spring of 1859, he held a stakeout outside Almeida's wine importing firm, Abranches, Almeida and Company. As he wrote to Archibald, he spotted the supercargo of the *Glamorgan* and the *Haidee*, José Cayetano, coming out "on 1st April about 3 pm."[32]

Although surveillance helped Sanchez identify traffickers and their associates, he had to employ a second tactic to determine how they were operating: recruit his own network of informants. The New York side of this network included dockworkers who helped prepare slavers for sea. Sanchez located

Memorandum of Sla

Name	Rig	Tons	Flag	Port of clearance	Destination
"Rosita" alias "Esperanza"	Barque	980	Mexican	New York Jan 9. 1857	Mazatlan
"Antelope" ×	Barque	244	U. States	New York Jany. 30th 59	San Juan de los Remedios
"Facony"	Barque	296	U. States	New York 11th Feby. 1859	Cadiz

Consul Archibald's "Memorandum of
Slavers Reported," October 1859.
(FO84/1086, f. 253, The National Archives, London)

vers reported by one Mitchell, at ....., with
.... the affairs here before.

Remarks

Formerly the "Indian Summer" purchased by John M.
Ceballos of New York who procured one Zavala (a Mexican)
to personate the Ownership. She was cleared ostensibly for
Mazatlan, discharged at Buenos Ayres and proceeded to
Mozambique. has made two voyages, the first voyage the
Spanish Authorities seized the Negroes. the Captain man-
aged to save the vessel and proceeded to Yucatan, where
the Mexican Authorities seized and detained her for three
months. proceeding to Marseilles she sailed thence for
Mozambique and arrives at Sagua laGrande in July
after a sixty days passage, and landed only some 90
Negroes out of 1200 to 1400 taken on board, caused by the
Small Pox; vessel proceeded to Yucatan and Captain
Bernadas left in the "Asia" for Liverpool on 31st August
to fit out again from Marseilles. Vessel and Cargo the
property of J Zulueta & C, and one Baro. original cost
of Vessel $17000. Purchased by A M Ros of New York for
one Valencia of Island of Cuba; sold by J McKie Ship
Broker, and chartered by H. S. Vining to A. M. Ros for
for Ian Euan de los Remedios. detained by United
States Marshall. arrives out. slips out of Port during
the night. mutilates the name off on her stern to "Ante-
captured by a British Cruizer after a long chase.

No 3   Reported sold by J de Calzada of
Havana and her projected voyage stated; from conscientious scruples on owners part sale and delivery
not carried out. vessel returned to New-York from
Palermo and has since been chartered to Rio Janeiro
via Richmond. correspondence of her being sold &c in
possession of H.B.M. Consul.

these individuals through commercial contacts, including a shipping master named Javier. When he located a potential spy, Sanchez would engage him in what he called "casual conversation." It was a deceiving description. Sanchez was hard at work in these exchanges, subtly plumbing witnesses for information on the slave trade. Many let details slip. Two leaky vessels were the sailmaker Jesse Braddick and a shipping master named Keefe. In April 1859 both men revealed that Almeida had held a stake in the voyage of the slaver *Putnam* the previous year. Another unwitting informant was Pierre L. Pierce, a ship chandler who, in addition to supplying vessels with stores, had a lucrative sideline taking ownership of slavers on behalf of Cunha Reis. In 1861, Pierce told Sanchez about the *Manuel Ortiz*, which had recently left New York under the British flag. According to Pierce, the vessel was actually a slaver and had only used British colors to "hoodwink" the U.S. marshal.[33]

Sanchez also drew information from New York investors and slave ship crews. Jonathan Dobson, who captained at least two slavers in the late 1850s, was one of his best sources. In April 1859, Sanchez reported: "Capt Dobson told me that the [slave ship] *Tyrant* was . . . Cunha Reis's" despite being owned, ostensibly, by Matthew Lind. In August of that year, a seasoned slave ship mate named John Macomber told Sanchez that the recently departed *Brookline* was a slaver. Macomber knew this, he said, because he had been offered the position of first mate but refused it. Sometimes Sanchez boldly played slave traders against one another. In December 1859, he approached José Lima Vianna, one of the principal slaving merchants and voyage investors in New York and told him that Dobson was about to denounce him to the local authorities for his involvement in the voyage of the *Isla de Cuba*. Vianna counterattacked: Dobson "was crazy" for he had also "invested in the affair."[34]

Sanchez was not prepared to limit his work to New York. Drawing on familial and commercial ties, he expanded his information network to Cuba. His brother Pedro was an important source on the island. The British vice consul for Nuevitas and the neighboring jurisdiction of Gibara since 1856, Pedro had already been active in reporting the local trade to Consul Joseph Crawford in Havana. In 1859, when Emilio became a spy, Pedro also sent intelligence to him in New York. His main reason for helping his brother was probably a sense of fraternal duty, although he may also have been hoping for a cut of the bounties and perhaps to "whiten" Cuba. In any case, unlike Emilio's unwitting informants in New York, Pedro clearly knew what he was doing. In the spring of 1859 Archibald remarked that Pedro had recently sent letters to his brother identifying "parties engaged in the traffic in slaves, and furnishing instructive details of some of their transactions." Much of this information probably related to the relatively small-traffic slave trade near Nuevitas, but it is possible that Pedro exposed aspects of the wider trade in Cuba. Emilio's reports were certainly replete with information regarding slave landings from all over the island.[35]

Sanchez's other Cuban informant, José de Calzada, was the source of at least some of that intelligence. He was based in Havana, at the heart of the island's traffic. Like Pedro, he was a merchant operating in the U.S.-Cuba market and sent his intelligence knowingly. His motives for helping Emilio are hard to assess. Unlike Pedro, he had no familial obligation to help Sanchez or attack the traffic; he probably knew Emilio through their legal trade. Financial reward was more likely to be the motivator behind his assistance. In 1859, Sanchez told Archibald that he had recently used "money and influence" to get information from Havana. He also stated, however, that Calzada sometimes volunteered intelligence. Whatever his motives may have been, Calzada did not share Sanchez's apparent concern about "Africanization": in 1861, he petitioned Madrid for the right to carry "free" African migrants from Fernando Po, Corisco, and Anabon to Cuba. Different views on these matters may been behind Sanchez's skepticism about Calzada's reports. In one note to Archibald, he said he had "faith" in Calzada's latest missive, but conceded "time alone will disclose the facts."[36]

Calzada was nevertheless well placed to help. His office was at 120 Obrapía Street, in the middle of the city's merchant district, close to the docks. Several important traffickers, including Julián Zulueta's father-in-law, Salvador Samá, were located nearby. Like Sanchez, Calzada was effective at engaging slave traders on the waterfront. In the summer of 1859, he spoke to a slaving captain named Ruiz, who was in command of the *Triton*. Ruiz told him, in Archibald's words, that he planned to sail to a U.S. port, "purchase necessaries, and sail direct for the African Coast." Calzada was also effective at identifying the owners of slavers plying the U.S.-Cuba route. In one instance, he wrote to Sanchez explaining that the *Tacony*, which had set sail from New York, was partly owned by same Havana-based merchants who had invested in the voyage of the *Haidee*.[37]

Sanchez's third strategy, researching shipping information printed in newspapers, registers, and gazettes, also had both local and international components. Much of these data originated in the New York Custom House, where U.S. law required shipowners to clear their vessels before heading to sea. Typically, slave traders complied, sending the false owners to clear the vessel on their behalf. Fortunately for Sanchez, the Custom House passed this clearance information to major daily newspapers such as the *New York Herald* and the *Journal of Commerce* via the Associated Press. Sanchez bought both these papers, checking for suspicious "owners" and destinations in their columns. When he found one, he would typically make a cutting and send it to Archibald, along with comments on the true nature of the voyage. He also scoured the pages of *The American Lloyd's Register*, *Boston Ship Lists*, *The New Orleans Ship List*, and the *Shipping and Mercantile Gazette* (London) for descriptions of vessels and included possible slavers in his missives to Archibald. These details would help the West Africa Squadron identify the vessels off the African coast.[38]

Sanchez cast his net wider by subscribing to a variety of domestic and foreign newspapers, including the *Baltimore American*, *Charleston Courier*, *Havana Weekly Report*, and *Diario de la Marina* (also in Havana). Like the New York papers, these sources contained clearance lists, which enabled Sanchez to identify when suspected vessels left distant ports. In July 1859, Sanchez used the *Diario de la Marina* to report the departure of the slaver *Eloisa* from Havana, enclosing a cutting from the paper as evidence. Foreign papers also helped Sanchez work around the slave traders' ploy of clearing vessels for false destinations. If a suspicious vessel cleared from New York for an unlikely port, he could check a local paper's "Arrivals" section to see whether it reached it. Sanchez was thus able to note in May 1859 that the barque *Antelope* had "cleared for St Juan de los Remedios," but there were "no report in the Cuban papers about her arrival."[39]

Despite Sanchez's adoption of these wide-ranging tactics, his access to the inner world of the slave trade was always limited, even in New York. He rarely got as close to the traffickers as Barreto, Alcoforado, or Rovirosa, his counterparts in other slaving regions, did. Although he talked with some leading investors, such as Vianna, he apparently had no direct contact with Almeida or Botelho, the principals in the *Haidee* affair. Indeed, that episode no doubt made it harder for him to strike up "casual conversation" with the most promising sources. Another problem was security. When he did talk with insiders, he was always wary of exposing himself. During one conversation with an unnamed informant, he learned that Cunha Reis was involved in the voyage of the *Panchita*. Rather than press on, however, he dropped the topic, deciding he "could procure no further particulars without subjecting one's self to suspicion." The New York Custom House could also be fruitless as a source. Clerks often failed to send full clearance information to the Associated Press, leaving the shipping lists without details on a vessel's owner, captain, or destination. When Sanchez attempted to access the originals at the Custom House, the staff would refuse to open the books. In other instances, slave trading vessels bypassed the Custom House completely and sailed straight out to sea. These moonlight departures left Sanchez scrambling.[40]

Sanchez's disclosures were nevertheless impressive. He gave information on 171 of the 223 voyages that took place around the Atlantic Basin between 1859 and 1862. In other words, he reported 77 percent of the voyages made during his tenure as a spy. As these figures suggest, his intelligence was strong not just in New York, or even the United States, but also in Cuba. On occasion, he learned snippets about the trade from Europe, where he also had ties through trade and family. His information from these regions was often superior to that offered by local British spies. In terms of slave trade shipping, Sanchez's knowledge was unmatched.[41]

THE INTELLIGENCE NETWORK
AND THE SLAVERS

With little help from American officials in New York, the British government had to send Sanchez's intelligence coursing around the Atlantic Basin before it could be put to use. The main flow followed a vast arc running from New York to London and from London to British cruisers off the African coast. Slave traders, however, were running international networks of their own. Like Sanchez's notes, the majority of their vessels began their journeys in the Americas and traveled to African waters. As a result, the slave trade and suppression networks broadly mirrored each other, as slavers sought to further the trade and suppressionists sought to end it. These networks can be traced through the voyage and interception of the slave ship *Pamphylia* in 1859.[42]

Like many midcentury slavers, the *Pamphylia* entered the traffic through the sugar route linking New York and Havana. Built in Brewer, Maine, in 1851, the vessel was a barque, and was for many years owned by a Boston merchant named Sewell, who had no apparent connection with the slave trade. In 1858, the *Pamphylia* was purchased by Mora Brothers and Navarro, a Cuban sugar-importing firm with offices in New York and Havana. Initially, Mora Brothers operated the vessel

CAPTURE OF A LARGE SLAVE-SHIP BY H.M.S. "PLUTO."—SEE NEXT PAGE

The *Pamphylia* was a barque, similar to the *Orion* (left),
here being captured by a British cruiser,
from *Illustrated London News*, April 28, 1860, 409.
(Image courtesy of University of Missouri Libraries)

in the sugar trade with Cuba. In June 1859 the *Pamphylia* sailed
to Havana, and in July it was back in New York undergoing
repairs. In August the barque was in Havana again. On this
occasion, however, it was chartered by the Cuban slave trading firm of Ximenes, Martínez, and Lafitte. The firm put a
new Spanish and Cuban crew aboard the vessel, and on September 21 they cleared it for Omoa, Honduras, under the
American flag.[43]

Sanchez had been keeping an eye on the *Pamphylia* since
the early summer. He first reported on the ship during its visit
to Havana in June. At that point, he noted that it had been sold
to Cuban traffickers and would eventually sail for the African

coast. He also gave Archibald a description taken from the *American Lloyd's Register*. He did not mention the vessel again until it had been repaired in New York in July and returned to Havana. On September 29, a week after the *Pamphylia* cleared Havana, he confirmed to Archibald that the vessel was a slaver. In a series of October missives he reported that the barque had set sail for the African coast. He also confirmed that the *Pamphylia* was "ostensibly under charter" but had actually been sold in Havana for $9,500. In other words, he was sure the slaver was no longer a bona-fide American vessel. This was exactly the information the West Africa Squadron required.[44]

After the vital information was confirmed, Archibald prepared Sanchez's intelligence for its long journey around the Atlantic Basin. Archibald's dispatches typically contained copies of Sanchez's notes, accompanied by a cover letter. It was six months into Sanchez's contract, however, and Archibald wanted to take stock of the work so far. He instructed a clerk to draw up a comprehensive list of all the slavers Sanchez had already reported. When news of the *Pamphylia* arrived, the clerk added it to the list, along with details on the barque's sale in Havana, its departure, flag, rigging, and tonnage. On October 10, the list was ready. Archibald wrote an introductory cover letter and enclosed a few of Sanchez's latest notes. He then bundled all the documents together and labeled them Slave Trade No. 31. It was the thirty-first "Slave Trade" dispatch of the year. He then sent Slave Trade No. 31 to New York Harbor, where the mail steamer *Asia* was about to depart for England.[45]

After a two-week passage across the North Atlantic aboard the *Asia*, Slave Trade No. 31 began the European leg of its journey. On October 25, it arrived at the Foreign Office in Downing Street, not far from Big Ben, which had been erected that summer. Archibald had addressed Slave Trade No. 31 to the foreign secretary, Lord Russell, but it was common practice for the relevant head clerks and undersecretaries, in this case, Wylde and Hammond, to read dispatches. Recognizing the value of Sanchez's information, these senior figures had a junior clerk make a copy of the dispatch and send it to the Admiralty, a few streets away in Whitehall. On November 4, William Romaine, the second secretary of the Admiralty, reviewed Sanchez's list and decided it should go to the West Africa Squadron. Composing a cover letter addressed to Frederick Grey, the commander of the British fleet, Romaine explained that the list contained "information respecting vessels which have from time to time been denounced by Her Majesty's Consul at New York." The Admiralty sent the list via train to Liverpool, 250 miles northwest of London. After its arrival on Merseyside, it was transferred to a mail steamer, *Cleopatra*, which was due to leave for West Africa. On November 24, the *Cleopatra* headed out into the Irish Sea.[46]

On December 30, five weeks after leaving Britain, the steamer arrived at its final destination, the Spanish colony of Fernando Po. Like many islands off mainland Africa, Fernando Po was an important waystation for passing vessels, and during the mid-nineteenth century, British and American cruisers stopped there for coal and provisions. They also came to receive mail from home. Thanks to the scheduling certainty introduced by steamships, they could expect the mail on specific days each month. Typically, one cruiser from each squadron collected the mail and headed south to its base in Luanda. In the case of the December 1859 mail, the name of the British runner is unknown, but the American warship

USS *Sumpter* can be used as a proxy. This vessel picked up the mail in Fernando Po on December 30 and spent the next week journeying to Luanda. As the *Sumpter* headed south toward the coast, its crew passed dispatches and news to their counterparts aboard passing American cruisers. It must have been during the British version of these exchanges that Sanchez's list arrived in the hands of British officers and word of the *Pamphylia* spread among the fleet.[47]

Sanchez's intelligence had reached the West Africa Squadron just in time. On January 9, 1860, Lieutenant Burton, captain of HMS *Triton*, spotted a barque matching the *Pamphylia*'s description and not displaying a flag standing off Landano about thirty miles north of the Congo River. Burton ordered his crew to fire a blank round. The vessel responded by raising the U.S. flag. Yet Burton was armed with Sanchez's information, and he approached the barque confidently. Realizing they were about to be captured, the *Pamphylia*'s thirty-strong crew hauled down the American flag, tossed the vessel's papers overboard, and surrendered. Burton and his men boarded the ship and promptly arraigned the crew. Dealing with the crew was legally complicated, however, because they had initially claimed U.S. protection. Neither Burton nor the Admiralty wanted to deal with potential American objections to the capture. Burton and his men would also have known their customary bounties on the capture were secure, regardless of whether they took the traffickers into custody. Under these influences, they decided to simply dump the crew ashore at Cabinda, near the mouth of the Congo River.[48]

In addition to the crew, Burton and his men discovered six hundred sick captives beneath the *Pamphylia*'s deck. Burton decided to bring two hundred of the Africans aboard the *Tri-*

ton and to leave the remainder on the barque. The two vessels then journeyed to the island of Saint Helena, where a British Vice Admiralty Court held jurisdiction over flagless vessels. On February 13, 1860, the court condemned the barque, and to prevent further use of it as a slaver, ordered it broken into pieces, with the parts sold to the highest bidder. The Africans, meanwhile, spent several months in cramped tents in Saint Helena's Rupert's Valley. In accordance with Britain's policy on "recaptives," in the spring of 1860 ships from Asia took the surviving *Pamphylia* Africans to Demerara, Trinidad, and other parts of the British Caribbean. Those who made it to the Americas entered "apprenticeships."[49]

Sanchez's information was clearly decisive in this instance, but was it a typical case? One way to assess Sanchez's overall effectiveness is to analyze his pay. The Foreign Office had agreed to reward him for vessels captured on his information and guaranteed him £400 annually, even if none were captured. Although the large number of slavers operating between 1859 and 1862 made this formula potentially lucrative, Sanchez did not do especially well from his intelligence. Despite laboring earnestly throughout his career and reporting on the majority of slavers, he never received more than his guaranteed annual salary. His total pay over the course of his three-year, four-month tenure was £1,400, a sum that included three annual £400 payments, plus £100 awarded retroactively in 1863. In fact, the Foreign Office only acknowledged that his information had been instrumental in the capture of four vessels: *Ardennes, Orion, Stephen H. Townsend,* and *Lillie Mills.*[50]

The Foreign Office's good faith on payouts was put to the test when positive news arrived from the African coast. A year into Sanchez's service, Commodore William Edmonstone reported glowingly about his intelligence. Summarizing Edmonstone's report for Wodehouse and Russell, Wylde noted that a single cruiser, HMS *Archer*, had captured the "Stephen H Townsend, Laura, Lillie Mills and Eloisa in consequence of information rec'd from the FO." Edmonstone had also said that British cruisers had intercepted the *Orion*, the *Tavernier*, and *Pamphylia* on Sanchez's intelligence. In addition, he mentioned that British officers were passing information directly to American officers and that "several other vessels" had been detained as result. Although Edmonstone did not specify how many vessels had been captured on Sanchez's intelligence, he clearly regarded it as valuable. According to Wylde, Edmonstone was "decidedly of the opinion that the information has been frequently the cause of vessels being captured which perhaps otherwise would not have been boarded." Edmonstone's successor, Commodore Frederick Grey, agreed. In 1860 he told the Foreign Office, "I have no doubt that the traffic has been considerably impeded [through Sanchez's information], & that a great advantage has resulted from it."[51]

Despite these favorable reports, the Foreign Office failed to pay Sanchez what it owed him. Edmonstone named seven vessels that had been captured on Sanchez's information in his 1860 report, but the Foreign Office acknowledged only three in a dispatch to Archibald. It was not that senior figures at the Foreign Office disputed the accuracy of Edmonstone's report. Rather, they did not consider it necessary to pass this information to Sanchez. Although Wylde wrote to Wodehouse and Russell in 1862 acknowledging that Sanchez's intelligence had "led to a considerable number of captures being made both by our own cruisers and Americans also," the Foreign Office only informed Sanchez that one other slaver, the *Ardennes*, had been captured through his intelligence. As a result, his pay never rose above the guaranteed annual salary. The Foreign Office seemed to consider that sum a maximum as well as a minimum.[52]

The Foreign Office's unscrupulous approach to Sanchez's pay was probably guided by financial constraints. The department was paying Sanchez and its other informants from a shrinking Secret Service budget. During Sanchez's tenure, Parliament approved the SSF at twenty-five thousand pounds annually. This sum was less than half the more than fifty thousand pounds allocated earlier in the century. The reduced allowance coincided with the expansion of British influence in the world and the Foreign Office's increasing use of undercover agents, especially in the slave trade. Making the budgetary situation worse, the Foreign Office paid many of its spies and their families substantial allowances from the SSF even after they had retired and was wary of dispensing with these payments. When Undersecretary Hammond expressed his alarm at the state of the SSF in May 1858, Malmesbury, the foreign secretary, instructed him not to trim the pensions. He may have been worried that unpaid pensioners would turn against their former masters. In the same note, he remarked that his major concern was "the unveiling [of] the Secret Service system to the public."[53]

Sanchez was aware that his information was making an important impact. While it may have failed to end the traffic, his intelligence probably led to the termination of around thirty voyages and kept at least 20,880 people from being forced to endure the Middle Passage to Cuba. By scouring his wide array of newspapers, he learned that British and U.S.

cruisers were intercepting many of the vessels he had reported. In the spring of 1860, he wrote angrily to Archibald: "When the writer accepted the terms offered by the F.O. he was under the impression that he would be paid according to the contract." Indeed, he contended that the Foreign Office was guilty of "nonfulfillment of their part of the contract" and was "thereby keeping him in a false position." Archibald forwarded Sanchez's complaints to the Foreign Office, but in response Wylde denied any wrongdoing and instructed Archibald not to pay Sanchez more than the annual fee. Sanchez did not drop the topic. In December 1860, he wrote to Archibald enclosing a "memorandum of captures" that listed the vessels on which he believed he was entitled to payment. The memo included sixteen slavers, and indicated arrears of £2,305. Archibald sent Sanchez's latest petition to London, but the Foreign Office again refused to pay up.[54]

Despite Sanchez's frustration, he kept working for the British government. Although he pursued his quest for fair pay until 1863 (after his final contract expired), he does not appear to have considered quitting his job. On several occasions, he wrote to Archibald asking if the Foreign Office planned to extend his contract for another year. It did so twice, and on both occasions he accepted the offer. It was perhaps surprising that he did not request amendments to the contract on either occasion, although by this point he may have presumed that the Foreign Office would never agree to them, given its approach to his rewards for captures. He continued working on the same terms as before. His ongoing dedication to the task despite the diminishing financial prospects, the personal risks, and the detrimental effect on his own business, suggests a deep commitment to suppressing the traffic.

Sanchez underlined this commitment in the summer of 1860 when he presented portions of his intelligence to the New York press. Between July and September, he wrote a series of detailed exposés of the trade for the New York *Evening Post*. Wishing to retain his anonymity but also to hint at his credentials, he wrote under the pseudonym "South Street," a main thoroughfare in Lower Manhattan where the trade was active. In his first note, he denounced several vessels as slavers and charged that twenty local firms were directly or indirectly involved in the trade. On July 28, "South Street" appeared again, presenting a list of eighty-five slavers that had sailed "under the American flag" since February 1859. The list, which included the names of the vessels' true owners, was one of the most detailed and accurate slave trade exposés ever published in the United States. Unprepared to stop there, "South Street" then attacked officials he thought were abetting the trade. In early August, he accused a clearance clerk at the New York Custom House, James De Graw, of knowingly clearing slavers and not passing full information to the Associated Press. As Sanchez explained to the readers of the *Evening Post*, he was determined to break up the slave trade in New York "single handed."[55]

Sanchez's stunning foray into the public sphere was unauthorized by the British government. He had not discussed his new tactic with Archibald, and the articles took the consul completely by surprise. As Archibald reported to the Foreign Office, it was only while he was reading "South Street"'s list of eighty-five vessels in the *Post* that it dawned on him that the information was "substantially the same as that already communicated by me [to London]." Sanchez did not say why he had embarked on his mission without telling Archibald. Perhaps he felt Britain might try to interfere with his efforts. In any case, Archibald and his superiors had few concerns about Sanchez's new tactic. The Foreign Office had financed the anti-slavery trade press in Rio, and it was not about to stop Sanchez attacking the traffic in New York at no cost to itself. When Sanchez admitted that he was, indeed, "South Street," Archibald gave him his blessing, and he continued to publish in the *Post*.[56]

Sanchez's newspaper articles temporarily put New York traffickers and their accomplices under increased scrutiny and forced some individuals into the public sphere to defend themselves. One anonymous writer used the *Evening Post* to ask "South Street" why he included the *Louisa* in his list of slavers and "what proof" he had "that the owner is a foreigner." Sanchez declined to substantiate his case, perhaps sensing this was an attempt to goad him into revealing his sources and thereby identify himself. He had, however, given notice to New York's slave traders that he had the power to expose them publicly. His articles even forced officials to publicly protest their innocence. The clearance clerk, De Graw, wrote to both the *Evening Post* and another New York newspaper, the *World*, denying that he was suppressing information on slavers. Sanchez responded by dismissing De Graw's defense as "twaddle" and leveling more accusations against him.[57]

Although Sanchez's letters were typically aimed at specific individuals such as De Graw, they quickly became wrapped up in the national political debate. His notes received attention from a wide range of New York newspapers. The topic of the illegal slave trade was attractive to publishers not just because it was secret and salacious, but because New York's press and the nation more broadly was deeply divided over the question of slavery within the United States. The slave trade was a useful proxy for debates about the issue. On one hand, Republican papers such as the *Post* opposed the expansion of slavery in the United States and blamed southern-friendly Democrats for abetting the trade from American ports. On August 7, the *Post* supported "South Street" and, referring to the presidential election in the fall, warned New York's slave traders that their time was "[al]most up." Other papers, however, more tied to mercantile interests, slavery, and the Democratic platform, were openly skeptical of the exposés. The *Journal of Commerce* slammed the "black Republican journals" for printing Sanchez's accusations and demanded that "South Street" unveil himself. The proslavery *Evening Express*, meanwhile, mocked "South Street," saying the trade was growing "the more he writes."[58]

Neither Sanchez nor the *Post* could win in the summer of 1860. The *Express* had been incorrect to say the slave trade was growing—it actually fell marginally in the summer and fall—but the traffic was still operating on a large scale, and Sanchez would be busy reporting departures from New York for another two years. In fact, U.S. officials in New York do not appear to have been any more active in the summer of 1860, when Sanchez was writing, than in previous months. The mainly Portuguese and Cuban traffickers mentioned in Sanchez's list remained at large. De Graw, meanwhile, not only retained his job at the Custom House, he convinced the U.S. government to allow him to start a suit against the *Post* to discover the identity of "South Street." This development may have ushered Sanchez out of the pages of the *Post* in September 1860.[59]

As Sanchez's failed campaign indicated, the demise of the

slave trade in New York would ultimately come when internal political circumstances changed in the country at large. Those changes led to the election of a Republican president, Abraham Lincoln, whose administration would finally root out the slave traders from New York in 1862 and make an enforceable treaty allowing British cruisers to intercept American vessels. Ironically, as it did so, the British government found little use for Sanchez. In the early spring of 1862, as the traffic faded from New York, Britain renewed his contract for only three months. When the contract elapsed at the end of May, Sanchez's career as a spy was over. He had failed to break the slave trade, something he had promised the readers of the *Post* he would do, but he had, at least, witnessed its demise. He continued to live in New York with his wife, Susan, until 1901, when he died, at the age of seventy-nine.[60]

When Sanchez retired from the world of spying in the early 1860s he may have reflected on what his efforts had achieved and what they had not. His information had helped check the trade, but it had not ended it. The only thing likely to do that was not his personal crusade, or even the ongoing efforts of the British, but the globalization of anti–slave trade sentiment. By 1860, most nations had taken serious action to suppress the traffic, but Spain, the United States, and several African polities had not joined them. As long as these powers failed to tackle the traffic in earnest, slave traders would continue to operate within their jurisdictions. Although he had helped turn New York into a battleground over the trade, it was not a war that Sanchez or the British could win without robust support from the U.S. government. Sanchez may have grasped that point in 1860, when he began writing his exposés. These missives played a small part in stirring the ongoing and fractious national debate about the future of slavery in the United States. It was the deep fissures over that question which would move the United States toward civil war and decisive American action against the trade in 1862.

CHAPTER FIVE

American Politics and
American Suppression

O N February 21, 1862, almost a year into the American Civil War, Nathaniel Gordon made his way to a specially erected scaffold at the Tombs, the city jail in New York. Gordon, a veteran slave trading captain, had completed at least four illegal voyages during the past decade, reputedly earning him the nickname "Lucky Nat" among his fellow traffickers in Manhattan. In 1860, however, Gordon's luck had run out. Upon leaving the Congo River aboard his ship, the *Erie*, with almost nine hundred slaves, he was caught by a U.S. cruiser. The navy returned Gordon to New York, and Delafield Smith, a vigorous and effective district attorney, prosecuted him under the federal anti-slave trade Act of 1820. The jury convicted him, and Gordon was sentenced to death. Despite pleas for mercy from scores of petitioners (including his wife) who were shocked by the severity of the sentence, President Abraham Lincoln declined to commute the sentence.

The crowd that gathered to witness Gordon's final moments reflected how seriously the state was taking the case. The execution yard was packed. Robert Murray, who was chief marshal and therefore the lead federal officer in New York, and his deputy, Adolphus Borst, were in charge of proceedings and appeared in full uniform. Two state governors were also present, as was a judge and the superintendent of police. Outside the Tombs, policemen guarded the streets. Inside, eighty-four Marines blocked the approach to the yard. Although groggy from ingesting poison the night before (a failed last-minute suicide attempt), Gordon used his last words to damn the federal government for pursuing him, giving special mention to District Attorney Smith. After he quieted down, the executioner covered his head and placed the noose around his neck. A few moments later his body flew up, then down, then hung suspended in air. Gordon had become the first and last slave trader to be executed under American law.[1]

When the Maine native first got into the business around 1850, the United States was becoming more deeply involved in the illegal slave trade. Migrant traffickers from all over the Atlantic Basin came to New York and other U.S. ports to set up their business. Gradually, American vessels such as the *Erie*, and American captains such as Gordon, became vital components in the wider illegal slave trade to Cuba. As this traffic grew, U.S. suppression measures remained tepid, with some of the most effective work being done undercover by Emilio Sanchez on behalf of the British, rather than by the American government. The traffic from New York and elsewhere grew to unprecedented levels. Yet by 1862, when Gordon was

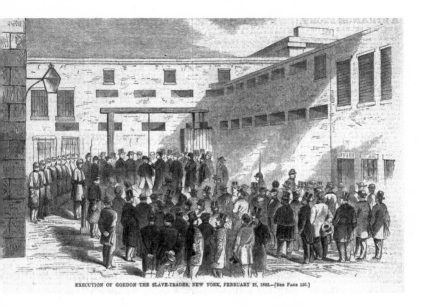

"Execution of Gordon the Slave-Trader, New York,
February 21, 1862," from *Harper's Weekly*, March 2, 1862.
(Prints and Photographs Division, Library of Congress,
Washington D.C., https://www.loc.gov/item/2011647819/)

executed, American suppression efforts had improved markedly. This change had not come about easily, but it would have
dramatic effects. Gordon's swinging body heralded the end
of U.S. involvement in the slave trade and suggested that the
traffic's days were numbered.

THE SCOPE AND LIMITS OF
U.S. SUPPRESSION MEASURES

The federal government held ultimate responsibility for suppressing American participation in the illegal slave trade. Al-

though several individual states took action against the traffic in the late eighteenth and early nineteenth centuries, federal statutes took precedence over state law. These federal acts dated back to the early republic and included the Act of 1807, which outlawed the traffic, and the Act of 1820, which declared the trade piracy. In combination, these laws prohibited Americans from participating in a wide range of slaving activity, including investing in voyages, owning slavers, and serving aboard them. They also stipulated punishments for offenders, ranging from fines to imprisonment and, in the case of the Act of 1820, execution. When Congress created federal anti–slave trade law, therefore, it was fairly broadly conceived, and in theory at least had teeth.

As U.S. connections to the trade increased after 1850, especially through the traffickers' use of American ports, several problems with the government's efforts at suppression became increasingly apparent. One accusation, leveled by several American newspapers and at least one U.S. senator, Henry Wilson of Massachusetts, was that federal marshals in U.S. ports were deeply complicit in the trade. These charges were given credence in the spring of 1860 when two deputy marshals in New York, Theodore Rynders and Henry Munn, were impeached and discharged for gross misconduct. The pair was found guilty of accepting a fifteen-hundred-dollar bribe from slave traders on the East River in exchange for letting the slaver *Storm King* sail safely out of port, bound for Africa. The episode caused a sensation in the New York press and inspired several newspapers to call for a general inquisition into the local marshal's office.[2]

Rynders's brother Isaiah Rynders, the chief marshal in New York, also came under the scrutiny of the press. In late

1860, Rynders was implicated in the escape from custody of a suspected slave trader named Morgan Fredericks, who had been first mate aboard the slaver *Cora*, captured by an American cruiser near the Congo River in the fall. After the interception, the navy dispatched the vessel and crew to New York for adjudication and trial. Upon their arrival, Rynders held the crew aboard the *Cora* in the Brooklyn Navy Yard. Late one December night Fredericks escaped and promptly disappeared. Rynders's implausible explanation was that Fredericks had leaped into the ice-laden waters and swum several hundred yards to shore. A subsequent investigation revealed that a boat had run alongside the *Cora* and spirited Fredericks away. Sensing a deeper conspiracy, the *New-York Times* called for Rynders's "instant removal" from office. Rynders survived, however, and completed his five-year tenure as chief marshal. During this period, the slave trade in New York reached its peak.[3]

Other functionaries also faced accusations of corruption, negligence, or incompetence. In 1861, the *Times* assailed the New York district attorney James Roosevelt for botching the prosecution of traffickers by drawing flawed indictments from grand juries, leading to problems in later trials. On one occasion, Roosevelt had even encouraged a trial jury to convict a defendant under the Act of 1820 on the basis that the president at the time, James Buchanan, would probably commute the death sentence. Although probably true, this entreaty not only smacked of desperation, it suggested that the federal government believed its own laws were too severe. The episode led the lawyer George Templeton Strong to question in his diary: "Is Judge Roosevelt more deficient in common sense or in moral sense?" Meanwhile, the *New-York Daily Tribune* accused judges, especially Samuel Betts in New York, of blocking the confiscation of slaving vessels and the conviction of slave traders because they were sympathetic to the traffickers. Other observers, including, as we have seen, Emilio Sanchez, accused clearance clerks in the Custom House of deliberately concealing information about when slavers were leaving port. These omissions, he argued in his "South Street" exposés, were made at the behest of local traffickers and prevented marshals from stopping vessels before they left port.[4]

Although some officials did fail to execute their duties honestly or adroitly, most were struggling with the shortcomings of anti–slave trade laws. District attorneys, especially, were hampered by the broad construction of the federal statutes. One particular problem was that none of the federal statutes specifically banned ships from carrying items (or "equipment," as it was then known) designed for slave trading. Much of this equipment, including extra lumber and large quantities of food and water, was essential for these voyages and was easily recognizable to authorities. Indeed, other nations had incorporated so-called equipment clauses into their anti–slave trade laws and treaties precisely for this reason. The absence of such clauses in the U.S. statutes had a detrimental effect on suppression measures. Although district attorneys brought up the presence of this equipment in their prosecutions, it was considered insufficient evidence on which to base a criminal conviction or even the condemnation of a slaver. As a result, marshals in New York and elsewhere often let vessels sail from port even though they knew they were fully equipped for the trade.[5]

A libel case filed by the United States government against the *Isla de Cuba* in 1858 for being engaged in the slave trade indicates the challenges faced by federal prosecutors. In this instance, the *Isla de Cuba*, a barque, had reached the African coast when the crew decided they did not want to go through with the slaving voyage. Instead, they launched a remarkable rebellion against the Portuguese supercargo, setting him adrift in a small boat, and then sailing to Boston and surrendering the vessel. The barque was carrying a large quantity of lumber, barrels of water, and several large cauldrons. These items were clearly meant for building a slave deck and provisioning captives, but the counsel for the defense, acting for the owner, Manoel Cunha Reis, contended otherwise. Using testimony from several merchants engaged in the Africa trade from New York—who were involved directly and indirectly in the slave trade—the defense explained to the Boston court that the lumber was a common trade good on the African coast, the barrels were used merely to ballast ships as they crossed the ocean, and the cauldrons were meant for boiling African palm oil before it was carried back to the United States. The court rejected these arguments, thanks, mainly, to the extraordinary testimony of the crew, but few cases were as open and shut.[6]

Even after successful libel cases such as the one against the *Isla de Cuba*, slaving vessels often ended up back in the traffickers' hands. Once the courts had condemned these slavers, marshals were required to sell them in the open market on behalf of the state. In many cases, slave traders simply purchased them all over again. After the federal government confiscated the *Isla de Cuba* in 1859, for example, it was sold at auction and bought by its former owners. Some observers believed that slave traders had cornered the market for condemned slavers. After Fredericks's vessel, the *Cora*, was condemned in 1861, the *New-York Times* reported it was "sold at one of those practically private sales, only attended by our slave-trading merchants. She was at once refitted for another slave-trading voyage." Not long thereafter, the *Cora* was again captured near Virginia by a U.S. official, Captain Faunce, who, according to the *Times*, "discovered on board of her all the usual insignia of the traffic in human ebony." Slave traders were often able to purchase these vessels at low prices in New York, owing to the efforts of the Cuban-born merchant Albert Horn, whom the U.S. government hired to appraise them before they went to public auction. Horn was notorious for appraising the vessels below market value, which helped slave traders reclaim them at minimal cost.[7]

Another limitation of the federal statutes was their focus on citizenship. Section 5 of the Act of 1820 stipulated that criminal convictions could be sustained only against U.S. citizens or individuals serving aboard a slaver owned by a U.S. citizen. In many cases, district attorneys saw their cases fall apart because they could not prove that the defendant or the vessel's owners were Americans. Foreign nationals, especially the Portuguese immigrants, were typically not naturalized U.S. citizens. According to District Attorney John McKeon in New York, some traffickers, including José Pedro da Cunha, underlined the point by pretending in court that they could not speak English. The second part of Section 5, relating to U.S. ownership of vessels, was also difficult to prove. Some sham purchases of slavers were carried out by obscure individuals whose citizenship district attorneys found it difficult to ascertain. Other buyers were not U.S. citizens at all and had merely claimed to be Americans to gain U.S. papers for their vessels. Those claiming citizenship of another nation enjoyed an added protection: since the United States did not hold extradition treaties with Spain, Portugal, or Brazil, they could not be sent abroad for trial. As a result, they held a kind of international immunity from prosecution while they remained in the United States.[8]

The trial of Captain James Smith in 1854 illustrates how the citizenship issue complicated prosecutions. During opening remarks, District Attorney McKeon stated that Smith had been indicted under the Act of 1820. McKeon proceeded to lay out his case, arguing that Smith had captained the brig *Julia Moulton* from New York earlier that year and delivered around six hundred captive Africans to Cuba. McKeon also stressed that Smith was a U.S. citizen. In response, Smith's attorney, Charles O'Conor, strikingly ignored what McKeon said about the voyage but hotly disputed the citizenship issue. To bolster his case, he paraded a host of Smith's friends and relatives, who claimed he had been born in Germany and had lived in the United States for only three years. Since it took five years for an immigrant to be eligible for naturalization, Smith could not be a U.S. citizen. McKeon countered that Smith's American citizenship was proved by an oath he had taken at the New York Custom House before the voyage, but O'Conor responded that Smith had simply lied. After deliberating on the case, the jury found Smith guilty, but the magistrate, Justice Samuel Nelson, subsequently granted Smith a retrial on the grounds that Nelson had not been sufficiently clear in his charge to the jury that the central issue at hand was Smith's citizenship. Perhaps realizing that the citizenship question was quicksand, McKeon struck a deal with the defense, offering Smith a guilty plea related to the Act of 1800, which carried only weak penalties. Smith accepted McKeon's offer and served just two years in jail.[9]

Problems with federal law and its enforcers would dog suppression efforts in courtrooms up to the Civil War. As the historian Warren Howard has shown, from 1851 to 1860, 159 individuals were prosecuted under slave trade laws in U.S. courts. Of this number, 99 were tried and acquitted, found their jury deadlocked, or were released after the jury was unable to find a bill against them. Prosecutors failed to pursue cases against a further 21 prisoners, probably owing to the slim chances of conviction. Only 12 individuals were tried and convicted, often, as in the case of Smith, on minor charges and with relatively light punishments. All the defendants dodged execution, the penalty stipulated by the Act of 1820. Meanwhile, an additional 9 defendants, including Fredericks, escaped custody, either before trial, while released on bail, or after sentencing. The outcomes for the final 18 individuals is unclear. Prosecutors had more success in libel cases, largely because the evidentiary standards were lower than in criminal trials. Yet even here, only about half of libeled vessels were confiscated by courts: 33 of 67 between 1851 and 1860. In fact, many condemned vessels, such as the *Isla de Cuba*, simply ended up back in the hands of slave traders. This grim picture worsens when we consider that the statistics above do not take account of the large number of traffickers and vessels that escaped the justice system altogether.[10]

The U.S. suppression efforts fared little better overseas. Several federal statutes called for the abolition of American involvement in the slave trade at sea, and by the mid-1850s two of the navy's five squadrons included suppression of the trade within their remits. The first of these fleets, the Home Squadron, theoretically covered both U.S. waters and the Caribbean. The main field of labor clearly lay in the latter region, where Cuba, unlike the United States, remained a major importer of slaves and use of American vessels was rampant. Yet the navy rarely sent any of the squadron's eight vessels into Caribbean waters before 1859. The misdirection of resources rendered the fleet almost impotent. Of the hundreds of American vessels bringing captives to Cuba, the Home Squadron intercepted just two slavers between 1850 and 1860, the *Putnam* in 1858 and the *Cygnet* in 1859.[11]

The second U.S. fleet, the Africa Squadron, was only slightly more successful. Guided by the Act of 1819, which among other provisions authorized the president to send "armed vessels of the United States, to be employed to cruise on any of the coasts of the United States . . . or the coast of Africa" to interdict slave traders, American presidents had been sending cruisers to fight the slave trade in African waters since the 1820s. It was a puny force, usually one or two vessels, and it was also responsible for protecting American commerce and supporting the new colony of Liberia, which was closely tied to the American Colonization Society. In 1842, after years of neglect and in response to slave traders' growing use of the U.S. flag (as well as mounting international pressure), President John Tyler's administration signed the Webster-Ashburton Treaty. This accord did not grant British cruisers the right to search American vessels for slaves, a concession the British desperately sought, but it did pledge that both nations would maintain a "sufficient and adequate squadron" on the African coast, carrying at least eighty guns in total.[12]

Despite creating a formalized U.S. Africa Squadron, the Webster-Ashburton Treaty did not produce a robust American suppression force on the African coast. Successive navy secretaries, including Abel P. Upshur, who later became secretary of state, took advantage of the treaty's wording to minimize their outlay of vessels and men. Noting that the treaty stipulated a minimum number of guns, not cruisers, the U.S. Navy sent only three to five vessels rather than a larger and probably more effective fleet. By contrast, the British West Africa Squadron in the last quarter-century of the trade typically numbered around thirty vessels. Underlining the weak commitment of the United States to Webster-Ashburton, the Africa Squadron carried fewer than the stipulated eighty guns during much of the 1840s and 1850s.[13]

Successive U.S. administrations compounded the problem of the squadron's skimpiness by sending unsuitable vessels to patrol the coast. At a time when traffickers were using increasingly fast vessels, the navy deployed a few bulky frigates (which carried almost all the guns), as well as lightly armed brigs and sloops. Commander William McBlair, who toiled aboard the sloop USS *Dale* in 1857, complained bitterly about the inadequacy of the squadron's sailing vessels. Writing to his wife back in Maryland, McBlair noted that suspicious vessels bolted as soon as they saw American cruisers. Since these cruisers were unable to catch the faster slavers in a chase, they were effectively "mere scarecrows." What McBlair and his fellow commanders sought, and regularly requested, were small steamers, which were both fast and maneuverable, but their pleas were routinely ignored in Washington. The frustrated McBlair, who managed to capture only one slaver, the *Wil-*

liam G. Lewis, during his two-year cruise, concluded frankly: "Our squadron is a farce."[14]

Another major deficiency was the location of the squadron's base at Porto Praya in the Cape Verde Islands. The navy chose this location off the upper Guinea coast in the early 1840s because it had a resident U.S. consul and was conveniently positioned along the shipping routes from the United States and Europe. Yet the islands were far from the main slaving grounds, especially as the slave trade shifted farther south and became more concentrated in West Central Africa. Cruisers had to sail for at least a month to reach the key slave embarkation zone and then return to resupply a few months later. As a result, only one or two U.S. cruisers were ever in the main slaving grounds at a time. Frederick Grey, commander of the West Africa Squadron, made the point to his brother, the former British secretary of war, in 1857, complaining that "instead of having a force of suitable vessels as they are bound [by treaty,] a [U.S.] cruiser is seldom seen on the coast." The navy recognized the problem and discussed moving the depot to Luanda or Saint Helena in the early 1850s, but navy secretary William Graham decided to wait and see whether the entire trade would collapse in the wake of Brazilian suppression of it before making a decision. The push to relocate the squadron waned even as the trade to Cuba continued into the 1850s. Meanwhile, the fleet continued its poor performance. Between its creation in 1843 and 1858, the Africa Squadron captured just twenty slavers. By contrast, the large British fleet, which was based in Luanda, captured over five hundred slavers during the same period.[15]

A final flawed element of America's overseas suppression

efforts was the constraints placed on U.S. officials. Like their British counterparts, these diplomats, including ministers, consuls, and vice consuls, were widely spread throughout the Atlantic Basin. Many operated in Cuba and the Iberian Peninsula, where the majority of American slavers stopped during the 1850s and 1860s before heading to the African coast, often to change owners and take on crew and supplies. Unlike their British counterparts, however, American consuls were generally not active combatants in the fight against the slave trade. Their approach was guided largely from Washington, where the State Department and the attorney general's office made it clear that consuls were not to interfere with the sale or clearance of vessels abroad if those transactions were not objected to by local authorities. American representatives were also often under considerable pressure in foreign ports, especially in Cuba, where public opinion was largely in favor of the trade. In this context, busy markets for American slave ships such as Havana were largely ignored by U.S. consuls. On occasion, an American official, such as Thomas Savage, acting consul general in Havana in 1858, would make an earnest attempt to check the traffic by refusing the clearances of a U.S. vessel, but they rarely blocked its departures.[16]

The U.S. suppression of the trade was therefore patchy at best in the 1850s. At home, marshals and district attorneys, though not faultless, struggled with the limitations imposed by the laws. Congress had not updated the anti–slave trade statutes since 1820, when the shape of the slave trade was very different. In 1859, after another failed trial against a slave captain and as the traffic rose to record levels, the *New York Tribune* charged: "At present, we can hardly be said to have any laws against the African slave-trade." The *Tribune* exaggerated; the acts had encountered some success and probably discouraged some Americans from entering the traffic. But they did not constitute effective legislation. Meanwhile, the U.S. efforts were struggling abroad. Successive administrations failed to make naval suppression a priority or to press their diplomats to take a firmer line against the traffic in foreign ports. The question on the lips of many critics was why Congress failed to take action to address these problems.[17]

AMERICAN EXPANSIONISM AND THE CUBAN SLAVE TRADE

For much of the 1850s, U.S. suppression efforts were powerfully shaped by American ambitions in Cuba. Encouraged by its westward and southward expansion during the 1830s and 1840s, and having witnessed the impressive development of the Cuban slave economy, many Americans, especially southerners, contended that Cuba ought to be incorporated into the United States. This view had been popular in policy circles since the early republic, but a new phase of Cuba agitation began at midcentury. Manifest Destiny, the belief that U.S. territorial expansion was both inevitable and ordained by God, was at its height. The Democratic Party, which supported American expansion, dominated the presidency and Congress during much of the 1840s and, especially, the 1850s. After the annexation of Texas in 1845, prominent Democrats, including President James K. Polk, argued forcefully that Spain should relinquish control of the island. They also offered to purchase the island, but Spain, having lost its mainland American empire a generation earlier and fully appreciating the value of the Pearl of the Antilles, rejected all U.S. proposals.[18]

Spain's refusal to sell Cuba led some American expansionists and frustrated Latin American revolutionaries to determine that it would have to be taken by force. To that end, in 1850, Narciso López, a Venezuelan who favored annexation, sailed from New Orleans to the island with a band of six hundred southern expansionists and Cuban revolutionaries and managed to take the town of Cárdenas before colonial troops forced their retreat back to Louisiana. The expedition had failed to inspire the Creole revolt López had envisioned, but he and his men enjoyed a rapturous welcome on their return to New Orleans. In 1851, López made another try, but this too failed and ended in his public garroting in Havana.[19]

Despite López's grisly demise, the "Cuba Question" would remain a central matter in American foreign policy for the rest of the decade. In 1853, President Franklin Pierce initially offered his tacit support to a López-style invasion by the pro-slavery Mississippi adventurer and imperialist John Quitman. Pierce eventually changed his mind, preferring to spend political capital on securing slavery in Kansas, a goal he achieved through the passage of the Kansas-Nebraska Act in 1854, but he was only temporarily sidetracked. The following year, Pierce authorized the Louisianan Pierre Soulé, his chief diplomat in Madrid, to offer Spain up to $130 million for Cuba. If Spain refused, he told Soulé, he should work toward "the next desirable object, which is to detach that island from the Spanish dominion." When Spain declined the offer, Soulé met with James Buchanan and John Mason, then U.S. diplomats in Britain and France, in Ostend, Belgium, and penned a memorandum, which became known as the Ostend Manifesto. The manifesto stated that the incorporation of Cuba into the United States was "necessary" and that should the Spanish crown refuse to sell the island, the United States would "by every law, human and divine . . . be justified in wresting it from Spain." Pierce's administration faced criticism at home and abroad when the manifesto became public, and he decided not to turn the threat into action, but Buchanan went on to become president from 1857 to 1861, and he, too, would make the acquisition of Cuba a key plank of his foreign policy.[20]

As agitation over Cuba intensified, many expansionists used the issue of the illegal slave trade to bolster their case for acquiring the island. They were building on a firm foundation. Americans were well aware that the traffic to Cuba was ongoing, since newspapers' foreign correspondents as well as travelers were reporting the latest clandestine landings. For much of the late 1840s and early to mid-1850s, almost all American commentators blamed Spain for allowing this trade to endure. According to the various reports, Spanish officials in Cuba were deeply involved in the traffic. Captains general were singled out for particularly strong criticism. In an article first printed in the fiery expansionist newspaper *New Orleans Delta* in 1850 and widely reprinted elsewhere, Captain General Conde Alcoy was accused of receiving a sack of money containing twenty thousand dollars in exchange for allowing six hundred slaves to land. The *Norfolk Democrat* of Dedham, Massachusetts, had a similar take. Referring to all senior Spanish officials in Cuba, the *Democrat* explained that after becoming "millionaires" through the slave trade, "these nabobs then generally return to Spain to spend their ill-gotten fortunes, leaving a crop of clerks to follow in the footsteps of their inhuman predecessors." According to this perspective, Spain was able, but unwilling, to suppress the traffic. As the *Constitution* of Middletown, Connecticut, argued: "Money has more than once prevailed over law, and no Government has been more susceptible to its influence than that of Spain."[21]

These arguments were given further weight by Cubans themselves. Creole exiles brought the message directly to American audiences. *La Verdad*, a newspaper founded by Cuban Creoles in New York in 1848 and published in both Spanish and English, consistently denounced the Spanish government for the slave trade, often deploying the arguments advanced by the reformist Cuban writer José Antonio Saco. In New Orleans, an associate of Narciso López, the Matanzas-born Ambrosio José Gonzales, published his *Manifesto on Cuban Affairs Addressed to the People of the United States* in 1853, calling for Cuban independence. Listing a series of grievances, including excessive taxation and the use of military courts for criminal offenses, he also complained about the ongoing slave trade to Cuba, which, he contended, continued "for the special benefit of the Queen Mother, the Captain-General, and a powerful Spanish clique in Havana." Back in New York, in January 1854, Lorenzo Allo, a professor of political economy, gave a speech to the Cuban Democratic Athenaeum of New York decrying Spanish rule in Cuba in general and its role in the slave trade in particular. Demanding the cessation of the traffic, Allo argued that the "trade will continue in Cuba whilst the Spanish government rules there, since it serves its policy and its treasury." The Spanish government took these critics seriously, responding with denials of its complicity in the trade through *La Crónica*, a newspaper it funded in New York, and banning unfriendly publications from entering Cuba. Behind the scenes, Spain also spent thousands of pesos on undercover spies to conduct what it called "direct and effective espionage" against exiled Creoles and annexationists in the United States.[22]

American expansionists and their Creole allies often placed evidence of Spain's responsibility for the traffic alongside testimonies of American virtue. The comparison was stark: while degraded Spain continued to deal in African slaves, the United States had taken early and stringent measures against the trade. Attendees at a meeting of Cuban annexationist in Columbus, Ohio, highlighted the contrast in 1851, resolving that while Spain offered "consent" to the slave trade, the United States was "the first of civilized governments to declare the slave trade Piracy." The following month, in an article titled "The Slave Trade in Cuba," the *New-York Times* noted that "one of the earliest legislative acts, on the part of the United States, was to abolish it and brand it as piracy." The *Times* went on to explain, "We have established it as a permanent and ineffaceable regulation, that the foreign slave trade shall never exist in any part of the United States." The newspaper's myopia was striking; within a few years, New York would be one of the great world centers for the trade.[23]

Newspapers underlined the distinction between the United States and Spain by emphasizing the cruelty of the latter's crime. In contrast to the United States, an apparently enlightened nation that had recognized the inhumanity of the traffic, Spain had no concern for the suffering Africans. After one Cuban landing, the *New Orleans Delta* described hundreds of "poor, miserable, half-dead shadows of men, who had been torn from their homes in Africa, and induced into the Island by consent and to the great profit of the Captain General of Cuba." Describing the international effects of the traffic, the *Daily Ohio Statesman* noted the "crimes of [Spain's] people who desolate towns in Africa, and run thousands of negroes into Cuba." After the appointment of a new captain general in 1860, the *Commercial Advertiser* in New York hoped that he would finally put down the "monstrous and inhuman traffic."[24]

Although Spain's responsibility for the trade was widely acknowledged in the United States, expansionists' emphasis on the luridness of the "Spanish" slave trade to Cuba led antislavery activists to compare the traffic with the domestic slave trade at home. Some writers could not tolerate the apparent hypocrisy of expansionists excoriating Spain for the Atlantic slave trade when the internal slave trade in the United States was running at record levels. An 1852 article in the *New York Tribune* wondered, "Wherein is the slave trade from Africa to Cuba worse than that from Richmond to New Orleans[?]. . . The more we seek to find such a difference, the more unreal and evanescent it appears." Pro-slavery writers strongly countered these critiques. In their defense they attempted to distinguish between the horrors of the slave trade from Africa and the supposedly benign nature of slavery in the United States. By midcentury, arguments in defense of American slavery were well honed and easily repurposed. Building on the contention of former vice president John C. Calhoun that slavery was "a positive good," pro-slavery expansionists minimized the scale and brutality of the domestic slave trade and noted that the slave population in the United States was growing through natural increase while Cuba still relied on the trade to replenish labor for the brutal cane fields.

In a nutshell, the argument was that American slavery was superior to Cuban slavery, and if the latter were to become more like the former, slaves and whites would benefit alike. In pro-slavery advocates' view, incorporating the island into the Union would allow this vision to become a reality.[25]

Aside from the afflictions the slave trade cast upon Africans, American expansionists argued the "Spanish" traffic to the island created security problems for the United States. On one hand, they pointed out that Britain's frustration with Spain's foot-dragging on the traffic could well lead it to take drastic action in Cuba. Their main fear was that Britain would force Spain to emancipate all its slaves and replace the slave trade with a free emigration scheme from Africa to Cuba. Rumors of this so-called Africanization scheme were rampant in the U.S. press throughout 1853 and 1854 and caused a frantic State Department to demand answers from U.S. consuls in Cuba. The prospect of Africanization was worrisome not only because it would diminish the economic rationale for acquiring Cuba, but also because it raised the specter of "another Haiti" on America's doorstep and the restiveness of the American slaves that would surely follow. In addition to the Africanization scare, some Americans argued that the slave trade to Cuba was offering Britain a pretext to send its warships into the island's waters. These cruisers, they argued, were really designed to accost American merchantmen and curtail American power in the Caribbean rather than stop the traffic. When British naval interceptions did occur, including a flurry in 1858, they caused serious diplomatic spats between the United States and Britain. In combination, these two concerns were potent. Understanding that the slave trade was threatening American independence, even the moderately antislavery *New-York Times* supported acquiring Cuba, at least in part on these grounds.[26]

According to American expansionists, the natural solution to ending the illegal slave trade and all its attendant problems was to remove the heinous power that was responsible for it. The *Daily Ohio Statesman* made the case explicitly in 1853: "If Spain cannot or will not put a stop to the baseness of her Viceroy, . . . the Island ought to be wrested from her forthwith." A more benevolent power, the United States, would then take control and put an immediate stop to the traffic. As the *New-York Times* argued, if Cuba was "annexed to this Union, the slave trade upon her coasts must cease." Indeed, the *Times* claimed, "The whole power of the Government would at once be enlisted in active measures for its suppression." Rhapsodizing over the allegedly fearsome U.S. laws against the trade, the *Cleveland Plain Dealer* argued, "Few will engage in the slave trade while capital punishment is the penalty of the crime." The paper implored bold lawmakers to seize the moment: "The statesman who should bring about the annexation of Cuba, would . . . enjoy the satisfaction of having at once and forever annihilated the Atlantic Slave Trade." The expansionist writer Cora Montgomery held similar views, writing in her book on Cuba, "If the United States receive [Cuba], humanity will at least rejoice over the suppression of the slave trade, and a mitigation of the horrors of the Spanish system of servitude."[27]

Leading policymakers made similar arguments. Slave trade suppression featured prominently among the various reasons James Buchanan, John Mason, and Pierre Soulé laid out for the immediate acquisition of Cuba in the Ostend Manifesto in 1854. According to the authors, "That infamous traffic remains an irresistible temptation and a source of immense profit to needy and avaricious officials, who, to attain their ends, scruple not to trample the most sacred principles under foot." Although they gave Spain some benefit of the doubt about its motives, they also raised the specter of an out-of-control colony. "The Spanish government, at home, may be well disposed," they noted, "but experience has proved that it cannot control these remote depositaries of its power." Their final argument was that Spain's inability to control the slave trade created security concerns that the United States could not ignore: "We should . . . commit base treason against our posterity should we permit Cuba to be Africanized and become a second St. Domingo, with all its attendant horrors to the white race, and suffer the flames to extend to our own neighboring shores, seriously to endanger or actually to consume the fair fabric of our Union."[28]

When Buchanan became president in 1856, he used his new platform to expand these arguments. The annual State of the Union address to Congress offered a key opportunity for the president to lay out foreign policy objectives, and Buchanan took the opportunity to tackle the issue directly. By 1858, the United States was deeply engaged in the slave trade, especially in New York, yet this did not prevent Buchanan from declaring in his State of the Union address that Cuba was "the only spot in the civilized world where the African slave trade is tolerated." This traffic, he claimed, posed myriad problems for the United States. Referencing the recent diplomatic spat with the British in the Gulf of Mexico, he explained that "the late serious difficulties between the United States and Great Britain respecting the right of search, now so happily terminated, could never have arisen if Cuba had not afforded a market for slaves." Then, striking a paternalistic tone, he turned to the wounds that the "Cuban" trade was inflicting upon Africa. "Whilst the demand for slaves continues in Cuba, wars will be waged among the petty and barbarous chiefs in Africa for the purpose of seizing subjects to supply this trade." The only solution was for Spain to sell Cuba to the United States. When that was accomplished, Buchanan assured the American people, "the last relic of the African slave trade would instantly disappear."[29]

The anti-Spanish narrative offered by Buchanan and some sections of the press deflected attention from U.S. participation in the trade during the 1850s. One clear example is the *New York Herald*'s reporting of the case of the *Lady Suffolk*, one of the first slave ships with strong U.S. connections, in the 1850s. This American-built vessel was bought in Baltimore on behalf of the Cuban slave trader Julián Zulueta, sent to New York for outfitting, and then moved on to Havana before departing for Mozambique. It subsequently returned to the Bay of Pigs in May 1853 with over a thousand captives. Several American sailors manned the decks. Although the American connections were clear, especially when the voyage came to light in the U.S. press, "Un Amigo," an anonymous writer in the New York *Weekly Herald*, cared only about the complicity of the captain general of Cuba. To "Un Amigo," Spanish law was nothing more than a "dead letter." Underscoring his position, when the daily version of the paper reported that the *Lady Suffolk* had again been sold to slave traders in Havana the following year, the writer argued not that the American government should prevent the sale of ships in Havana, but that Spain's obvious complicity in the trade justified the government's seizing the island.[30]

Senior policymakers followed the same reasoning as the *Herald*. Buchanan notably failed to address American participation in the traffic in any of his State of the Union addresses, even though he mentioned the slave trade in three of the four and American connections were by then impossible to deny. Some writers, often of a Republican bent, pointed out the omissions on Buchanan's part. The *New-York Times*, which by the late 1850s was acknowledging that both Spain and the United States were at fault for the slave trade, excoriated Buchanan for pinning the blame entirely on the Iberian power in his 1860 speech. His "attempt to fasten the whole blame on Spain unpleasantly resembles hypocritical cant." Yet Buchanan's narrative was powerful, at least until 1860, when the Republicans secured the presidency. Until that point, the Democratic view of Cuba, and the slave trade, held sway in the federal government and with a majority in Congress.[31]

The final result of pinning the blame on Spain was the not the acquisition of Cuba, which Spain continued to resist with British aid, but the effect it had on the slave trade itself. The ideology of blaming Spain encouraged Americans to downplay the role of the United States and sucked energy from efforts to suppress it. The *New Hampshire Patriot and State Gazette* made the case in 1858: "There is no use in keeping British and American cruisers on the African coast as long as faithless Spain keeps up a slave mart in the lovely Cuban isle." It was partly using this rationale that the Committee on Foreign Relations in the U.S. Senate proposed a bill in 1854 to openly break the Webster-Ashburton Treaty and withdraw American cruisers. The Senate did not pass the bill, but it settled for, effectively, undersupplying the fleet throughout the 1850s. Meanwhile, the few congressional efforts aimed at ending the U.S. trade, such as a bill introduced in the Senate by William Seward in 1859, were roundly defeated. Although not without flaws, Seward's bill would have introduced equipment restrictions aboard U.S. vessels, expanded the powers of police in U.S. ports, and beefed up the Africa Squadron. Certainly, merchants in cities such as New York had a part to play in opposing these restrictions, as Seward later acknowledged, but it was the Spain-blaming mantra, based on the undying pursuit of Cuba, that provided the underlying resistance to American suppression efforts during the 1850s. It was only when Republicans such as Seward ascended to power in the late 1850s that the abolition of U.S. involvement in the slave trade would become a priority.[32]

RISING TENSIONS

Like their Democratic opponents, the Republican Party approached the slave trade in the context of slavery in the United States and, more particularly, in the context of slavery expansion. The party was established in 1854 largely from the rump of the Whig Party, which had been a major national force in U.S. politics for a generation. Although many Whigs held reservations about slavery as a whole, they had been wary of inflaming disputes over the issue, which were increasingly breaking down along sectional lines. Their caution had alienated antislavery radicals, including Frederick Douglass and William Lloyd Garrison, who called for the immediate abolition of slavery throughout the United States, but it had kept the party together in a loose national coalition. By midcentury, however, the Whigs were struggling to maintain unity in the face of successive national crises over slavery, including the annexation of Texas, agitation over Cuba, and the Fugitive Slave Law, which forced northerners to return escaped slaves to the South. By the time the Kansas-Nebraska Act passed in 1854, repealing the Missouri Compromise's 1820 ban on slavery in Kansas, the party had come to the brink of collapse.[33]

Although the Kansas-Nebraska defeat proved to be the last straw for the Whigs, it was the genesis of the Republican Party, which emerged from "anti-Nebraska" meetings held throughout much of the Great Lakes region in 1854. Composed of many former Whigs and smaller remnants of the Free Soil and Know-Nothing Parties, the Republicans steadfastly opposed the extension of slavery in the United States. Founded chiefly on a commitment to free labor, and receiving its greatest support in the North and upper West, especially in rural communities and small towns, the Republicans were determined to keep slavery out of the territories. One of the leading Republican figures, Abraham Lincoln, set the tone for the party at a speech at Peoria, Illinois, in October 1854. Responding to the Kansas-Nebraska Act, Lincoln walked listeners through a litany of slavery extensions since the Louisiana Purchase before declaring: "We know the opening of new countries to slavery, tends to the perpetuation of the institution, and so does keep men in slavery who otherwise would be free. This result we do not feel like favoring, and we are under no legal obligation to suppress our feelings in this respect." As Lincoln made clear, the Republicans were no friend of slavery and would resist its extension. This strategy was different from that of Douglass and Garrison, who sought the immediate abolition of slavery, but the Republicans argued that the constriction of slavery would eventually lead to the same end.[34]

To explain the successes of slavery expansionism over previous years, the Republicans drew generously on the concept of the "Slave Power." This theory, first developed by the antislavery movement in the 1830s, argued that pro-slavery forces had taken over the federal government, were reinterpreting the Constitution as a pro-slavery document, and were determined to expand slavery at the expense of free labor. This interpretation gained currency during the 1840s, and by the time of the passage of the Kansas-Nebraska Act, the Slave Power was being commonly invoked in Republican as well as abolitionist speeches. Senator William Seward pumped the bellows in the buildup to the presidential election of 1856, which returned another Democrat, Buchanan, to the White House. In a speech titled "The Overthrow of the Constitution—Dangers from the Slave Power," Seward argued that the Slave Power had hijacked the nation's founding document in the interests of slavery. After listing the various extensions of slavery into the territories, he suggested that Cuba would be next. The following year, the Supreme Court's *Dred Scott* decision, which among other things ruled that the federal government had no right to prohibit slavery in the territories, seemed to imply that the Slave Power had even infiltrated the highest court of the land. These developments led George Templeton Strong to conclude: "Our federal government exists chiefly for the sake of nigger-owners."[35]

Both Seward's Republican Party and the antislavery radicals interpreted U.S. involvement in the slave trade through the lens of the Slave Power and slavery expansion. Their arguments began with an acknowledgement that although Spain was in many ways culpable, the United States also deserved a large portion of the blame for the slave trade. To that end,

Republican papers, particularly in New York, emphasized American connections to the latest slavers landing in Cuba, as well as offering fascinating exposés of the slave trade in U.S. ports. They also covered court proceedings against indicted slave traders in detail. For these papers, there was no minimizing the U.S. role in the trade. As the Republican *New-York Times* reminded its readers in 1856 (even before the main rash of U.S. slave trading began), "We have over and over again called public attention to the fact that the Slave-Trade, in spite of all the laws against it, is actively and constantly carried on from the ports of New York and Baltimore. No one familiar with the details of the shipping business in this City is ignorant of it. The recent revelations in our Courts of law place it beyond controversy." The following year, the *Barre* (Massachusetts) *Gazette*, announcing the arrival of two more American slavers in Cuba, explained, "Though we have pronounced slavery piracy, we are in fact the most successful slave-dealers, not even excepting the Cubans."[36]

According to these papers, the federal government, under the guidance of the Slave Power and Democratic Party, had simply abandoned the slave trade laws. The New York *Evening Post*, which kept a close eye on the trade and published Emilio Sanchez's exposés, repeatedly attacked Buchanan's administration. Arguing that the United States was more to blame for the slave trade than Spain, the *Post* posited, "But for the connivance of the federal government, it is almost certain that the African slave trade would have been entirely stopped years ago." According to the *Times*, the message filtered down through the ranks to local functionaries. Although the "traffic [is] condemned alike by our laws and by the public sentiment of the civilized world" it noted, "nothing is done by the officers of Government to enforce the law or vindicate the honor and dignity of the country." Bolstering the case, Marshal Isaiah Rynders, the head enforcement officer in New York, was not only widely reported to be a Democrat; he was an outspoken proponent of expanding American slavery into Cuba and central America.[37]

Democratic organs, especially in the South, but some also in the North, vigorously rejected these critiques. Sticking to a familiar line, an editorial in the *New York Herald* argued that although the trade was certainly active in U.S. ports, the "one thing" that was "certain" was that suppression could only be achieved by the annexation of Cuba. Democratic papers also attempted to make political capital out of slave trade involvement in the North, the supposed home of abolition. In an 1854 article titled "Slavers in New York," the New Orleans *Times-Picayune* noted that "in the midst of the public clamor there against the slaveholding South, as criminal enslavers of the black man, the slave trade is carried on to a great extent now, from the ports of the North." Until they were prepared to deal with the traffic "under their own eyes," the *Times-Picayune* argued, northerners should "cease to come abroad in order to find means for easing their consciences." The *Herald* agreed: "The country resounds with philippics and tirades against the South from Northern orators, and a Northern press, for one negro who may have been whipped to death at the hands of a brutal taskmaster, [but] we have nothing to say against the heartless and fiendish men by whom this traffic is carried on, and who live in our very midst upon their ill-gotten gains." These arguments were both a defense of weak Democratic suppression efforts and an attack on the Democrats' anti-slavery foes.[38]

Although Republicans could hardly deny that the trade was taking place mainly from northern ports, they countered that its emergence merely demonstrated the pervasive influence of the Slave Power. Republicans, who drew most of their support outside big cities, had long been skeptical of the sympathies that northern cities such as New York held for slavery and the South. In 1858, at the peak of slave trading in U.S. ports, the abolitionist Unitarian preacher Theodore Parker declared that the "four great commercial cities of the North"—New York, Cincinnati, Philadelphia, and Boston—voted as the "slave power" ordered them. "The Southernization of the North" as Parker termed it, apparently extended to the slave trade. One Republican newspaper underlined the point, using recent stories about the slave trade in New York to remind its readers that the city now belonged "as much to the South as to the North." The *Barre Gazette* took up the theme, suggesting the lack of slave trade enforcement was "chargeable to the southern proclivities of our judicial tribunals and executive officers." Anti-slavery observers were also appalled that the influence of slavery interests seemed to extend even to religious denominations, which by midcentury were splintering over the slavery issue. In 1859, the New York Diocesan Convention of the Episcopal Church rejected a resolution denouncing the slave trade at its general meeting, despite a passionate speech from John Jay, one of the delegates. The *London Christian Observer* in England reflected: "Even the Episcopal Church then, it appears, is quite prepared not merely to justify men stealers, but to add the weight of its authority to their hideous cause."[39]

For Republicans, the Democratic Party, under the direction of the Slave Power, was not only allowing the slave trade to flourish in the North, it was also using the issue to satisfy its ultimate goal of expanding slavery south and west. In Republican eyes, by blaming Spain for the trade, Democrats were brazenly using the traffic as an argument for taking Cuba into the Union. If they were successful in annexing the island, they would surely have to close the slave trade to its shores and replace it with the domestic slave trade from the United States. In other words, the slave trade from Africa to Cuba would merely be supplanted by a slave trade from Virginia to Cuba. A more radical interpretation was that after securing Cuba, a Democratic administration would continue to permit imports of slaves from Africa to Cuba to offset the steady erosion of slavery in the upper South through the domestic trade. "In this way," the *Hartford Republican* argued, "the planters mean to avail themselves of the African slave trade, to strengthen and spread their 'institution.'" This same premise could be applied to populating the West with slaves. With the retention of the trade to Cuba rendering the slave trade laws effectively repealed, southerners could reopen the traffic to their shores as well.[40]

Events in the South during the 1850s seemed to suggest that repealing the slave trade laws was not merely mischievous speculation. In 1853, South Carolinian Leonidas Spratt purchased a Charleston newspaper named the *Standard* in order to advocate for reopening the slave trade. Spratt quickly became what Horace Greeley, the editor of the antislavery *New York Tribune*, dubbed the "philosopher" of the reopening movement. Drawing on a common pro-slavery refrain, Spratt argued that slavery needed to expand in order to survive. His twist was that the Deep South should take its slaves not from the upper South but from the "teeming thousands from the plains of Africa." To Spratt and other "reopeners" the argument held a number of benefits: for slavery itself, which could now expand freely westward without sacrificing support in the upper South through slave depopulation; for whites, who could access slaves at low prices and broaden the base of slaveholders; and even for Africans, who would now enjoy the "blessing" of American slavery. Drawing on prevailing criticism of "northern" traffickers, Spratt argued that there could be a place in this traffic for Yankee slave traders, who, he claimed, would "bring [enslaved Africans] to us . . . as fast as we will be ready to receive them."[41]

Spratt's ideas were widely discussed in the South, but they attracted limited support. True, the reopening movement gained the favor of a few influential radical newspapers, including the *Charleston Mercury* and the *New Orleans Bee*, and some policymakers, such as Governor James H. Adams of South Carolina, backed the idea. The issue also became the major topic of debate at annual regional commercial conventions, with the majority of delegates eventually endorsing the position. And in the Louisiana legislature, the house passed a bill in 1858 to reopen the slave trade, but it was narrowly defeated in the senate. Even so, most southerners, including South Carolina's senator J. J. Pettigrew, opposed reopening, largely because it promised to divide the South, a fear sustained by the cold reception the idea received in Virginia and Maryland. Indeed, for many among the minority of southerners who did make the case for reopening, the ultimate goal was not to reopen the trade itself but to foster secessionism. William Yancey of Alabama, for example, sought to use the issue as a wedge to force a break from the Union. This angle was well understood by many southerners, including Roger

Pryor, editor of the *South* in Richmond, who rejected reopening and demanded of its advocates: "If you intend to dissolve the Union, say so, in manly and explicit language."[42]

Despite its limited traction in the South, the reopening movement had a considerable political impact among antislavery activists and in the North in general. Many commentators argued that reopening was not an idle threat but a genuine plan. The abolitionist *National Era* of Washington, D.C., noted, "From indications in prominent Southern journals, it would seem to be taking on the form of a settled opinion among certain portions of our Southern brethren." Then, borrowing Spratt's language, the *Era* asked, "And why not? If it be right to hold human beings as property, can it be wrong to transfer or exchange them as property? If it be right and decent to ship human beings at Norfolk, send them to New Orleans, and sell them in its public market, can it be wrong and indecent to ship them from Dahomey, and sell them to the planters of Louisiana?" The *Barre Gazette* similarly noted that "it is by no means strange that the friends of the repeal, encouraged by the success of their previous efforts to perpetuate the 'peculiar institution,' should advocate the measure with boldness, and with entire confidence in its ultimate success."[43]

To Republicans, the reopening agitation was not only an appalling violation of settled national policy but a serious, perhaps the most serious, blow to its strategy of containing slavery. Lincoln made the point in his first big slavery speech in 1854, in which he noted that slaveholders' arguments that they ought to be able to carry slaves into new territories in the West could just as easily be used to justify reopening the slave trade from Africa. Similarly, in Seward's "Slave Power" speech of 1856, the New York senator presented the "restoration of the African slave trade" as the culmination of westward expansion and the true aim of the dark forces at work in the federal government. The Boston abolitionist paper the *Liberator* shared this view. Contending that "the Slave Power will consummate its diabolical purposes to the uttermost," it posited, "The Northwest Territory, Nebraska, Mexico, Cuba, Hayti, the Sandwich Islands, and colonial possessions in the tropics—to seize and subjugate these to its accursed reign, and ultimately to reestablish the foreign Slave Trade as a lawful commerce, are among its settled designs." The *Albany Evening Journal* also tied the slave trade to expansion, arguing that to prevent the "slave oligarchy" from reopening it, "we must insist upon freedom for Kansas."[44]

These arguments took on much greater force when some southern radicals turned rhetoric into action. In 1858 the Georgia businessman Charles Lamar bought a yacht named the *Wanderer*. With help from others, but working largely outside the regular U.S. slaving network based in New York, Lamar organized a voyage and sent the vessel to West Central Africa for slaves. The *Wanderer* subsequently received almost five hundred captives at the Congo River, escaped coastal patrols, and landed the survivors on the south Georgia coast, from which they were transported inland and sold. U.S. authorities eventually captured the *Wanderer*, and it was condemned and auctioned, but the Africans were never located. Lamar, who was charged with violating federal law, was acquitted by a Georgia jury. This verdict came soon after the trial of the crew of another slaver, the *Echo*, which had been intercepted by a U.S. patrol off the coast of Cuba, and rerouted to Charleston, South Carolina. In this case, the crew, who were defended by none other than Leonidas Spratt, were also acquitted by a southern jury.[45]

These cases aroused a fierce reaction in the antislavery press. Although landings of enslaved Africans in the United States were isolated incidents (*Wanderer* and *Clotilda* are the only cases), antislavery newspapers were convinced they were just the tip of the iceberg. Rumors abounded that the slave trade laws had effectively been repealed by southern courts and the trade reopened. In 1858 the *National Era* published an article titled "Startling Discourses—African Slave Trade Reopened at the South" that contained details of numerous alleged landings. Meanwhile, in New York, the State Anti-Slavery Convention turned attention away from the slave trade at its door to declare that the slave trade to the South was "virtually now reopened." All that remained, the abolitionists argued, was the formal repeal of federal law. In 1859, the Republican-leaning *Commercial Advertiser* in New York proclaimed that such a move was afoot. "Southern members" of Congress "intend to make the repeal of that law the great issue at the coming Presidential election, and in all election of members of Congress."[46]

The Republicans were just as eager to bring the issues onto the national political stage. Both Lincoln and Seward warned of the likely repeal of the slave trade laws in their famous "house divided" and "irrepressible conflict" speeches in 1858. For both, reopening the trade was the culmination of all the Democratic Party's slavery-extending schemes that imperiled the Union. Seward and his allies also piled the pressure on Buchanan in Congress. In January 1859, Seward proposed a bill to amend the Act of 1819. Among the new bill's many provisions were the allocation of more cruisers for the African coast, larger bounties for the Africa Squadron and U.S.-based servicemen as well as civilian informants, a requirement that ships clearing American ports for the African coast be searched before departing, and the prohibition of U.S. vessels sailing from foreign ports to Africa. According to Seward, one million dollars would be required to enforce this act. The Democratic-controlled Senate rejected the bill.[47]

By the end of the 1850s, the slave trade issue had reached a crescendo. The traffic from U.S. ports, mainly in the North, had peaked, helping to deliver record levels of African captives to Cuban shores. New York, especially, had cemented its position as one of the chief slave trading cities in the world. The involvement of these ports was well known and passionately condemned by Democrats and Republicans alike. Radical southerners not only assailed federal slave trade laws; some openly defied them. Although most Democrats, North and South, distanced themselves from such schemes, Republicans argued that the reopening movement reflected the prevailing view in the South: the trade had effectively reopened already, and this state of affairs would soon be sanctioned by law. The slave trade issue was replete with meaning for both sides of the slavery debate and both sides of the sectional divide.

FEDERAL EFFORTS TO SUPPRESS THE SLAVE TRADE, 1859–1863

Facing increasing criticism from Republicans and with a view to the forthcoming presidential election in 1860, Buchanan revamped American suppression efforts in the late 1850s. He began modestly by distancing himself from pro-slavery extremists. In the fall of 1858, he secured a congressional appropriation to send the *Echo* Africans, who had been intercepted by an American cruiser in the Gulf of Mexico, to Liberia, despite objections from several Democrats, who baulked at the cost, and cries from pro-slavery radicals who argued that they should be retained in the South and re-enslaved. Buchanan vigorously defended his position a few months later in his State of the Union address. The next year, he went a step farther, using his annual address to openly denounce the reopening movement. Although he maintained that Cuba was ultimately responsible for the trade, he also declared his support for existing slave trade laws in the United States and reminded Congress that "the fathers of the Republic, in advance of all other nations, condemned the African slave trade." Positioning himself as a moderate and couching his argument in the paternalistic language familiar to defenders of slavery, he argued that reopening the trade would disturb the "sober, orderly, and quiet slaves" of the South, who would be exposed to the "wild, heathen, and ignorant barbarians" of Africa. To that end, Buchanan assured Congress, "All lawful means at my command have been employed, and shall continue to be employed, to execute the laws against the African slave trade."[48]

This statement embellished Buchanan's record on suppression, but his administration had indeed begun taking genuine measures to curtail the trade. One small initial step was to send a secret agent, Benjamin F. Slocumb, into the South in 1859 to report the rumors of illicit slave disembarkations. During his two-month trip, Slocumb traveled from North Carolina to Texas, gathering intelligence on illicit landings from officials, newspaper editors, and local slave dealers. Finding little evidence to support the rumors, he argued with some accuracy that they were "wholly founded upon the movements of the Wanderer negroes, or else they were mere fabrications, manufactured and circulated for political effect, or to fill a column in a sensation newspaper." Meanwhile, Buchanan's administration was taking serious steps to curb the genuine U.S. involvement in the slave trade to Cuba. In the summer of 1859, Secretary of the Navy Isaac Toucey doubled the size of the Africa Squadron, from four to eight vessels. All four additions were the oft-requested steamers. Toucey also moved the squadron's base from the Cape Verde Islands to Luanda. Finally joining the British and Portuguese, the American fleet was now positioned a few hundred, rather than a few thousand, miles from the epicenter of the trade on the African coast. In the Americas, Toucey bolstered the Home Squadron from five to thirteen vessels, including four steamers, which he dispatched to the Gulf of Mexico. No longer largely absent or lonely "scarecrows," the U.S. Navy suddenly became a much more effective force. Between 1859 and 1860, American cruisers captured twenty slavers, more than double the haul from 1851 to 1858. These slavers had been carrying around five thousand captives, whom the Buchanan administration now sent to Liberia, following the precedent laid down in the *Echo* case, although many perished en route.[49]

Although Buchanan's assault on the slave trade was a new departure in American suppression measures, it was still inadequate. Naval suppression actions had never been so successful, but 1859 and 1860 also marked the highest U.S. participation in the slave trade. In 1859, more slavers were fitted out in U.S. ports than ever before, helping deliver more Africans to Cuban shores than any other year in the island's history with the exception of 1817. Meanwhile, American consuls in Cuba continued to rubberstamp the sale of slavers before they sailed for the African coast. At sea, the majority of slavers dodged American cruisers, in part because the navy saw its priority as protecting American commerce rather than tackling the slave trade. The much larger British fleet was still denied the right to detain and search American slavers. It was true that the slave trade to the South was defunct, bar the landing of 150 Africans from the slaver *Clotilda* in Alabama in 1860, but this success had less to do with Buchanan's suppression measures than with the lack of appetite for reopening the trade in the South.[50]

As the ineffectiveness of the Democrats' assault on the trade became apparent, Republicans stepped up their attacks. The *New-York Times* suggested that the new approach was mere "tricks and schemes of the Buchananite Cabinet," and noted that the measures did little to tackle the trade at home. In particular, they failed to lower the burden of proof for prosecutors, which the *Times* saw as a critical impediment to securing convictions. In March 1860, Senator Henry Wilson attempted to push beyond Buchanan's measures by introducing a bill that among other provisions provided for the construction of five steamships for the African coast and authorized the president to open negotiations with foreign powers with a view toward permitting the right of search within two hundred miles of the African coast. The latter provision was a stark departure from traditional American policy, but as Wilson's colleague Seward told the Senate: "We are a powerful nation, and it is simply a point of duty to apply our power to bring this evil to an end." Underlining its commitment to suppression (and the Democrats' lack thereof), the Republican Party adopted the following platform for the 1860 presidential campaign: "We brand the recent reopening of the African slave trade, under the cover of our national flag, aided by perversions of judicial power, as a crime against humanity, and a burning shame to our country and age, and we call upon Congress to take prompt and efficient measures for the total and final suppression of that execrable traffic."[51]

Lincoln's subsequent victory in the presidential election of November 1860 would have important consequences for the slave trade, but its immediate impact was to raise national tensions over slavery to crisis levels. For the first time, a president was promising an end to the expansion of slavery in the United States, a policy that many southerners would not tolerate. Lincoln hardly shied away from the issue. During his Inaugural Address in Washington he declared: "One section of our country believes slavery is right, and ought to be extended, while the other believes it is wrong, and ought not to be extended." The new president argued that seceding states in the South would reopen the slave trade, while the North would refuse to return escaped slaves as required by the Fugitive Slave Act. He hoped to avoid war, he said, but he reminded the South that it did not have the right to break up the Union.[52]

Shortly before Lincoln painted this stark picture, others had desperately tried to prevent secession. In December 1860, John Crittenden, a senator from Kentucky, attempted to forge a compromise in Congress. His rescue plan included six amendments to the Constitution and four congressional resolutions. All concerned slavery in various ways. Perhaps sensing that suppression now had mainstream support on both sides of the aisle, Crittenden proposed in one resolution that the slave trade laws "ought to be made effectual, and ought to be thoroughly executed; and all further enactments necessary to those ends ought to be promptly made." Yet there was not enough common ground and the Senate rejected Crittenden's plan. All other attempts to stave off secession also failed, and in December 1860, South Carolina became the first state to secede from the Union. Ten others would follow, forming the Confederate States of America under the presidency of Jefferson Davis, with Montgomery, Alabama, as their temporary capital. In April 1861, the Confederate army fired shots at Union troops lodged in Fort Sumter in Charleston Harbor, not far from where the *Echo* Africans been held a few years before. The Civil War had begun.[53]

The outbreak of war created a new context that encouraged both the Union and the Confederacy to take action against the slave trade. Although many leading figures in the secession movement had urged reopening the trade to the South, the Confederacy rejected the traffic outright. Early in 1861, the newly created Confederate Constitution expressly outlawed the "importation of negroes of the African race from any foreign country other than the slaveholding States or Territories of the United States of America." As many southerners had previously pointed out, the issue divided the region's white inhabitants, and now that the Confederacy was at war, internal unity was especially critical. The Confederacy was also seeking to assure the British of its motives at a time when it sought Britain's support against the Union or, at the least, diplomatic recognition. In any case, with the Confederacy at war and Union warships gradually blockading southern ports, the chances of reviving the slave trade were slim. The British did discuss internally how they might deal with Confederate vessels if they showed up on the African coast, but none did.[54]

By contrast, some early signals from the Union did not appear to back up Republican rhetoric of previous years. As the Confederates were creating their Constitution in the spring of 1861, Lincoln was debating the withdrawal of U.S. cruisers from the African coast. Sensing that his priorities lay at home, Lincoln discussed the matter with his secretary of the navy, Gideon Welles, who assured the president that the vessels were "well adapted for service on our own coast." Lincoln subsequently instructed Welles to recall the entire Africa Squadron with the exception of one vessel, which was to remain for six months. The news was well received by American seamen on the African coast, where according to Willie Leonard, a sailor aboard the USS *Constellation*, there was "nothing talked of now, but the North, and the South, War to the death, Abolitionism, and Secession." After they returned to U.S. waters, these men would end up fighting on both sides of the conflict, while the cruisers were redeployed against the Confederacy. Although this shift of resources came under special circumstances, it was a radical step in American slave trade policy; this was the first time since a few years in the 1830s that the United States had not had even a nominal presence on the African coast to fight the traffic. The British, especially, harbored concerns about the impact of the president's decision, and even considered removing some of their own cruisers from the Mediterranean to West Africa to make up for the shortfall.[55]

Yet other steps taken by Lincoln's administration proved he was serious about suppression. The withdrawal of the cruisers notwithstanding, in spring 1861 Lincoln sent early signals that slave trade suppression was a priority. First he reorganized the Department of the Interior to create the Office for the Suppression of the African Slave Trade, similar to the British Foreign Office's Slave Trade Department, albeit with a domestic remit. Second, Lincoln charged his new secretary of the interior, Caleb Smith, with administering a new ten-thousand-dollar "secret fund" to suppress the slave trade in U.S. ports. The money, which was small but not inconsiderable given the imminent threat of war, was spent by the federal government's new district attorneys and marshals. These appointees had been carefully selected and proved to be committed to suppression. During the next few years, officials in every slaving port still within the United States, from Maine to Maryland, used the new secret funds; the largest sums were deployed in the traffic's major hub, New York.[56]

Robert Murray, the new chief marshal in New York, was particularly committed to suppression and judicious in his use of the extra funds. In contrast to his predecessors, Murray was determined to pursue "those iniquitous dealers in human flesh night and day." Murray also had intimate knowledge of the New York port. As a former harbormaster, he was familiar with the waterfront and its merchants, ships, and sailors. Upon his appointment, he launched a vigorous campaign against the trade. Operating much as the British did, he initiated a major surveillance campaign on slave traders, often co-opting local watermen, such as tugboat captains, into his operations (although apparently not Sanchez, who was still working for the Foreign Office). Between the spring of 1861 and the spring of 1862, Murray spent several thousand dollars on "watchers," including four men who kept an eye on the docks in New York and Brooklyn on a regular basis. He also sent deputies laden with cash to Portland and Baltimore to procure evidence for trials. In perhaps his clearest message to local traffickers, in the summer of 1861 he hosted a meeting of marshals from several Union states in New York to discuss suppression tactics. During their visit, Murray led the marshals around the docks and took them to visit imprisoned slave traders in the Tombs. Rattled by Murray's approach, the slave traders attempted to gain his favor, but apparently he was above reproach. In early 1862 he told the Department of the Interior that "barely two months ago, the Slave dealers held a meeting, and, unanimously decided to abandon the idea of influencing me." Meanwhile, Murray's efforts were met by high praise in the Republican press, as well as the London *Times*, which said he had done more to suppress the slave trade than both the U.S. and British fleets had done during the previous ten years.[57]

The energetic work of officials such as Murray and the new tone emanating from Washington set the stage for several important trials. None had a greater impact than that of the American slave ship captain Nathaniel Gordon. A seasoned trafficker, Gordon had been involved in the trade to Brazil in the 1840s and completed at least three voyages since 1850. In the summer of 1860, during the later days of Buchanan's administration, the U.S. Navy had arrested him aboard the *Erie* while it was leaving the Congo River. The *Erie*, which had sailed from the United States to Cuba and then to Africa, was captured with almost nine hundred captives aboard. After the interception, the Africa Squadron sent the Africans to Liberia and returned the *Erie* and Gordon to the United States for adjudication and trial. Having been caught with slaves aboard, the *Erie* was condemned and sold. Meanwhile, in July 1861, Gordon went on trial under the Act of 1820 in New York.[58]

Delafield Smith, a Republican Party member and the new

district attorney in the Southern District of New York, worked diligently and prudently to secure a conviction. Appreciating the high evidentiary threshold expected in these cases, he sent informants to Massachusetts to determine the ownership of the vessel, and to Maine, Gordon's home state, for testimony on his citizenship. Smith's efforts proved to be insufficient on the first attempt, for there was a hung jury. Yet Smith was convinced that he had "carried a majority" of the jury and redoubled his efforts. Casting the net wider, he gathered new information from Havana and tracked down several key witnesses to testify in court. Smith then initiated a second trial, which began in the fall of 1861. Understanding that some among the jury might be wary of convicting Gordon of a capital crime, he proceeded cautiously. As he later wrote to the Department of the Interior, he laid out his argument clearly, but dispensed with a second counsel to prevent the "idea of persecution" to the jury. He also tiptoed around the broader issue of slavery, which had many friends in New York City, by laboring "to separate the case from all questions as to slavery or slavery extension in this country." The defense countered in familiar terms—claiming that Gordon was not a U.S. citizen—but this time the argument failed to work. After just thirty minutes of deliberations the jury delivered a guilty verdict.[59]

Although the jury's decision was the first conviction under the Act of 1820 since 1854 and a great victory for the suppressionist cause, it remained to be seen what would happen next. Delafield Smith underscored the surprise of many Americans, noting that after the trial, "Persons crowded into my office, the following morning, and asked if it was really so." The Republican press cheered the news, which the *New-York Times* labeled another chapter in the "Dying Struggles of the

Slave Trade," but it was unclear whether Lincoln would grant Gordon a presidential pardon or allow the sentence to be carried out. The few prisoners who had previously been convicted under the act, including James Smith in 1854, had escaped with a few years in prison or been pardoned outright.[60]

Gordon's fate now became a matter of intense debate. Newspapers offered varying opinions on whether Lincoln would stay the execution or not; the Democratic press maintained that the punishment was harsh, and Lincoln would be merciful. Lincoln was inundated with advice. Rhoda White, the wife of a New York judge, wrote to the president arguing that Gordon had merely been involved in the slave trade "when many then in power upheld it, and engaged in it," and that the sentence really ought to be commuted to life in prison. Eleven thousand petitioners from New York, including lawyers, clergy, and state lawmakers, agreed that the punishment was too harsh. Meanwhile, Delafield Smith published a newspaper article, which soon reached Lincoln's hands, arguing for execution. Behind the scenes, Lincoln met with his new secretary of state, Seward, to discuss the matter and took advice from Attorney General Edward Bates. In the end, he decided to allow the execution. After a short reprieve, Gordon was hanged.[61]

A few months after Gordon's execution the United States entered into an international treaty that was unprecedented in American history. In 1861, Seward intimated to Britain's minister in Washington, Lord Lyons, that the United States would be prepared to be more flexible on right of search than previous administrations. Seward was following up on his arguments in the Senate the previous year, but his suggestion was also guided by realpolitik. Like the Confederacy, the United States was seeking British support for the war, an aim that had been jeopardized by the Trent Affair in 1861, in which a Union warship had arraigned a British vessel carrying two Confederate diplomats en route to London. Meanwhile, Prime Minister Palmerston sought to press home the advantage. In September 1861, he suggested to his foreign minister, John Russell, that the "north" should "prove their abhorrence of slavery, by joining and helping us heartily in our operations against slave trade, by giving us facilities for putting it down when carried under United States flag." The subsequent negotiations between Lyons and Seward were the polar opposite of the caustic exchanges that characterized Anglo-U.S. diplomacy during the Buchanan era. Buchanan's secretary of state, Lewis Cass, had been hostile to the British and bitterly opposed to right of search, whereas Seward was remarkably upbeat. Lyons wrote to Russell that Seward had told him that "a very great change . . . had taken place in public opinion concerning the Slave Trade" and that Lincoln and his cabinet were "warmly in favor" of a treaty. When Lyons queried what he would make of British cruisers bringing a captured American slaver into New York Harbor, Lyons reported that Seward said he would "see it with pleasure."[62]

Although Seward presented too rosy a picture of American attitudes toward the British navy, with some careful maneuvering he was able to guide a right of search agreement through the Senate. To clear the path, Seward requested that both nations publicly agree that it had been the United States that had first proposed a treaty, even though Britain had drawn up the initial draft. The reason, Lyons explained to the Foreign Office, was not that Congress was opposed to suppression but that there were "many who retained the old jealousy of Great Britain on the subject of the Right of Search." Presenting the accord as an American idea would, apparently, sweeten the pill. The ruse worked, and in April 1862 the Senate unanimously ratified the Lyons-Seward Treaty. Under its provisions, Britain was permitted to search American vessels within two hundred miles of the African coast and thirty leagues of Cuba, while the United States would be responsible for enforcing the treaty at home. The equipment clause, a long-absent feature of American slave trade law, was a central component of the treaty, with the essential items, including shackles, boilers, and cooking apparatus, all accounted for. Marking another radical departure, the United States joined the Court of Mixed Commission system. The United States even committed to establish a Mixed Commission Court in New York that would adjudicate vessels captured near Cuba. Reflecting on this great change in American policy, Seward wrote to Lincoln that the treaty would be "the most important act of your life and of mine." Two years later, in 1864, Lincoln's administration would cap its suppression efforts by extraditing José Agustín Argüelles, a Spanish official caught up in the slave trade, to Cuba, finally closing a legal loophole that had protected foreign traffickers for over a decade.[63]

The suppression measures introduced by the federal government up to the spring of 1862 had a decisive effect on U.S. participation in the illegal slave trade. In the wake of Gordon's execution and the vigorous efforts of U.S. officials, traffickers in New York and elsewhere reconsidered their options. District attorneys were busy pursuing indictments of outfitters and intermediaries in several U.S. ports, including Albert Horn in New York and Appleton Oaksmith in Boston. Some of these individuals avoided serious punishment, including

Oaksmith, who escaped custody, but these occurrences were now exceptional. Gordon's execution, especially, had a profound effect on slave traders. In the buildup to the execution, Consul Archibald in New York reported that the slave traders "are so alarmed that it is surmised that those who are under bonds will prefer forfeiting their bail rather than stand their trials." Among those taking action was João Machado, one of the most important intermediaries since the early 1850s, who was twice arrested and eventually skipped bail and fled, probably to Havana. Other prominent figures, including Abranches, Almeida, Antonio Ros, and José Lima Vianna, also left the United States for good.[64]

Some of these traffickers attempted to reinvigorate the trade elsewhere. One of these was Mary Watson, among the few American women mentioned in British and U.S. slave trade records. Watson was allegedly Machado's business partner and lover, and she appears to have taken on an expanded role in the slave trade toward its end. Under pressure in New York, she fled to Portugal and then to Spain, where she attempted to resume operations, perhaps hoping to link up with Machado in Cuba. Robert Murray was aware of her departure and sent his operatives in pursuit. Working with the U.S. consul in Cádiz and the U.S. minister in Madrid, Murray's team prevented Watson from dispatching four vessels to the African coast. Having now been shut down in the New York and Spain, and with the Lyons-Seward Treaty eradicating the utility of the American flag, Watson was out of options. Reports emerged from Spain that she had sought "solace in the cup" and died as a result. The news was well received by Murray back in New York. By then, the slave traders had all fled his jurisdiction or melted back into other pursuits, although he had three indictments waiting for Watson in case she returned.[65]

American involvement in the trade declined precipitously under Lincoln's presidency, especially as his new agents got to work in New York and other ports. After Gordon's execution and the ratification of the Lyons-Seward Treaty, U.S. participation in the trade finally petered out. In March 1863, the *Marquita* was captured by the British off the Congo River flying a Spanish flag and was condemned at Saint Helena. This vessel, which had departed New York the previous winter, was the last slave ship to set sail from American shores. A decade of slaving in Manhattan was over.[66]

In the summer of 1862, Gabriel Tassara, the Spanish minister in Washington, D.C., wrote to his superiors in Madrid about the great changes that were taking place in relation to the slave trade in the United States. In contrast to missives during previous years, in which he reported streams of slavers leaving U.S. ports, Tassara's latest message concerned the recently ratified Lyons-Seward Treaty, which promised to put an end to these departures. After leading his superiors through the main features of the accord, a copy of which he enclosed, Tassara determined that the right of search concession was a "great innovation" and that the treaty as a whole would probably increase pressure on Spain to ramp up its own suppression campaign. In an attempt to account for the important developments in the United States, Tassara noted the change of government in Washington. In his view: "It is more than likely that had the Democratic Party continued in power this treaty would never have been celebrated. The Republican Party on the contrary doesn't do more than obey its principle when celebrating it."[67]

Tassara's analysis captured the essence of the situation. The suppression measures that had culminated in the Lyons-Seward Treaty were indeed great innovations and were largely down to the change in administration. Throughout the 1850s, successive Democratic administrations had refused to grant Britain the right of search and generally failed to prioritize slave trade suppression at home or abroad. Although their approach was partly to do with long-standing opposition to British interference with American shipping, it was largely because Democrats had blamed Spain for the trade in order to bolster the case for acquiring Cuba and spreading American slavery. The Republican Party, by contrast, was committed to checking slavery in all its forms. For the Republicans, obeying their principles meant not only limiting the expansion of slavery to the places where it already existed but extinguishing the slave trade, which was threatening to drive the institution into new territories. Their work began during the mid-1850s and helped force Buchanan to take some suppression measures in 1859. With their ascent to power in 1860 and secession sweeping much Democratic opposition aside, Lincoln's administration was able to move decisively against U.S. participation in the traffic.

Atlantic Reverberations

ESPITE the twin losses of New York as a slave trading haven and the valuable protection of the U.S. flag, the traffic continued for another five years on a diminishing scale. During this period, Spain took a more prominent role in the logistics of the trade. Cádiz became an especially important embarkation point for slavers. In 1862, New York exiles Antonio Augusto Botelho and José Lima Vianna were key players in dispatching slavers from this port, although they were gradually supplanted by local merchants and shipowners such as Manuel Lloret. In 1864, the British consul in Cádiz, Alexander Dunlop, reported that Lloret and his allies had made the port "the European center of the trade." If Cádiz led the way, Barcelona and Bilbao were not far behind. Bilbao was particularly favored by the Basque native Julián Zulueta in Cuba. In 1863, one of Zulueta's vessels, the *Luiza*, sailed from Bilbao to the

Slave Steamer *Cicerón*
(FO84/1218, f. 320, The National Archives, London)

Bight of Benin for slaves. In a letter intercepted by the British, João Soares Pereira, a Portuguese trafficker on the African coast, informed Zulueta that a cargo of "oil" would be waiting for the *Luiza* when it arrived. The metaphor hardly needed careful deciphering.[1]

Zulueta was behind several voyages conducted under steam during this period. Traffickers in the North and South Atlantic had used steamships during the previous two decades, but very rarely. Sail had always been the mainstay. Now steamers took an increasing role in a dwindling trade—used in at least six voyages starting in 1862. These vessels, such as the *Noc Daqui* and *Cicerón*, were large and fast, and they were usually built in Europe and departed from Spain. They often carried over a thousand captives and made multiple voyages. The slave traders' use of these vessels shows not only how they capitalized on new industrial technologies but also how they changed to a new strategy involving fewer voyages using faster vessels as the winds of suppression grew stronger.[2]

As Spanish ports took on a greater role in dispatching vessels, their residents increased their financial stake in voyages. Although investors in Cádiz, Barcelona, and Bilbao had always had opportunities to finance illegal slaving voyages through their ties with Cuban traffickers and occasional departures from Spanish ports, the growing importance of Spanish shipping after 1861 created additional chances. Wealthy merchants with close ties to Cuba were best positioned to invest. The Portillo family of Cádiz became some of the most prominent Spanish slave traders in the 1860s, owing partly to a business partner in Havana. Iberian friends of Zulueta also stood to do well. In 1863, a telegram arrived in Bilbao from Cuba announcing the safe arrival of Zulueta's *Noc Daqui*. Zulueta had surely sent it to reassure nervous investors at home.[3]

As ties between slave traders based in Cuba and Spain became more important and the influence of the United States faded, the position of investors in West Central Africa also weakened. Now left to deal with the Cubans without their allies in New York, the most favorable arrangement they could forge was a normal "freighting" investment, coupled with a prayer that the Cubans would fairly remit the spoils. The 1863 voyages of the *Cicerón* and the *Haydee* are two examples of this approach, although in the latter case the British intercepted the vessel and no one made money. According to Joseph Crawford, the British consul in Havana, some investors in West Central Africa were prepared to make even less favorable arrangements. In 1862 he informed the Foreign Office that "desperate" West Central African traffickers had appeared on the island "offering slaves deliverable at certain points, so very cheap that they are hardly to be resisted." This proposal, which entailed shouldering all the risks at sea as well as offering a heavy discount, was highly unfavorable and reflected the increasingly weak position of West Central African investors as the 1860s wore on.[4]

The changing dynamics of voyage financing became irrelevant, however, as Spanish authorities in Cuba began to take serious action against the trade in the mid-1860s. The origins of this shift were partly external. The Lyons-Seward Treaty had isolated Spain as the final major power still unwilling to take aggressive measures against the traffic. Spanish officials in the Americas were certainly upset that the treaty seemed to imply that Spain was now solely at fault for the trade. Reporting on the treaty to Madrid, Gabriel Tassara complained that it was the "height of brazenness [for the United States] to make us responsible for a sin that at least was common to us." Yet Tassara also appreciated that post-treaty the international spotlight was now focused on Spain. In the same letter, he argued that "in the current state of things we must not allow ourselves to be overtaken by anyone in the repression of the trade." Tassara's instincts appeared to be astute, especially as other powers began increasing pressure on the Spanish government after the treaty was signed. In 1863, Britain sent six cruisers to Cuban waters to patrol for slavers, the largest deployment since 1858, when tensions with Buchanan's administration had forced the British to withdraw from the Gulf of Mexico. The following year, the United States and Britain requested a joint anti–slave trade treaty with Spain. Madrid rejected the proposal, still wary of foreign designs on Cuba, but the fact that even the United States was now asking for a slave trade treaty marked how isolated the Iberian power had become.[5]

As external pressures mounted, a series of reformist captains general in Cuba vigorously attempted to suppress the traffic. Each of these governors—Francisco Serrano, Domingo Dulce, and Francisco Lersundi—was more committed to suppression than were many of their predecessors. Serrano requested Madrid to declare the slave trade piracy, although his superiors rejected the proposal, fearing that such a move might anger Cuban planters. Dulce, his successor, departed from protocol by expelling two Cuban traffickers, Francisco Durañona and Antonio Tuero. Dulce also ejected several recently arrived Portuguese, at least some of whom were exiles from New York. More broadly, these governors sought to convince Madrid that the trade's days were numbered and that the future security of slavery on the island would not be imperiled by suppressing the traffic. In the summer of 1861, only a few months after the U.S. Civil War broke out, Serrano wrote to Madrid insisting that "the indisputable principle is laid, that the trade is going to decline in the world and that sooner or later it will have to be extinguished. It would be insanity for slavery in Cuba, an institution almost indispensable today for the development and maintenance of its prosperity, to depend upon it." Indeed, Serrano argued that given the international assault on the trade, continuing the traffic could endanger Cuban slavery itself. "The only means of keeping the one is to finish with the other," he explained to his superiors. Putting a more positive spin on the situation, he also argued that Cuba could become like United States, Brazil, and Puerto Rico, in which slavery had grown in strength even after slave importations had ceased.[6]

As Serrano's suggestions implied, full suppression of the trade to Cuba could come only with support from the Iberian Peninsula. By the mid-1860s, the conservative approach to suppression that had characterized previous Spanish governments began to change as a wave of liberalism swept Madrid. Colonial reform, including slave trade suppression, was an important element of this movement and was championed by new publications such as *Revista Hispano-Americana*, and by Cuban Creoles, who denounced it at home and in the metropole. Meanwhile, reformers created the Spanish Abolition Society, and former governors Serrano and Dulce, who had now returned to Spain, campaigned for suppression in the upper house of the Cortes. The end of the U.S. Civil War in 1865 and the demise of slavery in the American South multiplied and galvanized the critics. When General O'Donnell's Union Liberal government returned to power the same year, vigorous action against the traffic was all but assured. In 1866, O'Donnell's government introduced a strong new slave trade bill that, among other measures, broadened the definition of trafficking to include direct and indirect support for voyages, increased penalties for offenders, and negated Article 9 of the penal law, which had prevented the Cuban authorities from searching estates for newly arrived slaves. The Spanish Senate passed the bill the following year. It was fully implemented in Cuba by Captain General Joaquín Manzano, who demonstrated his desire to end the traffic by making an additional proclamation in Havana, which contained even sterner regulations and punishments.[7]

The end of U.S. participation in the slave trade, Spain's growing international isolation, and the stronger efforts of the Spanish government to suppress the traffic were reflected in the demise of the trade in the 1860s. In contrast to what happened in Brazil in 1850, when a dramatic death blow almost instantaneously ended a large branch of the trade, the decline of the Cuban traffic was gradual and the result of several wounds that were collectively fatal. In 1861, when Lincoln's administration first began to take action, around twenty-four thousand captives were driven aboard slave ships in Africa. That number was roughly halved every year until 1866. Although it emerged from various sources, government action in the United States, Spain, and Britain gradually took its toll on the traffic. Despite the fact that world sugar and Cuban slave prices remained high, action by these states effectively raised the risk of voyages to the point where traffickers were unwilling to send their ships to sea. According to Manzano, one slaver arrived in Cuba in the summer of 1867, although this voyage is difficult to corroborate. There were no reliable reports of further disembarkations.[8]

The suppression of the slave trade to Cuba signaled that the final phase of the traffic was over. The midcentury trade had always been in some ways fragile. After several generations of sustained assault by a growing cast of opponents, the traffic had few open defenders. The collapse of the Brazilian trade in 1850 had been a particularly significant victory for global antislavery. As the international web of suppression stretched wider, the traffic became confined to three main zones: the United States, West Central Africa, and Cuba. Yet even here it was not totally secure. The United States, Spain, and Portugal made various efforts to suppress it, while the British, having precipitated the closure of the Brazilian trade, drove especially hard to extinguish it altogether. Slave traders and sugar barons in Cuba were well aware that the trade might not last much longer. For this reason, many Cuba-based traffickers, including the infamous Cunha Reis, who had operated on the island since 1858, promoted "free" emigration schemes from Africa in the early 1860s.[9]

Yet the traffic not only survived, it thrived for much of the midcentury period. Planters' demand for slave labor in Cuba was strong, while Spain, wary of their political loyalties and shielded from British pressure by the United States, failed to prosecute the traffic vigorously or consistently. On the other side of the Atlantic, several African societies remained strongly attached to the trade and saw limited demand for alternative exports. The British themselves aided the traffic indirectly by selling slave trading goods on the African coast and by importing vast amounts of Cuban sugar. The British government acknowledged this problem internally, but never resolved it. Meanwhile, slave traders proved remarkably adept at adjusting to the new scenarios. Under increased international pressure, they migrated to locations where suppression was weaker and forged new transatlantic alliances. By the close of the traffic in 1867, they had brought over two hundred thousand captives aboard their vessels since 1850.

As slave traders and their opponents warred, they turned their battleground into a strikingly modern arena. Although the traffic was more geographically constricted than previously, it had probably never been as internationalized. Unlike the fairly discrete North and South Atlantic trades of earlier times, the traffic now crossed even more jurisdictional, legal, and linguistic boundaries. Slave traders themselves were a particularly multiethnic and transient group, largely because of the new international networks but also because suppression measures forced them to be on the move. Regular shipping patterns and faster vessels also allowed them to travel more quickly. Although their work was as brutal as it had ever been, in many ways it was more technically advanced. Slave traders used larger, faster vessels, often built in the United States, and harnessed new technologies such as the telegram and steamships. In Cuba, traffickers occasionally transported slaves inland using railroads and found new ways of laundering and transferring capital, including through Cuba's first bank, Banco Español. Antislavery forces responded with modern weapons of their own. The British created a vast intelligence web stretching from the Americas across Europe to Africa, using steamers and railways and a growing network of spies and consuls who were now spread throughout the Atlantic world thanks to increasing global trade. On a smaller scale, Manzano and his regional lieutenants began communicating across Cuba by telegram during the final crackdown in the mid-1860s. By midcentury the traffic and its suppression bore the hallmarks of the modern world.[10]

The United States proved to be critical to both the slave trade and its eventual suppression. The country's growing commercial and diplomatic strength was particularly important in sustaining the trade. American shipbuilders produced an abundance of large vessels, which were ideal for traffickers such as the members of the Portuguese Company. U.S. ports were home to merchants who already operated in the long-distance trade to slaving zones and proved to be useful allies to slave traders. New York City, a huge shipping and financial center, was an especially attractive hub for the traffickers owing to its large international trade, many overseas merchants, and surfeit of dockworkers and seamen. The government's ability to resist British diplomatic pressure to concede the right of search made the American flag particularly appealing. Despite the fact that Britain had compelled all other major slaving nations to yield to this demand, and that the trade was now almost completely conducted under the U.S. flag, Washington refused to go along. The British did occasionally violate American sovereignty by intercepting vessels flying U.S. colors, but the strong reaction to such moves in the United States limited these interventions. With little help from the United States, Britain turned to Sanchez, whom the Foreign Office believed could provide sufficient evidence of non-U.S. ownership to sustain their captures and to tackle the continued use of the American flag.

The politics of slavery and the slave trade in the United States would have an even greater impact on the traffic and its suppression. During the early and mid-nineteenth century, the United States expanded territorially into many parts of North America, often introducing slavery along the way. By the late 1840s, Cuba was a major target of expansionists, especially among those with ties to slavery. Many Americans, including leading policymakers in the ruling Democratic Party, supported this position. These individuals did not have a vested interest in the slave trade except as a tool to delegitimize Spanish rule in Cuba. By the time the dozen or so migrant traffickers from the South Atlantic trade had arrived in New York in the early and mid-1850s, many newspaper editors and senior policymakers were already committed to blaming Spain for the traffic to Cuba. The effect of this argument, which held sway in the White House and in Congress for much of the 1850s, was the neglect of suppression measures at home, although they increased substantially later in the decade.

The emergent Republican Party viewed the slave trade very differently. Favoring free labor and free soil over slavery expansion, the Republicans considered the rising role of the United States in the slave trade as further evidence of the Slave Power's hold over the federal government and the seemingly inexorably spread of slavery throughout the nation. Radical southerners' suggestion that U.S. anti–slave trade laws ought to be repealed and the arrival of a few hundred captive Africans on American soil made these dangers tangible. The Republicans, including Abraham Lincoln and William Seward, would make such arguments central to their national antislavery platform in the late 1850s, which in turn stoked sectional tensions between North and South. When they came into power and the Civil War erupted, the Republican leadership moved swiftly to concede the right of search to the British and to shut down the slave trade in New York and other U.S. ports.

The effect of the U.S. departure from the trade was considerable. With U.S. ports no longer active in the trade and no protection from the American flag, traffickers in Europe, Africa, and Cuba struggled. Meanwhile, in the diplomatic sphere, the Lyons-Seward Treaty further highlighted the growing isolation of Spain, as the sole promoter of the traffic. The course of the Civil War also suggested that slavery itself might be imperiled if Spain did not finally suppress the trade. These factors, in alliance with a new approach to the traffic by Cuban governors and growing liberalism in Spain, resulted in vigorous attempts to suppress it in Cuba and reluctance by slave traders to conduct further voyages. The United States, therefore, was in many ways the linchpin in the triangular route sustaining the traffic, despite the fact that only a few hundred African slaves landed there. Although slavery would survive in Cuba and in Brazil until the 1880s, the U.S. withdrawal from the trade played a major part in finally ending the slave trade to the Americas.[11]

The traffickers who were responsible for the slave trade were rarely punished. The execution of Gordon was a powerful example to other slave traders, but his case was unique. As the slave trade crumbled and his African emigration plans failed to get off the ground, Manoel Cunha Reis, who had once been the main trafficker in New York, left Cuba and immigrated to Mexico, where he invested in railroads. In the late 1860s he returned to New York with his family and became a naturalized citizen, apparently without difficulty. His partner, José Maia Ferreira, returned to New York from Cuba during the early days of the Civil War and served in a northern cavalry regiment in 1864. By the late 1860s he appears to have finally ended his turbulent marriage to Margaret and moved to Brazil, where he died in 1867. Appleton Oaksmith, the merchant ally of the slave traders in New York who had escaped custody during the crackdown in 1862, fled to England during the Civil War and afterward settled in coastal North Carolina. He was granted a presidential pardon for his crimes in the 1870s. Mirroring the forgiveness offered to Confederates after the War, the U.S. government absolved illegal slave traders. Like Cunha Reis, many pirates of New York simply slipped back into American society.

The last word should go to the Africans who endured the "final triangle." These men, women, and children were forced

Oluale Kossola
(N-3448, Erik Overbey Collection, The Doy
Leale McCall Rare Book and Manuscript
Library, University of South Alabama)

out of their homes and cast around the Atlantic world on brutal odysseys that claimed lives every mile of the way. Most of
those who survived their transportation ended up in slavery
in the Americas. Few detailed accounts of their lives remain,
although we do have testimonies from some of the Africans
from the *Clotilda*, which reached Alabama in 1860. One of
these was the account of Oluale Kossola, who was interviewed
several times by the anthropologist and novelist Zora Neale
Hurston around 1930. Now an elderly man, Kossola described

the suffering he had endured as a captive and then an enslaved man, and how he and other *Clotilda* survivors had gained their freedom as the Civil War closed and tried to rebuild their lives thereafter. Their postwar dream, he explained, was to return to Africa, but they viewed this as impossible. Instead they saved their earnings and eventually bought land from their former enslaver, Timothy Meaher, who had organized their transatlantic voyage in 1860. Finally able to turn their back on Meaher, the *Clotilda* survivors divided the land among themselves, and Kossola received a humble 1.5-acre plot. Here they built houses, formed a church, and appointed a leader and judges. In remembrance of their homes, they named their new community Africa Town, Alabama.[12]

Notes

ABBREVIATIONS

AHN — Archivo Histórico Nacional, Madrid

ANC — Archivo Nacional de la República de Cuba, Havana

BL — British Library

CRLM — Chancellor Robert R. Livingston Masonic Library, New York

DUA — Durham University Archives, Durham, England

JSMFP — José da Silva Maia Ferreira Papers, Arquivo Nacional Torre do Tombo, Lisbon

LoC — Library of Congress, Washington, D.C.

NARA — National Archives and Records Administration, Washington, D.C.

NYH — *New York Herald*

NYT — *New York Times* (previously *New-York Daily Times*; *New-York Times*)

RLDU — David M. Rubenstein Rare Book and Manuscript Library, Duke University, Durham, North Carolina

TNA — The National Archives, Kew, England

TSTD2 — Voyages: The Trans-Atlantic Slave Trade Database, www .slavevoyages.org

INTRODUCTION. THE MIDCENTURY MOMENT

1. For Kossola's story and the quote, see Zora Neale Hurston, *Barracoon: The Story of the Last "Black Cargo,"* ed. Deborah G. Plant (Lon-

don: Harper Collins, 2018), 45–57. For more on this voyage and its after-math see Sylviane A. Diouf, *Dreams of Africa in Alabama: The Story of the "Clotilda" and the Last Enslaved African Brought to America* (New York: Oxford University Press, 2007); TSTD2: *Clotilda* (voyage id 36990).

2. For overviews of pro- and antislavery clashes discussed in this and the following paragraph, see Seymour Drescher, *Abolition: A History of Slavery and Antislavery* (New York: Cambridge University Press, 2009); Robin Blackburn, *The American Crucible: Slavery, Emancipation and Human Rights* (London: Verso, 2011); David Brion Davis, *The Problem of Slavery in the Age of Emancipation* (New York: Knopf, 2014); David Eltis, *Economic Growth and the Ending of the Transatlantic Slave Trade* (New York: Oxford University Press, 1987).

3. Hurston, *Barracoon*, 44–45, 161–62. See also estimates page of TSTD2.

4. For these transitions see Leonardo Marques, *The United States and the Transatlantic Slave Trade to the Americas, 1776–1867* (New Haven: Yale University Press, 2016), 56–184; "Um último triângulo notório: contrabandistas portugueses, senhores cubanos e portos norte-americanos na fase final do tráfico transatlântico de escravos, 1850–1867," *Afro-Ásia* 53 (2016): 50–63.

5. The database interface of TSTD2 identifies 460 voyages that took place after 1852, when almost every voyage aimed to bring captives to Cuba. The researchers behind the database suggest they have accounted for 97 percent of all voyages to the Spanish Americas after 1835, and although I have found documentation of several additional Cuba-bound voyages after 1852, including trips by the *Braman* (1856), *Isla de Cuba* (1859), *Ottowa* (1859), *Comoro* (1859), and *Atlantic* (1859), I have not found enough to substantially alter their accounting. The resulting post-1852 estimate is 474. See David Eltis and David Richardson, "A New Assessment of the Transatlantic Slave Trade," in *Extending the Frontiers: Essays on the New Transatlantic Slave Trade Database*, ed. Eltis and Richardson (New Haven: Yale University Press, 2008), 37. For number of voyages see TSTD2: https://slavevoyages.org/voyages/R6EAY9Dp. For number of captives see estimates page of TSTD2.

6. Walt Whitman, *Leaves of Grass*, in *The Complete Poems*, ed. Francis Murphy (London: Penguin, 2005), 319. For a detailed overview of New York during this period, see Edwin G. Burrows and Mike Wallace, *Gotham: A History of New York City to 1898* (New York: Oxford University Press, 1999), 620–1039. See also Catherine McNeur, *Taming Manhattan:*

Environmental Battles in the Antebellum City (Cambridge: Harvard University Press, 2014), 6–42, 170–91.

7. For an introduction to these figures see Marques, *The United States*, 189–218.

8. On right of search and the Webster-Ashburton Treaty see Don E. Fehrenbacher, *The Slaveholding Republic: An Account of the United States Government's Relations to Slavery* (Oxford: Oxford University Press, 2001), 157–72.

9. For an overview of the politics of the midcentury slave trade, see Marques, *The United States*, 219–55.

10. *Frederick Douglass: Selected Speeches and Writings*, ed. Philip S. Foner (Chicago: Lawrence Hill, 1999), 188–206. See also David W. Blight, *Frederick Douglass: Prophet of Freedom* (New York: Simon and Schuster, 2018), 228–36.

11. Douglass borrowed this line from another abolitionist, William Lloyd Garrison. *Douglass: Selected Speeches*, 197, 204–5.

CHAPTER 1. THE FINAL TRIANGLE TAKES SHAPE

1. Clarendon to Crampton, Mar. 6, 1854, FO84/948, TNA; Crampton to Clarendon, Feb. 19, 1854, FO84/948, TNA; Crampton to Barclay, Mar. 30, 1854, FO84/948, TNA; Barclay to Crampton, Apr. 5, 1854, FO84/948, TNA.

2. Important recent work on British antislavery includes Christopher Leslie Brown, *Moral Capital: Foundations of British Abolitionism* (Chapel Hill: University of North Carolina Press for the Omohundro Institute, 2006); Richard Huzzey, *Freedom Burning: Anti-Slavery and Empire in Victorian Britain* (Ithaca: Cornell University Press, 2012).

3. See estimates page of TSTD2; James McMillin, *The Final Victims: Foreign Slave Trade to North America, 1783–1810* (Columbia: University of South Carolina Press, 2004); Jay Coughtry, *The Notorious Triangle: Rhode Island and the African Slave Trade, 1700–1807* (Philadelphia: Temple University Press, 1981). For more on these views and the shift from the international to internal slave trade, see Adam Rothman, "The Domestication of the Slave Trade in the United States," in *The Chattel Principle: Internal Slave Trades in the Americas*, ed. Walter Johnson (New Haven: Yale University Press, 2004), 32–54. Leonardo Marques, *The United States and the Transatlantic Slave Trade to the Americas, 1776–1867* (New Haven: Yale University Press, 2016), 12–55; Don E. Fehrenbacher, *The Slaveholding Republic: An Account of the United States Government's Re-*

lations to Slavery (Oxford: Oxford University Press, 2001), 135–46. The acts were "An Act to Prohibit the Carrying on the Slave Trade from the United States to Any Foreign Place or Country" (1794), "An Act in Addition to the Act Intituled 'An Act to Prohibit the Carrying on the Slave Trade from the United States to any Foreign Place or Country'" (1800), and "An Act to Prohibit the Importation of Slaves into any Port or Place Within the Jurisdiction of the United States, from and After the First Day of January, in the Year of Our Lord One Thousand Eight Hundred and Eight" (1807).

4. On slave trading in the early Republic see Marques, *The United States*, 56–90; David Head, "Slave Smuggling by Foreign Privateers: The Illegal Slave Trade and the Geopolitics of the Early Republic," *Journal of the Early Republic* 33, no. 3 (2013): 433–62; Jorge Felipe Gonzáles, "Foundation and Growth of the Cuban-Based Transatlantic Slave Trade, 1790–1820" (Ph.D. diss., Michigan State University, 2019), 86–111, 246–47. On slave trade legislation, see Paul Finkelman, "Regulating the African Slave Trade," *Civil War History* 54, no. 4 (2008): 379–405; Marques, *The United States*, 91–101; Craig Hollander, "Against a Sea of Troubles: Slave Trade Suppressionism During the Early Republic" (Ph.D. diss., Johns Hopkins University, 2013), 90–136. The 1820 act was "An Act to Continue in Force 'An Act to Protect the Commerce of the United States, and Punish the Crime of Piracy,' and Also to Make Further Provisions for Punishing the Crime of Piracy."

5. For the French, Portuguese, and Spanish cases, see Lawrence Jennings, *French Anti-Slavery: The Movement for the Abolition of Slavery in France, 1802–1848* (Cambridge: Cambridge University Press, 2000); João Pedro Marques, *The Sounds of Silence: Nineteenth-Century Portugal and the Abolition of the Slave Trade*, trans. Richard Wall (Oxford: Berghahn, 2006); Christopher Schmidt-Nowara, *Empire and Antislavery: Spain, Cuba, and Puerto Rico, 1833–1874* (Pittsburgh: University of Pittsburgh Press, 1999); Arthur F. Corwin, *Spain and the Abolition of Slavery in Cuba, 1817–1886* (Austin: University of Texas Press, 1967). On the impact of the Haitian Revolution on Cuban slavery, see Ada Ferrer, *Freedom's Mirror: Cuba and Haiti in the Age of Revolution* (New York: Cambridge University Press, 2014).

6. David Eltis, *Economic Growth and the Ending of the Transatlantic Slave Trade* (New York: Oxford University Press, 1987), 81–91.

7. For a comparative perspective on the crucial Brazilian and Cuban cases see Márcia Regina Berbel, Rafael de Bivar Marquese, and Tâmis

Parron, *Slavery and Politics: Brazil and Cuba, 1790–1850*, trans. Leonardo Marques (Albuquerque: University of New Mexico Press, 2016), 129–260. On the metropolitan context in Portugal, see João Pedro Marques, *The Sounds of Silence*, 99–157. See also Eltis, *Economic Growth*, 86–88; Leslie Bethell, *The Abolition of the Brazilian Slave Trade: Britain, Brazil and the Slave Trade Question, 1807–1869* (Cambridge: Cambridge University Press, 1970), 70, 242–95. The measures taken by the British foreign secretaries were the Palmerston Act ("An Act for the Suppression of the Slave Trade," 1839) and the Aberdeen Act ("An Act to Amend an Act, Intituled 'An Act to Carry into Execution a Convention Between His Majesty and the Emperor of Brazil, for the Regulation and final Abolition of the African Slave Trade,'" 1845).

8. See estimates page of TSTD2.

9. See estimates page of TSTD2.

10. Eltis, *Economic Growth*, 145–63; Marques, *The United States*, 147–49. For Cuban speculators and traces of foreign investment in the Cuban slave trade in the 1810s, see Gonzáles, "Foundation and Growth," 122–25.

11. Marques, *The United States*, 143–47.

12. See also Leonardo Marques, "US Shipbuilding, Atlantic Markets, and the Structures of the Contraband Slave Trade," in *The Rise and Demise of Slavery and the Slave Trade in the Atlantic World*, ed. Philip Misevich and Kristin Mann (Rochester, N.Y.: University of Rochester Press, 2016), 196–219.

13. Marques, *The United States*, 143–47, 154–55, 168–76.

14. On Anglo-American tensions over the right of search and the Webster-Ashburton Treaty, see Fehrenbacher, *Slaveholding Republic*, 157–72; David Waldstreicher and Matthew Mason, eds., *John Quincy Adams and the Politics of Slavery: Selections from the Diary* (New York: Oxford University Press, 2017), 103.

15. Warren S. Howard, *American Slavers and the Federal Law, 1837–1862* (Berkeley: University of California Press, 1963), 42–43; Fehrenbacher, *Slaveholding Republic*, 173.

16. Gorham Parks to John Clayton, July 20, 1849, Roll 14, June 5, 1849-Dec. 27, 1850, Microfilm, T-172, NARA.

17. On United States—Cuba trade see Roland Ely, "The Old Cuba Trade: Highlights and Case Studies of Cuban-American Interdependence During the Nineteenth Century," *Business History Review* 38, no. 4 (1964): 456–78. On United States—Africa trade see George

Brooks, *Yankee Traders, Old Coasters and African Middlemen: A History of American Legitimate Trade with West Africa in the Nineteenth Century* (Boston: Boston University Press, 1970), 79–125. For British contributions to the slave trade see David Eltis, "The British Contribution to the Nineteenth-Century Trans-Atlantic Slave Trade," *Economic History Review* 32, no. 2 (1979): 211–27; Marques, *The United States*, 134–35.

18. For these roles before 1850 see Marques, *The United States*, 132–34, 154–55, 166–76; Robert Conrad, *A World of Sorrow: The African Slave Trade to Brazil* (Baton Rouge: Louisiana State University Press, 1986), 126–53. Gerald Horne, *The Deepest South: The United States, Brazil, and the African Slave Trade* (New York: New York University Press, 2007), 8–9, 29–30.

19. For Portugal see João Pedro Marques, *The Sounds of Silence*, 158–92. On Angola and Brazil see Mariana Candido, "South Atlantic Exchanges: The Role of Brazilian-Born Agents in Benguela, 1650–1850," *Luso-Brazilian Review* 50, no. 1 (2013): 53–82; Roquinaldo Ferreira, *Cross-Cultural Exchange in the Atlantic World: Angola and Brazil During the Era of the Slave Trade* (Cambridge: Cambridge University Press, 2012), 203–41.

20. João Pedro Marques, *The Sounds of Silence*, 167–70, 258–64; Leslie Bethell, "The Mixed Commissions for the Suppression of the Transatlantic Slave Trade in the Nineteenth Century," *Journal of African History* 7, no. 1 (1966): 90–91; Jenny Martinez, *The Slave Trade and the Origins of International Human Rights Law* (New York: Oxford University Press, 2012), 76.

21. On transitions in West Central Africa see Roquinaldo Ferreira, "The Suppression of the Slave Trade and Slave Departures from Angola, 1830s–1860s," in *Extending the Frontiers: Essays on the New Transatlantic Slave Trade Database*, ed., David Eltis and David Richardson (New Haven: Yale University Press, 2008), 313–34; Roquinaldo Ferreira, *Dos sertões ao atlântico: tráfico ilegal de escravos e comércio lícito em Angola, 1830–1860* (Luanda: Kilombelombe, 2012), 137–46; Roquinaldo Ferreira, "The Conquest of Ambriz: Colonial Expansion and Imperial Competition in Central Africa," *Mulemba: Revista Angolana de Ciências Sociais* 5, no. 9, (2015), available online at https://journals.openedition.org /mulemba/439. See also estimates page of TSTD2.

22. Bethell, *The Abolition of the Brazilian Slave Trade*, 309–31. Recent contributions to the long-running debate about Brazil's suppression of the trade include Sidney Chalhoub, *A Força da Escravidão: Ilegalidade e Costume no Brasil Oitocentista* (São Paulo: Cia. das Letras, 2012), 109–40;

Beatriz G. Mamigonian, *Africanos Livres: A Abolição do Tráfico de Escravos No Brasil* (São Paulo: Cia. das Letras, 2017), 209–84; Tâmis Parron, "The British Empire and the Suppression of the Slave Trade to Brazil: A Global History Analysis," *Journal of World History* 29, no. 1, (Mar. 2018): 1–36.

23. See estimates on TSTD2; Bethell, *The Abolition of the Brazilian Slave Trade*, 331–63; Eltis, *Economic Growth*, 214–16.

24. For a summary of the Brazilian measures and quote see Edward Kent to Daniel Webster, Apr. 10, 1852, Roll 15, Feb. 8, 1851–Aug. 16, 1854, Microfilm, T-172, NARA. For developments in Portugal, see William Smith to Palmerston, Mar. 19, 1851, FO84/841, TNA; Edwin Johnston to Palmerston, July 21, 1851, FO84/841, TNA.

25. George Brand to Palmerston, Jan. 13, 1851, FO84/841, TNA.

26. For the 1853 treaty with Francisco Franque at Cabinda see FO881/503, TNA. For the treaty with Cangala, see Henry Need, Sept. 15, 1855, ART/10, National Maritime Museum, Greenwich, England. See also Ferreira, "The Conquest of Ambriz," 6.

27. Appleton Oaksmith Journal, 1851–52, Apr. 18–July 4, 1852, Appleton Oaksmith Papers, RLDU. Guilherme José da Silva Correa to João José Vianna, Apr. 21, 1855, enc. in John Morgan to Clarendon, June 13, 1856, in *Accounts and Papers of the House of Commons*, vol. 44: *Session 30 April–28 August 1857* (London: Harrison and Sons, 1857), 132.

28. Appleton Oaksmith Journal, 1851–1852, July 4, 1852, Oaksmith Papers, RLDU. Undated, unnamed newspaper clipping (original in *Cornwall Gazette*), Box 1, Folder 1840–1852, Oaksmith Papers, RLDU.

29. George Brand to Palmerston, Jan. 13, 1851, FO84/841, TNA.

30. On British actions see Peter Grindal, *Opposing the Slavers: The Royal Navy's Campaign Against the Atlantic Slave Trade* (London: Tauris, 2016), 748; Eltis, *Economic Growth*, 121, 166; James Hudson to Palmerston, Mar. 23, 1850, FO84/803, TNA; Christopher Lloyd, *The Navy and the Slave Trade: The Suppression of the African Slave Trade in the Nineteenth Century* (London: Routledge, 1968), 117. For Blanco and Gallinas see Théophilus Conneau, *A Slaver's Log Book: or 20 Years' Residence in Africa; The Original 1853 Manuscript by Captain Théophilus Conneau*, ed. Mabel M. Smythe (London: Prentice-Hall International, 1976), 243–47. For quote see Conneau, *A Slaver's Log Book*, 246. On Sierra Leone and the Windward Coast see estimates page of TSTD2. The vessel departing after 1850 was TSTD2: *Paquete de Trinidad* (Voyage id 4219).

31. Robin Law, *Ouidah: The Social History of a West African Slav-*

ing "Port," *1727–1892* (Athens: Ohio University Press, 2004), 216–21; Olatunji Ojo, "Correspondence of the Lagos Slave Trade," in *Slavery in Africa and the Caribbean: A History of Enslavement and Identity Since the Eighteenth Century,* ed. Ojo and Nadine Hunt (New York: Tauris, 2012), 93–94. On the 1851 attack, see Lloyd, *The Navy and the Slave Trade,* 149–62; Kristin Mann, *Slavery and the Birth of an African City: Lagos, 1760–1900* (Bloomington: Indiana University Press, 2007), 84–102. See estimates page of TSTD2.

32. See estimates page of TSTD2; Lisa Yun, *The Coolie Speaks: Chinese Indentured Laborers and African Slaves of Cuba* (Philadelphia: Temple University Press, 2008), 14–21; Michele Reid-Vazquez, *The Year of the Lash: Free People of Color in Cuba and the Nineteenth-Century Atlantic World* (Athens: University of Georgia Press, 2011); Robert Paquette, *Sugar Is Made with Blood: The Conspiracy of "La Escalera" and the Conflict Between Empires over Slavery in Cuba* (Middletown, Conn.: Wesleyan University Press, 1990).

33. Louis A. Pérez, *Winds of Change: Hurricanes and the Transformation of Nineteenth-Century Cuba* (Chapel Hill: University of North Carolina Press, 2001), 97–98.

34. Christopher Schmidt-Nowara, *Empire and Antislavery: Spain, Cuba, and Puerto Rico, 1833–1874* (Pittsburgh: University of Pittsburgh Press, 1999), 70–71; Martín Rodrigo, "Spanish Merchants and the Slave Trade: From Legality to Illegality, 1814–1870," in *Slavery and Antislavery in Spain's Atlantic Empire,* ed. Josep M. Fradera and Christopher Schmidt Nowara (New York: Berghahn, 2013), 176–99.

35. David Murray, *Odious Commerce: Britain, Spain and the Abolition of the Cuban Slave Trade* (New York: Cambridge University Press, 1980), 222–40.

36. Gefatura Principal de Policía to Gobr. Supr. Civil, Jan. 2 and Feb. 1, 1854, Legajo 427/20575, Gobierno General, ANC; Secretaría Politica to Teniente Gobernador de Cárdenas, Feb. 17, 1854, Legajo 427/20575, Gobierno General, ANC. For more on Avellar, see Ferreira, *Dos sertões ao atlântico,* 146–52. See also enclosures in Crawford to Foreign Office, June 27, 1853, FO84/905, TNA.

37. Consul Archibald gave the number of ten to twelve traffickers in New York. Archibald to Malmesbury, July 11, 1859, FO84/1086, TNA; Marques, *The United States,* 181–82; Eltis, *Economic Growth,* 157–58.

38. T. Ward in memo respecting expulsion of Cunha Reis, July 7, 1854, FO84/955, TNA (quote); Passport Applications, 1795–1905, Roll

162, 2739, Aug. 7, 1869, RG59, NARA; Andres Cassard, *Cincuenta años de la vida de Andres Cassard, escrita por un amigo y hermano, con presencia de documentos auténticos* (New York: G. R. Lockwood, 1875), 216; Passenger Lists of Vessels Arriving at New Orleans, Louisiana, 1820–1902, 44, RG85, NARA; José Maia Ferreira to Cunha Reis, Mar. 9, 1855, Ex 1, PT 2, JSMFP; Alien Depositions of Intent to Become U.S. Citizens, 1825–1913, New York, Vol. 27, Box 28, Folder 2, Book 12, Page 170, Department of State, Series A1869, New York State Archives, Albany.

39. Many of these individuals are discussed in the correspondence of the spy Emilio Sanchez. For example, see memo enclosed in Edward Archibald to Malmesbury, May 3, 1859, FO84/1086, TNA. On Maia Ferreira see José Maia Ferreira to Margaret Butler, Dec. 11, 1852, cx. 1, pt. 13, No. 66, JSMFP; José Maia Ferreira to Margaret Maia Ferreira, Aug. 19, 1855, cx. 1, pt. 13, no. 50, JSMFP; Marriage announcement in cx. 1, pt. 6, no. 2, JSMFP; George Jackson to Earl Clarendon, Sept. 29, 1856, FO84/985, TNA; William P. Rougle, "José da Silva Maia Ferreira: Poeta angolano, correspondente brasileiro, homem de negócios Americano," *Revista Colóquio/Letras, Notas e Comentários* 120 (1991): 184–88; Carlos Pacheco, *José da Silva Maia Ferreira: O Homem e a Sua Época* (Luanda: União dos Escritores Angolanos, 1990), 128–30, 257–58; Carlos Pacheco, *O nativismo na poesia de José da Silva Maia Ferreira* (Évora: Pendor, 1996); Jacopo Corrado, *The Creole Elite and the Rise of Angolan Porto-Nationalism: 1870–1920* (Amherst, N.Y.: Cambria, 2008), 161–66; Marques, *The United States*, 194–95.

40. John G. Willis to Lewis Cass, Jan. 26, 1859, Dispatches from United States Consuls in St. Paul de Loanda, 1854–93, T430, Roll 1, RG59, NARA. On New York port see Robert Greenhalgh Albion, *The Rise of New York Port, 1815–1860* (New York: Scribner's, 1939). On New York's Cuban connections see Louis A. Pérez, *Cuba and the United States: Ties of Singular Intimacy*, 3rd ed. (Athens: University of Georgia Press, 2003), 1–28.

41. For these addresses, see *New York City Directory* (New York: John Trow, 1859). See also Sven Beckert, *The Monied Metropolis: New York City and the Consolidation of the American Bourgeoisie, 1850–1896* (New York: Cambridge University Press, 2001), 17–45.

42. On Machado and quote see enclosure in Benjamin Campbell to Clarendon, Dec. 19, 1854, FO84/950, TNA. For Cunha Reis–Figanière connections see John S. Lumley to Clarendon, Oct. 7, 1856, FO84/999, TNA; John O'Sullivan to William Marcy, Aug. 24, 1856, M43: Dis-

patches from U.S. Ministers to Portugal, 1790–1906, Roll 16, NARA. For Lopes Baptista see enclosures in John O'Sullivan to William Marcy, Aug. 28, 1856, M43: Dispatches from U.S. Ministers to Portugal, 1790–1906, Roll 16, NARA. For Maia Ferreira's frustration about consular position see José Maia Ferreira to Cecilia Butler, Jan. 18, 1861, cx. 1, pt. 13, JSMFP. On the *Susan* case see Frederico Figanière to John Clayton, Apr. 27, May 5, 1849, M57: Notes from the Portuguese Legation in the United States to the Department of State, 1796–1906, Roll T4, Feb. 8 1842–Dec. 21, 1860, NARA; William Marcy to John O'Sullivan, June 21, July 21, 1856, M77: Diplomatic Instructions of the Department of State, 1801–1906, Roll 134, RG59, NARA.

43. John Bassett Moore, *History and Digest of the International Arbitrations to Which the United States Has Been a Party*, vol. 3 (Washington, D.C.: Government Printing Office, 1898), 2886–2900. For Charleston see Robert Bunch to Russell, July 28, 1859, FO84/1086, TNA. On Horn see Howard, *American Slavers*, 189. On the Moras see *NYT*, Apr. 26, 1897; Gloria Pilar Totoricaguena, *The Basques of New York: A Cosmopolitan Experience* (Reno: University of Nevada Press, 2011), 68–69.

44. Lodge Returns, La Fraternidad, Lodge No. 387, and La Fraternidad, Minutes, 1855–1858, Chancellor Robert R. Livingston Masonic Library, New York; Cassard, *Cincuenta años*, 208–17; Thomas Smith Webb and Rob Morris, eds., *The Freemasons' Monitor* (Cincinnati: Moore, Wilstach, Keys, 1859), 18.

45. José Maia Ferreira to Margaret Maia Ferreira, n.d., cx. 1, pt. 13, no. 1, 15, 43, 67, 70, JSMFP; José Maia Ferreira to Cecile Butler, Aug. 20, 1853, cx. 1, pt. 13, JSMFP; José Maia Ferreira to Margaret Maia Ferreira, Nov. 2, 5, 7, 21, 28 (quote), 1860, cx. 1, pt. 13, JSMFP.

46. Andrew Hull Foote, *Africa and the American Flag* (New York: Appleton, 1854), 300; Fehrenbacher, *Slaveholding Republic*, 183–87.

47. For a rejection of incorporation of Cuba into the United States on antislavery grounds, see *Hartford Republican*, ca. Aug. 1851, reprinted in *National Era*, Aug. 14, 1851. See also Robert E. May, *Manifest Destiny's Underworld: Filibustering in Antebellum America* (Chapel Hill: University of North Carolina Press, 2002); Walter Johnson, *River of Dark Dreams: Slavery and Empire in the Cotton Kingdom* (Cambridge: Harvard University Press, 2013), 303–29; Jonathan H. Earle, *Jacksonian Antislavery and the Politics of Free Soil, 1824–1854* (Chapel Hill: University of North Carolina Press, 2004).

48. Davis quote in James M. McPherson, *Battle Cry of Freedom*

(New York: Oxford University Press, 1988), 104. For rising annexation-ism from the mid-1840s, see Hermino Portell Villa, *Narcisco López y su epoca*, 3 vols. (Havana: Cultural and Compañía Editora de Libros, 1930–58); Tom Chaffin, *Fatal Glory: Narciso López and the First Clandestine U.S. War Against Cuba* (Charlottesville: University of Virginia Press, 1996). See also May, *Manifest Destiny's Underworld*.

49. Cora Montgomery, *The Queen of Islands and the King of Rivers* (New York: Charles Wood, 1850), 23; *NYH*, Aug. 22, 1858; *NYT*, Apr. 7, 1852.

CHAPTER 2. SLAVE TRADERS AT WORK

1. *NYH*, Apr. 1, 1857.

2. For an introduction to this circuit see Leonardo Marques, *The United States and the Transatlantic Slave Trade to the Americas, 1776–1867* (New Haven: Yale University Press, 2016), 185–218; John A. E. Harris, "Circuits of Wealth, Circuits of Sorrow: Financing the Illegal Trans-atlantic Slave Trade in the Age of Suppression, 1850–66," *Journal of Global History* 11, no. 3 (2016): 409–29.

3. For Spanish diplomats see Legajo 451/7891, Embajada de España en Washington, Archivo General de la Administración, Alcalá de Henares, Spain; Legajos 3549 and 4686, Ultramar, AHN; FO84/1197, TNA. For the Sanchez correspondence see FO84/1086, FO84/1111, FO84/1138, TNA. For the Lisbon spy see M43: Dispatches from U.S. Ministers to Portugal, 1790–1906, Roll 16, RG59, NARA. For destroy-ing papers and vessels see *NYT*, Mar. 17, 1860.

4. I define U.S. involvement broadly and include U.S. ports, Ameri-can citizens and noncitizens living in those ports, and vessels and capital flowing within and across U.S. borders. Some of this activity could also be described as Portuguese or Cuban participation, for there was plenty of overlap in this highly internationalized traffic.

5. See notebook in Legajo 451/7891, Embajada de España en Wash-ington, Archivo General de la Administración, Alcalá de Henares, Spain.

6. For this trade see Calvin Schermerhorn, "Capitalism's Captives: The Maritime United States Slave Trade, 1807–1850," *Journal of Social History* 47, no. 4 (2014): 897–921. The percentage is based on voyages that took place in vessels for which place of construction is known (111 of 474). Sources: TSTD2, https://slavevoyages.org/voyages/R6EAY9Dp; *American Lloyds' Registry of American and Foreign Shipping* (New York: E. and G. W. Blunt, 1859).

7. Estimates are based on voyages for which flag designation is known (200 of all 474 voyages, 1853–66). See TSTD2: https://slavevoyages.org/voyages/FMVPBMPP.

8. Estimates are based on data for which port of departure information is known (229 of 474 voyages). See TSTD2, https://slavevoyages.org/voyages/sMCeQXIA. Havana was the single most important point of departure during this era, although it was barely ahead of New York.

9. Guilherme José da Silva Correa to João José Vianna, Apr. 21, 1855, enclosed in John Morgan to Clarendon, June 13, 1856, *Accounts and Papers of the House of Commons*, vol. 44: *Session 30 April–28 August 1857* (London: Harrison and Sons, 1857), 132. See also Leonardo Marques, "US Shipbuilding, Atlantic Markets, and the Structures of the Contraband Slave Trade," in *The Rise and Demise of Slavery and the Slave Trade in the Atlantic World*, ed. Philip Misevich and Kristin Mann (Rochester, N.Y.: University of Rochester Press, 2016), 201.

10. For Valentine see *NYT*, Dec. 2, 1854. For Dobson and Vining, see Sanchez to Archibald enclosed in Archibald to Malmesbury, Apr. 5, 1859; Archibald to Malmesbury, July 25, 1859, FO84/1086, TNA. For Shufeldt quote see "Secret History of the Slave Trade to Cuba Written by an American Naval Officer, Robert Wilson Shufeldt, 1861," ed. Frederick C. Drake, *Journal of Negro History* 55, no. 3 (1970): 229.

11. See the cases of *Isla de Cuba*, which cleared New York for the Azores, and *Cora* (TSTD2: voyage id 4655), which cleared for Luanda; Sanchez to Archibald enclosed in Archibald to Malmesbury, Mar. 29, 1859, FO84/1086, TNA; Sanchez to Archibald, enclosed in Archibald to Foreign Office, July 6, 1860, FO84/1111, TNA. For more on the cover of the Africa trade, see Archibald to Foreign Office, Dec. 31, 1863, FO84/1197, TNA.

12. For *Altivie*, see John O'Sullivan to William Marcy, Aug. 24, 1856, and Mar. 28, 1857, M43, Roll 16, RG59, NARA; TSTD2: *Altivie* (Voyage id 42930). For *Storm King*, see *NYT*, May 7, 1860; TSTD2: *Storm King* (Voyage id 4654).

13. For *Mary E. Smith* see W. Stafford Jerningham to Clarendon, June 13, 1856, FO84/995, and John Morgan to Clarendon, Aug. 11, 1856, FO84/995, TNA; *NYT*, June 28, 1856. For *Haidee*, see Sanchez to Archibald, enclosed in Archibald to Malmesbury, Mar. 8, 1859, FO84/1086, TNA and TSTD2: voyage id 4285. For *North Hand*, see *NYT*, Sept. 13, 1857.

14. On da Costa, see José Lucas Henriques da Costa to Bento

Pacheco dos Santos, May 20, 1856 enclosed in O'Sullivan to State Department, July 28, 1856, and Mar. 28, 1857, Roll 16, M43, RG59, NARA. On the *Charles*, see Commodore Charles Wise to Rear-Admiral Sir F. Grey, Sept. 20, 1857, and Commander Moresby to Grey, Sept., n.d., 1857, enclosed in Grey to Secretary of the Admiralty, Sept. 23, 1857, *Accounts and Papers of the House of Commons*, vol. 61: *Session 3 December 1857–2 August 1858* (London: Harrison and Sons, 1858), 137–38.

15. John J. Cisco to Caleb Smith, June 5, 1861, Misc. Letters Relating to the Suppression of the Slave Trade, Dec. 30, 1858–Feb. 3, 1871, *Records of the Office of the Secretary of the Interior Relating to the Suppression of the African Slave Trade and Negro Colonization, 1854–72*, Publication M-160, NARA. On *Echo* and *Antelope* see Archibald to Russell, Oct. 10, 1859, FO84/1086, TNA, and TSTD2: voyage ids 4284 and 4839.

16. Sanchez to Archibald enclosed in Archibald to Malmesbury, Mar. 8, 1859, FO84/1086, TNA (quote). On the Horns, see Deposition of Jose Curvelo Paez, The United States vs. Albert Horn, Criminal Case Files, 1790–1912, RG21, NARA, available online at https://catalog.archives.gov/id/278446, and Marques, *The United States*, 215–16, 246–51. For the Mora vessels *Antelope*, *JJ Cobb*, and *Panfilia* see TSTD2: voyage ids 4389, 4304, 4809. On the Ximenes, Martínez, and Lafitte firm see Lieutenant J. W. Pike to Charles Wise, June 20, 1859, in *Correspondence with British Commissioners* (London: Harrison and Sons, 1860), 113.

17. "Secret History of the Slave Trade," 221; José Maia Ferreira to Margaret Maia Ferreira, ca. 1860, Ex 1, PT 13, number unspecified, JSMFP. Sanchez to Archibald, enc. in Archibald to Malmesbury, Mar. 8, 1859, FO84/1086, TNA. Solomon Beale to Caleb B Smith, Nov. 7, 28, Dec. 11, 1862, Misc. Letters Relating to the Suppression of the Slave Trade, Dec. 30, 1858–Feb. 3, 1871, Publication M-160, NARA.

18. On Pezuela's unusually robust administration, see María de los Ángeles Meriño Fuentes and Aisnara Perera Díaz, *Contrabando de bozales en Cuba: perseguir el tráfico y mantener la esclavitud, 1845–1866* (Mayabeque, Cuba: Ediciones Montecallado, 2015), 104–10; Arthur Corwin, *Spain and the Abolition of Slavery, 1817–1886* (Austin: University of Texas Press, 1967), 114–23. For bribes, see Francisco Serrano to Ministro de la Guerra y Ultramar, Sept. 6, 1861, Legajo 3549/3, Ultramar, AHN. On the impact of bribes on slave prices see David Eltis, *Economic Growth and the Ending of the Transatlantic Slave Trade* (New York: Oxford University Press, 1987), 140–41, and for profit rates, captures, and slave prices in Africa, ibid., 97–101, 161, 269–82. For Cuban prices, see Laird W. Bergad,

Fe Iglesias García, and María del Carmen Barcia, *The Cuban Slave Market: 1790–1880* (New York: Cambridge University Press, 1995), 47–52.

19. The Portuguese in New York also had links with Portuguese traffickers in the Bight of Benin, though these connections were not as strong and Benin was a much smaller source of captives. See Robin Law, *Ouidah: The Social History of a West African Slaving "Port," 1727–1892* (Athens: Ohio University Press, 2004), 235–36.

20. On Cunha Reis see Andres Cassard, *Cincuenta años de la vida de Andres Cassard, escrita por un amigo y hermano, con presencia de documentos auténticos* (New York: G. R. Lockwood, 1875), 216, and Sanchez to Archibald, May 16, 30, 1859, FO84/1059, TNA. For Brazilian slave traders in Cuba see Concha to Ministro, Aug. 12, 1855, Legajo 3549/4, Ultramar, AHN. On Maia Ferreira see José Maia Ferreira to Margaret Maia Ferreira, Oct. 25, 1860, Ex 1, PT 13, No. 34, JSMFP.

21. For examples of these business and political connections, see David Murray, *Odious Commerce: Britain, Spain and the Abolition of the Cuban Slave Trade* (New York: Cambridge University Press, 1980), 186–87; Martín Rodrigo, "Spanish Merchants and the Slave Trade: From Legality to Illegality, 1814-1870," in *Slavery and Antislavery in Spain's Atlantic Empire*, ed. Josep Maria Fradera and Christopher Schmidt-Nowara (New York: Berghahn, 2013), 176–99. On bribes see Joseph Crawford to Clarendon, June 10, 1853, FO84/905, TNA. On estates see Francisco Serrano to Ministro de la Guerra y Ultramar, Sept. 6, 1861, Legajo 3549/3, Ultramar, AHN.

22. These details are drawn from José Luciano Franco, *Comercio clandestine de esclavos* (Havana: Editorial de Ciencias Sociales, 1980), 246–49, and Laird W. Bergad, *Cuban Rural Society in the Nineteenth Century: The Social and Economic History of Monoculture in Matanzas* (Princeton: Princeton University Press, 1990), 51, 126–30. See also Marques, *The United States*, 191–93; Manuel Barcia Paz, "'Fully Capable of Any Iniquity': The Atlantic Human Trafficking Network of the Zangroniz Family," *Americas* 73, no. 3 (2016): 303–24.

23. On the trade to Spanish America see Alex Borucki, David Eltis, and David Wheat, "Atlantic History and the Slave Trade to Spanish America," *American Historical Review* 120, no. 2 (2015): 433–61. For Spanish reliance on the Portuguese on the African coast see William Gervase Clarence-Smith, "The Portuguese Contribution to the Cuban Slave and Coolie Trades in the Nineteenth Century," *Slavery and Abolition* 5, no. 1 (1984): 25–27. For the expansion of Cuban networks, see Manuel Bar-

cia and Effie Kesidou, "Innovation and Entrepreneurship as Strategies for Success Among Cuban-based Firms in the Late Years of the Transatlantic Slave Trade," *Business History* 60, no. 4, (May 2018): 547-50; Jorge Felipe Gonzáles, "Foundation and Growth of the Cuban-Based Transatlantic Slave Trade, 1790-1820" (Ph.D. diss., Michigan State University, 2019), 75-120, 174-223. See also Theodore Canot, *Adventures of an African Slaver* (New York: Dover, 1928).

24. José Suárez Argudín, Manuel Basilio da Cunha Reis, y Luciano Fernández Perdones, *Proyecto de Inmigración Africana presentado al superior gobierno de esta isla* (Havana: Imprenta de la Habanera, 1860). Lisa Yun, *The Coolie Speaks: Chinese Indentured Laborers and African Slaves of Cuba* (Philadelphia: Temple University Press, 2008), 15-16, 45-46. On Lusitania see the newspaper *Diario de la Marina* (Havana), May 3, 1861. Eltis, *Economic Growth*, 152-53.

25. Sanchez memo in Archibald to Malmesbury, May 3, 1859, FO84/1086, TNA; John O'Sullivan to William L. Marcy, Aug. 24, 1856, RG59, NARA.

26. On freighting see Joseph Miller, *Way of Death: Merchant Capitalism and the Angolan Slave Trade, 1730-1830* (Madison: University of Wisconsin Press, 1988), 314-78. For the British trade see Kenneth Morgan, "Remittance Procedures in the Eighteenth-Century British Slave Trade," *Business History Review* 79, no. 4 (Jan. 2005): 715-49. For the French trade see Robert Louis Stein, *The French Slave Trade in the Eighteenth Century: An Old Regime Business* (Madison: University of Wisconsin Press, 1979), 51-94.

27. John Beecroft to Clarendon, Feb. 20, 1854, FO84/950, TNA.

28. On *Dolores* see W. Stafford Jerningham to Clarendon, Mar. 8, 1856, FO84/995, TNA. For Domingo Mustich, a rare Spanish resident of the African coast who helped with some of these shipments and was himself a supplier of captives, see Benjamin Campbell to Clarendon, Aug. 12, 1854, FO84/950, TNA, and Law, *Ouidah*, 222.

29. Harris "Circuits of Wealth," 428, table 2. For more on *Mary E. Smith* see Yuko Miki, "In the Trial of the Ship: Narrating the Archives of Illegal Slavery," *Social Text* 37, no. 1 (Mar. 2019): 87-105, and TSTD2: voyage id 4968.

30. Da Costa to João Soares, May 20, 1856, enclosed in John O'Sullivan to Lewis Cass, Mar. 28, 1857, RG59, NARA.

31. José Maia Ferreira to Margaret Maia Ferreira, Nov. 2, 30, 1855, Ex 1, PT 13, No. 34, JSMFP.

32. TSTD2: *Mary E. Smith* (voyage id 4968).

33. In addition to the *Haidee*, we have information for the *Tacony* and the *William H. Stewart*. See Sanchez to Archibald, enclosed in Archibald to Malmesbury, Mar. 8, 1859, FO84/1086, TNA.

34. John O'Sullivan to Lewis Cass, Mar. 28, 1857, M43, RG59, NARA.

35. José Maia Ferreira to Margaret Maia Ferreira, Oct. 24, 25, Nov. 28, 1860, and Jan. 20, 1861, Ex 1, PT 13, JSMFP. On Plá, see Juan J. Burgoa Fernández, *El Marqués de Amboage, Ramón Plá y Monge, Un Ilustre Ferrolano* (Ferrol: Vision Libros, 2011), 30–31.

36. See John O'Sullivan to William Marcy, Aug. 24, 1856, and O'Sullivan to Lewis Cass, Mar. 28, 1857, M43, RG59, NARA; Sanchez to Archibald, Dec. 16, 1859, FO84/1086, TNA. For cost estimates see *De Bow's Review* in Roquinaldo Ferreira, *Dos sertões ao atlântico: tráfico ilegal de escravos e comércio lícito em Angola, 1830–1860* (Luanda: Kilombelombe, 2012), 173; Sanchez to Archibald enclosed in Archibald to Malmesbury, Mar. 8, 1859, FO84/1086, TNA.

37. Sanchez to Archibald enclosed in Archibald to Malmesbury, Mar. 8, 1859, FO84/1086 TNA.

38. Archibald to Malmesbury, Mar. 8, 1859, FO84/1086, TNA. For the background and business of Juan Miguel Ceballos, see *NYT*, Feb. 23, 1886.

39. For a damning portrait of Spain's failure to suppress the trade in Cádiz, see Alexander Graham Dunlop to William H. Wylde, Sept. 20, 1864, WYL/27/38–40, Wylde Papers, DUA. For the role of gold see O'Sullivan to Marcy, Aug. 24, 1856, M43, RG59, NARA.

40. Sanchez to Archibald enc. in Edward Archibald to Malmesbury, Mar. 8, 1859, FO84/1086. For growth of U.S.-Cuba trade see Louis Perez, *Cuba and the United States: Ties of Singular Intimacy* (Athens: University of Georgia Press, 2003), 1–28.

41. On New York–Spain trade see Robert Greenhalgh Albion, *The Rise of New York Port, 1815–1860* (New York: Scribner's, 1939), 394–95, 399. On Cádiz see Patrick O'Flanagan, *Port Cities of Atlantic Iberia, c. 1500–1900* (Aldershot: Ashgate, 2008), 112–15.

42. Domingo Dulce to Ministro de Ultramar, Aug. 30, 1863, Legajo 4686/52, caja 1, Ultramar, AHN. On the Banco Español, see *Estatutos y reglamento del Banco Español de la Habana* (Havana: Imprenta del Gobierno y Capitanía General por S.M., 1856); *Directorio de artes, comercio e industrias de la Habana, 1859* (Havana: Litografia de T. Cuesta, 1859),

tercera parte, 8–9. See also John O'Sullivan to Lewis Cass, Mar. 28, 1857, M43, RG59, NARA.

43. R. Drake to H. Coit, Jan. 14, 1854, Box 220, Folder 2, Moses Taylor Collection, New York Public Library; Sanchez to Archibald enclosed in Archibald to Malmesbury, Apr. 5, 1859, FO84/1086, TNA; *NYT*, Nov. 30, 1860; Cunha Reis to João José Vianna, Oct. 2, 1855, enclosed in John Morgan to Clarendon, June 13, 1856, *Accounts and Papers of the House of Commons*, vol. 44, 132; Appleton Oaksmith and Mason and Company Daybook, page 43, Oaksmith Papers, RLDU. At least some of this money circulated through Figanière, Reis and Company. Cesar Figanière to Joaquim Figanière y Morao, Nov. 11, 1854, M57: Notes from the Portuguese Legation in the United States to the Dept. of State, 1796–1906, Roll T4, RG59, NARA.

44. John O'Sullivan to State Department, July 28, 1856, and Mar. 28, 1857, M43, RG59, NARA.

45. José Maia Ferreira to Ferreira Reis, n.d. 1855, Maia Ferreira to Soares, n.d. 1855, Ex 1, PT 2, JSMFP.

46. Sebastião Lopes de Calheiros e Meneses to Edmund Gabriel, Aug. 28, 1862, enclosed in Gabriel to Lord Russell, Sept. 17, 1862. FO84/1167, TNA; Palmerston to William H. Wylde, May 16, 1862, Wylde Papers, DUA. For more on this issue, see Harris, "Circuits of Wealth," 423–25. See also David Eltis, "The British Contribution to the Transatlantic Slave Trade After 1807," *Economic History Review* 32, no. 2, (1979): 211–27; Marika Sherwood, *After Abolition: Britain and the Slave Trade Since 1807* (New York: Tauris, 2007), 111–42.

47. Willis to Marcy, Jan. 9, 1857, Dispatches from United States Consuls in St. Paul de Loanda, 1854–1893, T430, Roll 1, NARA.

48. Archibald to Russell, Dec. 31, 1863, FO84/1197, TNA.

CHAPTER 3. ABOARD AN ILLEGAL AMERICAN SLAVER

1. *Life Illustrated*, Aug. 2, 1856.

2. For short analyses of this voyage, see Warren S. Howard, *American Slavers and the Federal Law, 1837–1862* (Berkeley: University of California Press, 1963), 192–96; Leonardo Marques, *The United States and the Transatlantic Slave Trade to the Americas, 1776–1867* (New Haven: Yale University Press, 2016), 209–10.

3. On Lemos see Cesar Figanière to Joaquim Figanière y Morao, enclosed in Figanière y Morao to Secretary of State Marcy, Nov. 17, 1854, M57, Roll T4, NARA; *NYT*, June 3, 1854; Dulce to Ministro de

Ultramar, Aug. 30, 1863, Legajo 4686/52, Ultramar, AHN. For Maia Ferreira-Cunha Reis correspondence, see José Maia Ferreira to Cunha Reis, Mar. 9, 1855, Ex 1, PT 2, JSMFP.

4. See also New York Passenger Lists, 1820–1957, M237, Roll 136, List number 112, Year 1854, NARA; Roquinaldo Ferreira, *Dos sertões ao atlântico: tráfico ilegal de escravos e comércio lícito em Angola, 1830–1860* (Luanda: Kilombelombe, 2012), 223.

5. For an introduction to Trinidad and adjacent jurisdictions, see Manuel Moreno Fraginals, *The Sugarmill: The Socioeconomic Complex of Sugar in Cuba, 1760–1860*, trans. Cedric Belfrage (New York: Monthly Review Press, 1976), 66–70. TSTD2 (General Variables>Itinerary> Principal Place of Slave Landing). On the Castros, see Gefaturia principal de policía to Gobr Supr Civil, Feb. 1, 1854, Legajo 427/20575, gobierno general, ANC; María de los Ángeles Meriño Fuentes and Aisnara Perera Díaz, *Contrabando de bozales en Cuba: perseguir el tráfico y mantener la esclavitud, 1845–1866* (Mayabeque: Ediciones Montecallado, 2015), 165.

6. David Eltis, *Economic Growth and the Ending of the Transatlantic Slave Trade* (New York: Oxford University Press, 1987), 127–31. Leonardo Marques, "US Shipbuilding, Atlantic Markets, and the Structures of the Contraband Slave Trade," in *The Rise and Demise of Slavery and the Slave Trade in the Atlantic World*, ed. Philip Misevich and Kristin Mann (Rochester, N.Y.: University of Rochester Press, 2016), 196–219; TSTD2 (General Variables>Ship, nation, owner>Rig, tonnage, and guns mounted>tonnage).

7. New York *Evening Post*, Aug. 17, 1846, Apr. 5, 1848; *Times-Picayune*, Aug. 26, 1846; *Boston Evening Transcript*, Apr. 4, 1851; *Charleston Courier*, July 7, 1851; *Daily Atlas* (Boston), Aug. 5, 1853; *Portland* (Maine) *Weekly Advertiser*, Oct. 25, Dec. 6, 1853, Jan. 3, 1854.

8. For the composition of crews see Joseph Miller, *Way of Death: Merchant Capitalism and the Angolan Slave Trade, 1730–1830* (Madison: University of Wisconsin Press, 1988), 371, 389–90; Jay Coughtry, *The Notorious Triangle: Rhode Island and the African Slave Trade, 1700–1807* (Philadelphia: Temple University Press, 1981), 51–57; Marcus Rediker, *The Slave Ship: A Human History* (New York: Viking, 2007), 157–221. For Maia Ferreira as supercargo, see José Maia Ferreira to Margaret Maia Ferreira, Nov. 28, 1860, cx. 1, pt. 13, no. 58, JSMFP.

9. *New York Evangelist* reprinted in *Liberator*, Dec. 15, 1854 (quote). On crew sizes, see Eltis, *Economic Growth*, 131–33; Sean M. Kelley, *The Voyage of the Slave Ship "Hare": A Journey into Captivity from Sierra Leone*

to *South Carolina* (Chapel Hill: University of North Carolina Press, 2016), 36–51; TSTD2 (General Variables>Captain and crew>Crew at voyage outset).

10. Coughtry, *Notorious Triangle*, 58–59.

11. Coughtry, *Notorious Triangle*, 45–66; Rediker, *The Slave Ship*, 136–42, 222–30; *Illustrated London News*, Sept. 19, 1857, 284 (quote).

12. *NYH*, Nov. 9, 1854; *NYT*, Nov. 9, Dec. 29, 1854.

13. *NYH*, Nov. 9, 1854, *NYT*, Dec. 2, 29, 1854, Feb. 8, 1855. On the *Republic* see *NYT*, Feb. 8, 1855, and TSTD2: voyage id 46497. On shipping masters see Dorothy Denneen Volo and James M. Volo, *Daily Life in the Age of Sail* (Westport, Conn.: Greenwood, 2002), 93–103.

14. *New York Evangelist* reprinted in *The Liberator*, Dec. 15, 1854 (quote); *NYH*, Nov. 9, 1854.

15. *NYT*, Feb. 9, 1854; *New-York Daily Tribune*, July 15, 1856; Stephen D. Behrendt, "Human Capital in the British Slave Trade," in *Liverpool and Transatlantic Slavery*, ed. David Richardson, Suzanna Schwarz, and Anthony Tibbles (Liverpool: Liverpool University Press, 2007), 66–97; Coughtry, *Notorious Triangle*, 66–70. On Dobson, see Sanchez's Memo on *Panchita*, Apr. 5, 1859, FO84/1086, TNA.

16. *NYH*, Nov. 9, 1854; *NYT*, Nov. 7, 1854 (quote).

17. Sanchez to Archibald, Dec. 24, 1859, FO84/1086, TNA; *NYT*, Nov. 7, 1854 (quote); *NYH*, Nov. 9, 1854.

18. *NYH*, Nov. 9, 1854; *NYT*, Feb. 13, Nov. 7, 1854.

19. *NYH*, Nov. 9, 1854.

20. Roquinaldo Ferreira, "The Suppression of the Slave Trade and Slave Departures from Angola, 1830s–1860s," in *Extending the Frontiers: Essays on the New Transatlantic Slave Trade Database*, ed., David Eltis and David Richardson (New Haven: Yale University Press, 2008), 313–34. For imperial tensions see diplomatic correspondence between the British and the Portuguese in FO96/31/4, FO881/553, TNA; Ferreira, "The Conquest of Ambriz: Colonial Expansion and Imperial Competition in Central Africa," *Mulemba: Revista Angolana de Ciências Sociais* 5, no. 9, (2015): 221–23, available online at https://journals.openedition.org/mulemba/439. See also Ferreira, *The Costs of Freedom: Central Africa in the Age of Abolition, 1820–1880* (forthcoming, Princeton University Press).

21. TSTD2, estimates page.

22. Daniel Domingues da Silva has performed the most in-depth research on the origins of captives taken from this region during the nineteenth century. Domingues da Silva, *The Atlantic Slave Trade from*

West Central Africa, 1780–1867 (New York: Cambridge University Press, 2017), 73–99.

23. Jelmer Vos, '"Without the Slave Trade, No Recruitment": From Slave Trading to 'Migrant Recruitment' in the Lower Congo, 1830–90," in *Trafficking in Slavery's Wake: Law and the Experience of Women and Children*, ed. Benjamin N. Lawrance and Richard L. Roberts (Athens: Ohio University Press, 2012), 45–64. Domingues da Silva, *The Atlantic Slave Trade*, 87–93. For British officer Richard Burton's assessment of the French emigration scheme in 1863, see his memo "Reports by Consul Burton of His Ascent of the Congo River, in September 1863," in FO881/1294, TNA.

24. Zora Neale Hurston, *Barracoon: The Story of the Last "Black Cargo,"* ed. Deborah G. Plant (London: Harper Collins, 2018), 43–49; Hannah Durkin, "Finding Last Middle Passage Survivor Sally 'Redoshi' Smith on Page and Screen," *Slavery and Abolition* 40, no. 4 (Mar. 2019): 638–39.

25. George B. Matthew to Clarendon, Aug. 20, 1854, FO84/948, TNA; Edward Manning, *Six Months on a Slaver: A True Narrative* (New York: Harper and Brothers, 1879), 73; Domingues da Silva, *The Atlantic Slave Trade*, 103–11, 115–19; Hurston, *Barracoon*, 41–42.

26. Domingues da Silva, *The Atlantic Slave Trade*, 109–115; Joachim John Monteiro, *Angola and the River Congo*, 2 vols. (New York: Macmillan, 1875), 1:58.

27. David Eltis and David Richardson, *Atlas of the Transatlantic Slave Trade* (New Haven: Yale University Press, 2010), 166; Nicholas Radburn and David Eltis, "Visualizing the Middle Passage: The *Brooks* and the Reality of Ship Crowding in the Transatlantic Slave Trade," *Journal of Interdisciplinary History* 49, no. 4 (Spring 2019): 558; Domingues da Silva, *The Atlantic Slave Trade*, 118–19; Benjamin N. Lawrence, *Amistad's Orphans: An Atlantic Story of Children, Slavery, and Smuggling* (New Haven: Yale University Press, 2014), 36–37.

28. *NYH*, Nov. 9, 1854 (quote); Domingues da Silva, *The Atlantic Slave Trade*, 67–72.

29. *New York Evangelist* reprinted in *The Liberator*, Dec. 15, 1854.

30. For these routes and a description of Boma, see "Reports by Consul Burton of His Ascent of the Congo River, in September 1863," FO881/1294, TNA. For more on Boma, see Norm Schrag, "Mboma and the Lower Zaire: A Socioeconomic Study of a Kongo Trading Com-

munity, c. 1785–1885" (Ph.D. diss., Indiana University, 1985), 62–65. On transporters and caravans, see Miller, *Way of Death*, 189–206; David Livingstone to Edmund Gabriel, Oct. 28, 1854, Add. MS. 37410, British Library, London.

31. *NYT*, June 28, 1856 (Wilson quote); João Soares, May 20, 1856, enc. in John O'Sullivan to Lewis Cass, Mar. 28, 1857, RG59, NARA. On branding see also Yuko Miki, "In the Trial of the Ship: Narrating the Archives of Illegal Slavery," *Social Text* 37, no. 1 (Mar. 2019): 93–94.

32. Hurston, *Barracoon*, 54; William McBlair to Mrs. William McBlair, Oct. 29, 1857, William McBlair Papers, Mariners' Museum Library, Newport News, Virginia.

33. Hurston, *Barracoon*, 55.

34. *NYT*, Dec. 2, 1854, Jan. 26, 1855. For the *Glamorgan*, see TSTD2: voyage id 4924. For jurisdictional issues over sailors on captured slavers, see Don E. Fehrenbacher, *The Slaveholding Republic: An Account of the United States Government's Relations to Slavery* (Oxford: Oxford University Press, 2001), 175.

35. For *Echo* see J. Woodruff, *Report of the Trials in the Echo Cases in Federal Court, Charleston, S.C., April 1859; Together with Arguments of Counsel and Charge of Court* (Columbia, S.C.: Steam-Power Press, 1859), 8. For *Julia Moulton* see *NYH*, Nov. 9, 1854 (quote). For *Thomas Acorn* see Manning, *Six Months*, 55, 61. For *Grey Eagle* see Joseph Town in George B. Matthew to Clarendon, Aug. 20, 1854, FO84/948, TNA.

36. *New York Evangelist* reprinted in *The Liberator*, Dec. 15, 1854; *NYT*, Nov. 9, 1854.

37. Durkin, "Finding Last Middle Passage Survivor," 639; Hurston, *Barracoon*, 55–56; Joseph Town in George B. Matthew to Clarendon, Aug. 20, 1854, FO84/948, TNA; *New York Evangelist* in *The Liberator*, Dec. 15, 1854.

38. *NYH*, Nov. 9, 1854; *New York Evangelist* reprinted in *The Liberator*, Dec. 15, 1854; Manning, *Six Months*, 71.

39. For dimensions of *Julia Moulton* see *NYT*, Nov. 7, 1854. Multiplying the length and breadth gives a rough square footage of the main deck of 2,208. Given the inward curve of the vessel, the slave deck of *Julia Moulton* would have been smaller, perhaps around 2,000 square feet. For *Abbot Devereux*, see *Illustrated London News*, Sept. 19, 1857, 284 (quote); TSTD2: voyage id 4247.

40. Nicholas Radburn, "The Long Middle Passage: The Enslave-

ment of Africans and the Trans-Atlantic Slave Trade, 1640–1808" (Ph.D. diss., Johns Hopkins University, 2016), 137–38, 143; Radburn and Eltis, "Visualizing the Middle Passage," 554–62; *New York Evangelist* reprinted in *The Liberator*, Dec. 15, 1854.

41. Radburn, "The Long Middle Passage," 145–46; TSTD2 (General Variables>Dates>view Summary Statistics).

42. For the *Wildfire* see *Harper's Weekly*, June 2, 1860; TSTD2: *Wildfire* (voyage id 4362). For Liberia vessels see *NYH*, Oct. 4, 1860. For Manning quote see Manning, *Six Months*, 59–60. For burials of Africans liberated from slave ships see Andrew Pearson, *Distant Freedom: St Helena and the Abolition of the Slave Trade* (Liverpool: Liverpool University Press, 2016), 148–153. For more on disease in the slave trade during this period see Manuel Barcia, *The Yellow Demon of Fever: Fighting Disease in the Nineteenth-Century Transatlantic Slave Trade* (New Haven: Yale University Press, 2020).

43. *New York Evangelist* reprinted in *The Liberator*, Dec. 15, 1854; *NYT*, Dec. 2, 1854; *NYT*, Jan. 26, 1855.

44. David Eltis, "Mortality and Voyage Lengths in the Middle Passage: New Evidence from the Nineteenth Century," *Journal of Economic History* 44, no. 2 (June 1984): 301–8. Figures from TSTD2 (General Variables>Itinerary+Dates>see Summary Statistics).

45. *NYT*, June 28, 1856 (Wilson quote); Commodore Wise to Rear-Admiral Sir F. Grey, July 20, 1859, enclosed in Wise to Sec. of Admiralty, July 26, 1859, *Accounts and Papers of the House of Commons*, vol. 70: *Session 24 January–28 August 1860* (London: Harrison and Sons, 1860), 122; William McBlair to Virginia Myers McBlair, Oct. 29, 1857, William McBlair Papers, Mariners' Museum Library, Newport News, Virginia. For *Nightingale* see *NYH*, June 17, 1861. For more on long confinement in barracoons, see Eltis, *Economic Growth*, 135–38.

46. *New York Evangelist* reprinted in *The Liberator*, Dec. 15, 1854. On provisioning see David Eltis, "The Slave Trade and Commercial Agriculture in an African Context," in *Commercial Agriculture, the Slave Trade and Slavery in Atlantic Africa*, ed. Suzanne Schwarz, Robin Law, and Silke Strickrodt (Oxford: Boydell and Brewer, 2013), 28–53.

47. The *Brutus* for instance, took in beans, corn, pork, and beef near the Congo River on the same day it took captives. See *Whaleman's Shipping List and Merchant's Transcript* (New Bedford, Mass.), Aug. 27, 1861. Guilherme José da Silva Correa to João José Vianna, Apr. 21, 1855, enc. in John Morgan to Clarendon, June 13, 1856, in *Accounts and Papers*

of the House of Commons, vol. 44: *Session 30 April—28 August 1857* (London: Harrison and Sons, 1857), 132.

48. Hurston, *Barracoon*, 55; McCarthy in Thomas Savage to William Seward, May 14, 1864, enclosed in Lyons to Russell, Aug. 15, 1864, FO84/1222, TNA. On running out of provisions see Miller, *Way of Death*, 351–55. For dehydration in the Middle Passage, see Kenneth F. Kiple and Brian T. Higgins, "Mortality Caused by Dehydration During the Middle Passage," *Social Science History* 13, no. 4 (1989): 421–37; Sowande' Mustakeem, "'I Never Have Such a Sickly Ship Before': Diet, Disease, and Mortality in 18th-Century Atlantic Slaving Voyages," *Journal of African American History* 93, no. 4 (Fall 2008), 474–96.

49. Manning, *Six Months*, 66, 74–77. Sowande' M. Mustakeem, *Slavery at Sea: Terror, Sex, and Sickness in the Middle Passage* (Urbana: University of Illinois Press, 2016), 82–90, 122–29.

50. *New-York Daily Times*, n.d., 1853, enclosed in Crawford to Clarendon, Apr. 28, 1853, FO84/905, TNA. TSTD2 lists three cases of "slave insurrection" after 1850 (General Variables>Outcome>African Resistance). The vessel that lost all captives is unnamed in TSTD2 but its voyage id is recorded as 4313. For the shorter voyages argument, see Eltis, *Economic Growth*, 133. On violent resistance in the legal slave trade, see Eric Robert Taylor, *If We Must Die: Shipboard Insurrections in the Era of the Atlantic Slave Trade* (Baton Rouge: Louisiana State University Press, 2006).

51. Sylviane A. Diouf, *Dreams of Africa in Alabama: The Story of the "Clotilda" and the Last Enslaved African Brought to America* (New York: Oxford University Press, 2007), 68; Pearson, *Distant Freedom*, 142.

52. For the number of slavers see TSTD2: Database>Year Range> Itinerary, at https://slavevoyages.org/voyages/CIWGYd1o. For the number of captives see TSTD2, estimates page, at http://slavevoyages.org/estimates/ehKGVhqi.

53. The 1851–63 data derive from TSTD2 (General Variables>Outcome). See also Daniel Domingues da Silva, David Eltis, Philip Misevich, and Olatunji Ojo, "The Diaspora of Africans Liberated from Slave Ships in the Nineteenth Century," *Journal of African History* 55, no. 3 (2014): 347–49, 367; Jake Christopher Richards, "Anti-Slave-Trade Law, 'Liberated Africans' and the State in the South Atlantic World, c. 1839–1852," *Past and Present* 241, no. 1 (Nov. 2018): 204–15. On interceptions see Eltis, *Economic Growth*, 100.

54. The Colonial Office, Foreign Office, Admiralty, and Treasury

all had a say in the fate of liberated Africans, as did the British anti-slavery lobby and West Indian planters. Interception data derived from 1851–63 data in TSTD2 (General Variables>Outcome).

55. Rosanne Marion Adderley, *"New Negroes from Africa": Slave Trade Abolition and Free African Settlement in the Nineteenth-Century Caribbean* (Bloomington: Indiana University Press, 2006), 72–75. Around 364 Africans also ended up in the Bahamas due to the shipwreck of a slaver, *Heroina* (also known as *Peter Mowell*, TSTD2: voyage id 4365), in 1860 that was bound for Cuba. See Adderley, *New Negroes*, 61–62, 129–30. For cases in Saint Helena and pathways to the British Caribbean, see Pearson, *Distant Freedom*, 278–290.

56. The intercepted vessels and the number of captives liberated were: *Echo*, 318, *Wildfire*, 559, *William*, 570, *Bogota*, 441, *Erie*, 897, *Storm King*, 619, *Cora*, 709, *Bonito*, 750, *Delicica*, 673, *Nightingale*, 916. See Sharla M. Fett, *Recaptured Africans: Surviving Slave Ships, Detention, and Dislocation in the Final Years of the Slave Trade* (Chapel Hill: University of North Carolina Press, 2017), 140. For the U.S. reception to transportation to Liberia see Ted Maris-Wolf, "'Of Blood and Treasure': Recaptive Africans and the Politics of Slave Trade Suppression," *Journal of the Civil War Era* 4, no. 1 (Mar. 2014): 53–83. For the broader context for free people of color in the United States see David Brion Davis, *The Problem of Slavery in the Age of Emancipation* (New York: Knopf, 2014).

57. On captures see Joseph Crawford to Clarendon, Sept. 27, 1854, FO84/937, TNA, with additional captures computed from Angeles and Perera, 251–59. On Cunha Reis, see "Expediente de solicitud de Manuel Basilio Reis pidiendo emancipados para su finca," 4676, Exp. 64, Ultramar, AHN. On emancipados see Inés Roldán de Montaud, "On the Blurred Boundaries of Freedom: Liberated Africans in Cuba, 1817–1870" in *New Frontiers of Slavery*, ed. Dale W. Tomich (Albany: State University of New York Press, 2016), 159–92; David Murray, *Odious Commerce: Britain, Spain and the Abolition of the Cuban Slave Trade* (New York: Cambridge University Press, 1980), 271–97.

58. *NYT*, Nov. 7, 1854; *NYH*, Nov. 9, 1854.

59. Murray, *Odious Commerce*, 233–39.

60. Joseph Crawford to Clarendon, July 6, 14, Sept. 27, 1854, FO84/937, TNA; John Backhouse to Clarendon, Jan. 1, 1854, FO84/959, TNA.

61. John Backhouse to Clarendon (*Gaceta* enclosed), Aug. 3, 1854, FO84/930, TNA.

62. Roldán de Montaud, "On the Blurred Boundaries," 144-46; Murray, *Odious Commerce*, 238.

63. For more on this case see United States v. James Smith, Criminal Case Files, United States Circuit Court for the Southern District of New York, RG 21, NARA, New York office; Robert McClelland to John McKeon, Oct. 7, 1854, July 18, 1855, RG48, Letters Sent Concerning the Judiciary, 1854-1869, Box 1, NARA; *NYT*, Nov. 7, 9, 10, 1854.

CHAPTER 4. RING OF SPIES

1. Palmerston to Russell, Mar. 14, 1860, PRO/32/22/21, Russell Papers, TNA. Figure from TSTD2, estimates page.

2. On U.S. spies see Paul Finkelman, "The American Suppression of the African Slave Trade: Lessons on Legal Change, Social Policy, and Legislation," *Akron Law Review* 42, no. 2 (2009): 464-65. On Pezeula see Joseph Crawford to Clarendon, July 25, 1854, FO84/937, TNA. On Alcoforado, see Leslie Bethell, *The Abolition of the Brazilian Slave Trade: Britain, Brazil and the Slave Trade Question, 1807-1869* (Cambridge: Cambridge University Press, 1970), 310-11, 351-52; Joaquim de Paula Guedes Alcoforado, "História sobre o infame negócio de africanos da África Oriental e Ocidental, com todas as ocorrências desde 1831 a 1853," transcribed by Roquinaldo Ferreira in *Estudos Afro-Asiáticos* 28 (1995): 219-29. Act of 1819: "An Act in Addition to the Acts Prohibiting the Slave Trade," Act of Mar. 3, 1819, 3 Stat. 532.

3. Richard Huzzey, *Freedom Burning: Anti-Slavery and Empire in Victorian Britain* (Ithaca: Cornell University Press, 2012), 42-43; David Eltis, *Economic Growth and the Ending of the Transatlantic Slave Trade* (New York: Oxford University Press, 1987), 91-97.

4. Keith Hamilton, "Zealots and Helots: The Slave Trade Department of the Nineteenth-Century Foreign Office," in *Slavery, Diplomacy and Empire: Britain and the Suppression of the Slave Trade, 1807-1975*, ed. Keith Hamilton and Patrick Salmon (Eastbourne: Sussex Academic Press, 2009), 20-41; Ray Jones, *The Nineteenth-Century Foreign Office: An Administrative History* (London: Weidenfield and Nicolson, 1971), 12-14; Keith Neilson and T. G. Otte, *The Permanent Under-Secretary* (New York: Routledge, 2009), 5-31; Richard Huzzey, *Freedom Burning*, 42-44, 70-74; Eltis, *Economic Growth*, 91-97, 114-16, 212-14.

5. Archibald to Foreign Office, Dec. 28, 1858, FO5/697, TNA. On the SSF see Neilson and Otte, *The Permanent Under-Secretary*, 8. On SSF

allowance see Memos and correspondence in HD3/142, TNA. On criticism of the naval campaign see Huzzey, *Freedom Burning*, 112–24.

6. For the functions and expansion of British consuls in the nineteenth century, see D. C. M. Platt, *The Cinderella Service: British Consuls Since 1825* (London: Longman, 1971), 16–67.

7. On these broad developments see C. A. Bayly, *The Birth of the Modern World, 1780–1914* (Oxford: Wiley-Blackwell, 2004), 445–64; Jürgen Osterhammel, *The Transformation of the Modern World: A Global History of the Nineteenth Century*, trans. Patrick Camiller (Princeton: Princeton University Press, 2014), 77–113, 710–29.

8. Palmerston to Henry Hudson, Oct. 29, 1849, FO84/766, TNA; Eltis, *Economic Growth*, 114–16.

9. On Britain's hiring of Alcoforado in 1849, and earlier work in the 1840s, see Hudson to Palmerston, July 27, 1850, FO84/804, TNA. For bounties paid to British and U.S. crews see Peter Grindal, *Opposing the Slavers: The Royal Navy's Campaign Against the Atlantic Slave Trade* (London: Tauris, 2016), 109–10, 203, 205, 371, 449–50, 531, 537, 543, 624; George Brooks, *Yankee Traders, Old Coasters and African Middlemen: A History of Legitimate American Trade with West Africa in the Nineteenth Century* (Boston: Boston University Press, 1970), 109.

10. Memo from Commander Grey Skipwith, ca. spring 1850, ADM 123/173, TNA. For payments see Hudson to Palmerston, July 27, 1850, FO84/804, TNA; Earl Granville to Henry Southern, Jan. 31, 1852, Earl Malmesbury to Southern, May 3, 1852, Malmesbury to Southern, Nov. 11, 1852, Malmesbury to Southern, Dec. 20, 1852, FO84/877, TNA; Clarendon to Jerningham, Mar. 24, 1853, FO84/910, TNA. Palmerston to Russell, Mar. 14, 1860, PRO/32/22/21, Russell Papers, TNA. TSTD2 (General Variables>Itinerary>Place of Departure+Year Range).

11. Wylde Memo, May 26, 1859, FO84/1082, TNA.

12. For report, see Appendix B in Jones, *The Nineteenth-Century Foreign Office*, 151–52. Archibald to Malmesbury, Oct. 9, 1858, FO84/1059, TNA; Edwards to Archibald, Sept. 20, 1859, enclosed in Archibald to Malmesbury, Oct. 9, 1858, FO84/1059, TNA.

13. Campbell to Clarendon, Dec. 19, 1854, FO84/950, TNA; John V. Crawford to William Henry Wylde, Aug. 25, 1864, Oct. 4, 1865, WYL/27/33-34, Wylde Family Papers, DUA; Hudson to Wylde, Aug. 22, 1859, FO84/1095, TNA.

14. For Rio de Janeiro, see James Hudson to Wylde, Aug. 22, 1859, FO84/1095, TNA. For Havana, see John V. Crawford to William Henry

Wylde, Aug. 25, 1864, Oct. 4, 1865, WYL/27/33–34, Wylde Family Papers, DUA. For Santander, see "Pensions and allowances paid out of Secret Service Fund," June 29, 1859, HD3/27; "Statement of Annual Charges on the Secret Service Fund," Nov. 9, 1865, HD3/33, TNA. For Cádiz, see Dunlop to Wylde, Jan. 28, 1865, FO84/1241, TNA.

15. For Thomes, see Crawford to Clarendon, May 30, 1853, FO84/905, TNA. For New York, see John Crampton to Clarendon, Mar. 30, Apr. 10, 1854, FO84/948, TNA. For West Central Africa see Eltis, *Economic Growth*, 114; Roquinaldo Ferreira, "The Conquest of Ambriz: Colonial Expansion and Imperial Competition in Central Africa," *Mulemba: Revista Angolana de Ciências Sociais* 5, no. 9, (2015), available online at https://journals.openedition.org/mulemba/439. For Barreto, see Campbell to Clarendon, Dec. 19, 1854, FO84/950, TNA. For Carvalho, see Campbell to Russell, Jan. 8, 1864, ADM123/184, TNA. On Alcoforado and Brito, see James Hudson to Wylde, Aug. 22, 1859, FO84/1095, TNA.

16. Sanchez's full name was Emilio Francisco Sanchez y Dolz. Bernabé died sometime before 1831, when Emilio was still a boy. See Escribanías, Legajo 639/10, ANC; Francisco Xavier de Santa Cruz y Mallen, *Historia de Familias Cubanas*, vol. 2 (Havana: Ed. Hercules, 1940), 344–45, 354.

17. On Nuevitas see Jacobo de la Pezuela, *Diccionario geográfico, estadístico, histórico, de la isla de Cuba*, vol. 4 (Madrid: Imprenta del Banco Industrial y Mercantil, 1866), 133–48. For the growth of the slave trade and slave society in Cuba see David Murray, *Odious Commerce*; Manuel Moreno Fraginals, *The Sugar Mill: The Socioeconomic Complex of Sugar in Cuba, 1760–1860*, trans. Cedric Belfrage (New York: Monthly Review Press, 1976); Ada Ferrer, *Freedom's Mirror: Cuba and Haiti in the Age of Revolution* (New York: Cambridge University Press, 2014).

18. On Adolfo see *Philly Public Ledger*, July 18, 1843; *NYT*, July 25, 1898. On José see José Sanchez to Daniel Webster, Apr. 7, 1843, T588, RG59, NARA. On Pedro's lands and slaves in 1869 see Sanchez to Comandante General del Departamento Central, Nuevitas, Aug. 5 1869, Legajo 4356/21, Ultramar, AHN. For trade see *NYT*, July 17, 1860, May 28, 1861.

19. *Times-Picayune*, Dec. 12, 1846; New York State Census, 1855, New York City, Ward 20, E.D. 2; *NYH*, Nov. 30, 1858; Sanchez to Archibald, July 12, 1859, FO84/1086, TNA. On Taylor see Roland Taylor Ely, "From Counting-House to Cane Field: Moses Taylor and the Cuban

Sugar Planter in the Reign of Isabel II, 1833–1868" (Ph.D. diss., Harvard University, 1958).

20. Archibald to Malmesbury, Mar. 29, May 3, 1859, FO84/1086, TNA.

21. Archibald to Secretary of State for Foreign Affairs, July 11, 1859, FO84/1086, TNA; Barreto to Campbell enclosed in Campbell to Clarendon, Dec. 19, 1854, FO84/950, TNA; Dunlop to Wylde, May 8, 1865, FO84/1241, TNA; Crawford to Clarendon, May 30, 1853, FO84/905, TNA. See also Luis Martínez-Fernández, *Fighting Slavery in the Caribbean: The Life and Times of a British Family in Nineteenth-Century Havana* (Armonk, N.Y.: Sharpe, 1998), 143–51.

22. Archibald to Wylde, Mar. 31, 1862, FO84/1172, TNA; Archibald to Secretary of State, July 11, 1859, FO84/1086, TNA.

23. See Sanchez memo enclosed in Archibald to Malmesbury, May 3, 1859, FO84/1086, TNA.

24. For the Portuguese–slave trade connection see *New-York Daily Tribune*, Mar. 19, 1856. Robert Ernst counts only 1,176 Portuguese natives arriving in New York between May 5, 1847, and December 31, 1860. See Ernst, *Immigrant Life in New York City, 1825–1863* (New York: King's Crown Press, 1949), 188. Archibald to Malmesbury, May 3, 1859, FO84/1086, TNA.

25. Archibald to Malmesbury, June 14, 1859, FO84/1086, TNA; John V. Crawford to Wylde, Aug. 25, 1864, WYL/27/33-34, Wylde Family Papers, DUA.

26. Archibald to Malmesbury, May 3, 1859, FO84/1086, TNA.

27. Wylde Memo, May 26, 1859, FO84/1082, TNA; Archibald to Malmesbury, Mar. 8, 29, 1859, FO84/1086, TNA; Malmesbury to Archibald, June 10, Aug. 6, 1859, FO84/1086, TNA. For ships intercepted by the British, Sanchez was to earn £5. 10s. per ton if it was empty and £1. 10s. per ton plus £5 per captive if it was carrying slaves.

28. On Saco see Olga Portuondo Zúñiga, *José Antonio Saco: Eternamente Polémico* (Santiago de Cuba: Editorial Oriente, 2005); Christopher Schmidt-Nowara, *Empire and Antislavery: Spain, Cuba, and Puerto Rico, 1833–1874* (Pittsburgh: University of Pittsburgh Press, 1999), 18–21.

29. On Bernabé Sanchez in Philadelphia see Geoffrey Scott Mitchell, "Blacks, the White Elite, and the Politics of Nation Building: Inter and Intraracial Relationships" (Ph.D. diss., Tulane, 2006), 191; Levi Marrero, *Cuba: Economía y Sociedad: Azúcar, Ilustración y Conciencia, 1763–1868*, vol. 15 (Río Piedras: Editorial San Juan, 1972), 47–48, 354.

On a tantalizing letter written by a Bernabé Sanchez (possibly Emilio's father) to President James Monroe in 1822 requesting U.S. annexation of Cuba, see John Quincy Adams, *Memoirs of John Quincy Adams, Comprising Portions of His Diary from 1795 to 1848*, vol. 6 (Philadelphia: Lippincott, 1875), 69–74. On Sanchez during the War for Independence see Sanchez to Comandante General del Departamento Central, Nuevitas, Aug. 5, 1869, Legajo 4356/21, Ultramar, AHN.

30. John V. Crawford to Clarendon, Sept. 30, 1869, FO84/1303, TNA.

31. Archibald to Lord Lyons, Oct. 4, 1859, FO84/1086, TNA.

32. Archibald to Malmesbury, Mar. 29, 1859, FO84/1086, TNA; Sanchez to Archibald, Apr. 5, 30, 1859, FO84/1086, TNA.

33. Sanchez to Archibald, May 9, July 27, Aug. 2, 1859, FO84/1086, TNA; Archibald to Malmesbury, May 17, 1859, FO84/1086, TNA; Sanchez to Archibald, Sept. 17, 1861, FO/84/1138, TNA. For Braddick and Keefe see Sanchez's Memo on *Panchita*, Apr. 5, 1859, FO84/1086, TNA.

34. Sanchez's Memo on *Panchita*, Apr. 5, 1859, FO84/1086, TNA; Sanchez to Archibald, Aug. 2, 1859, FO84/1086, TNA.

35. Archibald to Sanchez, Mar. 8, 1859, FO84/1086, TNA.

36. Sanchez to Archibald, May 9 ("money and influence"), 13 ("time alone"), 1859, FO84/1086, TNA; Gabriel Enriquez to Captain General, July 6, 1861, Reales Ordenes y Cédulas, Legajo 222/428, ANC.

37. *Directorio de artes, comercio e industrias de la Habana, 1859* (Habana: Litografia de T. Cuesta, 1859), segunda parte, 26; Archibald to Secretary of State, Aug. 29, 1859, FO84/1086, TNA (quote); Sanchez to Archibald, May 9, 1859, FO84/1086, TNA; TSTD2: *Tacony* (voyage id 5125).

38. For a full list of Sanchez's newspapers, see enclosure in Archibald to Secretary of State, July 11, 1859, FO84/1086, TNA.

39. On *Eloisa* see Sanchez to Archibald, July 19, 1859, FO84/1086, TNA. For *Antelope* and quote see enclosure in Archibald to Secretary of State, May 17, 1859, TNA.

40. On Vianna, see Sanchez memo enclosed in Archibald to Malmesbury, May 3, 1859, FO84/1086, TNA. Sanchez to Archibald, Apr. 30 ("suspicion" quote), May 9 (customhouse), July 27 ("casual conversation" quote) 1859, FO84/1086, TNA.

41. TSTD2 indicates that 216 total voyages took place in 1859–1862. Accepting TSTD2's estimation that they have accounted for 97 percent of all voyages to the Spanish Americas during this period, we can

project that 223 voyages took place in 1859-1862. See TSTD2, http://slavevoyages.org/voyages/BVnRRbrF. Sanchez documented 171 voyages: see FO84/1086, FO84/1111, FO84/1138, FO84/1172, TNA.

42. TSTD2: *Pamphylia* (voyage id 4809).

43. For construction and Sewell ownership, see *New-York Marine Register, 1857*, 105. For Mora Bros. and Navarro ownership, see *New-York Marine Register, 1858*, 113. For voyages in the sugar trade, see *Boston Courier*, Apr. 18, May 26, 1859. For repairs, see *American Lloyd's Register of American and Foreign Shipping* (New York: E. & G. W. Blunt, 1861), 196. For preparations in Havana and clearance, see Sanchez to Archibald, Oct. 21, 1859, FO84/1086, TNA; U.S. Consul John Appleton to Assistant Secretary of State, Oct. 6, 1859, *House Executive Documents, 36th Congress* (Washington, D.C., 1861), 373-74.

44. For details of these reports, see list of slavers in Archibald to Secretary of State, Oct. 10, 1859; Sanchez to Archibald, Sept. 29, Oct. 21, 1859, FO84/1086, TNA.

45. See notes on cover of Archibald to Secretary of State, Oct. 10, 1859, FO84/1086, TNA.

46. For the journey of information, see *Economist*, Feb. 18, 1860; W. G. Romaine to Grey, Nov. 4, 1859, ADM123/179, TNA; notes on cover of Archibald to Secretary of State, Oct. 10, 1859, FO84/1096, TNA. On the mechanical role of junior clerks, see Otte, *The Permanent Under-Secretary*, 8. See also, Jones, *The Administration of the Nineteenth-Century Foreign Office*, 11, 20-40, 149-50.

47. For the arrival of *Sumpter* in Luanda on Jan. 5, 1860, see Log of HMS *Pluto*, ADM53/6499, TNA. For USS *Sumpter* at Fernando Po see London *Times*, Mar. 13, 1860. For more on mail pickup see Donald L. Canney, *Africa Squadron: The U.S. Navy and the Slave Trade, 1843-1861* (Dulles, Va.: Potomac Books, 2006), 214; C. Herbert Gilliland, ed., *USS "Constellation" on the Dismal Coast: Willie Leonard's Journal, 1859-1861* (Columbia: University of South Carolina Press, 2013), 30, 40.

48. For payout for the *Pamphylia* capture, which totaled £2,930, see High Court of Admiralty, and Supreme Court of Judicature, High Court of Justice, Probate, Divorce and Admiralty Division: Admiralty Miscellanea; Naval prize account register, vol. 1, 1855-62, no. 16, in HCA30/988, TNA. Burton had been communicating frequently with other British cruisers during early January. See Log of HMS *Triton*, ADM53/6621, TNA.

49. On Burton's description of the *Pamphylia* see Lt. Burton to

Admiralty, Jan. 9, 1860, in *Accounts and Papers of the House of Commons*, vol. 70: *Session 24 January—28 August 1860* (London: Harrison and Sons, 1860), 149. On the *Pamphylia* decision see Judge Wilde to Russell, Feb. 28, 1860, FO84/121, TNA. For the *Pamphylia* Africans' voyages to the Americas, see E. H. Drummond Hay to Duke of Newcastle, Feb. 29, 1860, CO247/93, TNA. I am indebted to Andrew Pearson for sharing this source. For the experiences of Africans freed from slave ships at Saint Helena, see Pearson, *Distant Freedom*, 106–200, 211–41.

50. The Foreign Office renewed Sanchez's contract annually in the spring. For the final three-month renewal in 1862, see Wylde Memo, Feb. 20, 1862, FO84/1172, TNA. The Foreign Office paid £100 on the capture of the *Stephen H. Townsend* and *Lillie Mills* retroactively in 1863. For the payments on the four vessels, see Foreign Office to Archibald, Aug. 5, 1859, FO84/1086, TNA and W. G. Romaine to E. Hammond, May 14, 1863, and enclosures, FO84/1208, TNA.

51. Edmonstone note, June 18, 1860, enclosed in Wylde Memo, Feb. 1, 1861, FO84/1138, TNA; Grey to Secretary of Admiralty, May 18, 1860, enclosed in Romaine to Wodehouse, June 28, 1860, FO84/1123.

52. Wylde Memo, Feb. 20, 1862, FO84/1172, TNA.

53. Hammond Memo (with response by Malmesbury), May 1858, HD3/142, TNA. For budget and annual expenses, see Hammond to Russell, June 29, 1859, HD3/27, TNA. For the SSF account in 1862 and 1865, see annual expense memos in HD3/31 and HD3/33, TNA, respectively. For further budgetary pressure on the Foreign Office from the Treasury between 1853 and 1858, see Jones, *The Nineteenth-Century Foreign Office*, 22–40.

54. Sanchez to Archibald, Feb. 26, 1860, FO84/1111, TNA. The Foreign Office also blamed the Admiralty for "neglect[ing] to state on what information they made." Wylde Memo, Mar. 21, 1860, FO84/1111, TNA. For Sanchez's memo, see Sanchez to Archibald, Dec. 4, 1860, FO84/1111, TNA. Although the Foreign Office's approach to Sanchez's pay makes an assessment of his effectiveness difficult, it is possible to give rough estimates of the number of ships and captives intercepted on his intelligence by extending Edmonstone's one-year assessment over the entire length of Sanchez's career and adjusting for his slightly diminishing reportage over time. That calculation produces a total of 30 slavers captured on his information between 1859 and 1862. To estimate how many captives traffickers would have forced across the Atlantic Basin on these ships, we can multiply the 30 slavers be multiplied by 696, the aver-

age number of captives carried between 1859 and 1862, which produces a figure of 20,880. Although it is difficult to calculate the extra risk that Sanchez's information created for slave traders, his intelligence presumably reduced their willingness to send more vessels into the traffic, and thus prevented even more Africans from entering the trade.

55. For Sanchez's first note, see New York *Evening Post*, July 26, 1860. For the list of eighty-five slavers, see New York *Evening Post*, July 28, 1860. For Sanchez's accusations against De Graw, see clipping from New York *Evening Post*, ca. Aug. 7, 1860, enclosed in Archibald to Secretary of State, June 5, 1860, FO84/1111, TNA. For the "single handed" quote, see clipping from New York *Evening Post*, ca. Sept. 1, 1860 enclosed in Archibald to Secretary of State, Sept. 4, 1860, FO84/1111, TNA.

56. Archibald to Russell, July 31, 1860, FO84/1111, TNA.

57. For *Louisa*, see clipping of New York *Evening Post*, ca. Aug. 1860, enclosed in Archibald to Secretary of State, Feb. 5, 1861, FO84/1138, TNA. For De Graw, see the *World*, Aug. 11, 1860; New York *Evening Post*, Aug. 14, 1860. For Sanchez's response to De Graw, see New York *Evening Post*, Aug. 16, 1860.

58. New York *Evening Post*, Aug. 7, 1860; *Journal of Commerce*, reprinted in *Evening Express*, Aug. 9, 1860; *Evening Express*, Sept. 3, 1860.

59. Sanchez to Archibald, Aug. 18, 1860, FO84/1111, TNA.

60. *New York City Deaths*, 1892–1902; Deaths Reported in 1901 (M–Z). Borough of Manhattan; Certificate no. 3443.

CHAPTER 5. AMERICAN POLITICS
AND AMERICAN SUPPRESSION

1. *NYT*, Feb. 22, 1862. See also Ron Soodalter, *Hanging Captain Gordon: The Life and Trial of an American Slave Trader* (New York: Atria, 2006); James A. Rawley, "Captain Nathaniel Gordon, the Only American Executed for Violating the Slave Trade Laws," *Civil War History* 39, no. 3 (1993): 216–24.

2. See slips in Archibald to Secretary of State, May 8, 1860, FO84/1111, TNA. For Wilson, see *NYT*, June 16, 1860. The United States v. Theodore Rynders and Henry Munn: Indictment, United States Circuit Court for the Southern District of New York, Criminal Case Files, RG 21, NARA, New York office; *NYT*, May 7, 1860.

3. Isaiah Rynders to Abraham Lincoln, Mar. 25, 1861, RG60, Let-

ters Received, 1809–1870, Box 115: NY 1856–1861, NARA; *NYT,* Mar. 18, 1861.

4. *NYT,* Mar. 18, 1861; *NYT,* Dec. 27, 1860; George Templeton Strong, diary entry of Nov. 2, 1860, in *Writing New York: A Literary Anthology,* ed. Phillip Lopate (New York: Washington Square Press, 1998), 219. On Betts, see *New-York Daily Tribune,* July 10, 1857; Warren S. Howard, *American Slavers and the Federal Law, 1837–1862* (Berkeley: University of California Press, 1963), 155–59.

5. Don E. Fehrenbacher, *The Slaveholding Republic: An Account of the United States Government's Relations to Slavery* (Oxford: Oxford University Press, 2001), 175–76; Leonardo Marques, *The United States and the Transatlantic Slave Trade to the Americas, 1776–1867* (New Haven: Yale University Press, 2016), 207–16; Peter Graham Fish, *Federal Justice in the Mid-Atlantic South: United States Courts from Maryland to the Carolinas, 1836–1861* (Durham: Carolina Academic Press, 2015); Randy J. Sparks, "Blind Justice: The United States's Failure to Curb the Illegal Slave Trade," *Law and History Review* 35, no. 1 (Feb. 2017): 53–79, esp. 71–72.

6. United States v. Island of Cuba, Bark et al., Case Files, 1790–1917, RG21; NARA, Waltham, Massachusetts, office.

7. For sale of *Isla de Cuba* see enclosure in Archibald to Malmesbury, Apr. 5, 1859, FO84/1086, TNA. On *Cora,* see *NYT,* Mar. 18, 1861. On Horn, see Sanchez to Archibald Aug. 9, Dec. 16, 1859, FO84/1086, TNA.

8. John McKeon to J. B. Sheeter, Mar. 29, 1856, New York Southern District, Box 80, 1856–1860, RG206, Letters Received from U.S. District Attorneys, Marshals, and Clerks of Court, 1801–1898, NARA; McKeon to Caleb Cushing, Oct. 31, 1854, Box 113, RG60, Letters Received, 1809–1870, NARA. See also Marques, *The United States,* 219–22.

9. For more on this case see United States v. James Smith, Criminal Case Files, United States Circuit Court for the Southern District of New York, RG 21, NARA, New York office; Robert McClelland to John McKeon, Oct. 7, 1854, July 18, 1855, RG48, Letters Sent Concerning the Judiciary, 1854–1869, Box 1, NARA; *NYT,* Nov. 7, 9, 10, 1854.

10. Howard, *American Slavers,* 213–35.

11. On American naval suppression, see Donald L. Canney, *Africa Squadron: The U.S. Navy and the Slave Trade, 1843–1861* (Dulles, Va.: Potomac Books, 2006); Howard, *American Slavers,* 41–44, 70–84, and appendixes; John Randolph Spears, *The American Slave-Trade: An Ac-*

count of Its Origin, Growth and Suppression (New York: Scribner's, 1900), 148–59. A third fleet, the Brazil Squadron, wound down its suppression operations in South American waters after the closure of the Brazilian traffic in 1850. On this squadron, see Canney, *Africa Squadron*, 111–20, 234.

12. Act of 1819: "An Act in Addition to the Acts Prohibiting the Slave Trade," Act of Mar. 3, 1819, 3 Stat. 532. On the Webster-Ashburton Treaty, see Fehrenbacher, *Slaveholding Republic*, 165–72; Richard Mac-Master, "The United States, Great Britain and the Suppression of the Cuban Slave Trade" (Ph.D. diss., Georgetown University, 1968), 154–203.

13. Canney, *Africa Squadron*, 41, 50–51. Howard, *American Slavers*, 239–40.

14. William McBlair to Virginia Myers McBlair, Oct. 29, Sept. 25, 1857, William McBlair Papers, Mariners' Museum Library, Newport News, Virginia.

15. Howard, *American Slavers*, 42–43, 48; Andrew Hull Foote, *Africa and the American Flag* (New York: Appleton, 1854), 351–53; F. W. Grey to 3rd Earl Grey, Aug. 11, 1857, GRE/B98/4/5–7, Papers of Henry George, 3rd Earl Grey, DUA; Canney, *Africa Squadron*, 138, 233; Christopher Lloyd, *The Navy and the Slave Trade: The Suppression of the African Slave Trade in the Nineteenth Century* (London: Routledge, 1968), 275–76.

16. On consuls during this period, including the role of Savage, see Marques, *The United States*, 207–9; Howard, *American Slavers*, 45–46, 111–123.

17. *New York Tribune*, May 30, 1859, enclosed in Archibald to Malmesbury, May 30, 1859, FO84/1086, TNA.

18. Basil Rauch, *American Interest in Cuba: 1848–1855* (New York: Columbia University Press, 1948), 55–101. For the relationship between annexationism and broader U.S. concerns for the security of Cuba's slave system, see Matthew Karp, *This Vast Southern Empire: Slaveholders at the Helm of American Foreign Policy* (Cambridge: Harvard University Press, 2016), 59–69, 187–98.

19. On López, see Tom Chaffin, *Fatal Glory: Narciso López and the First Clandestine U.S. War Against Cuba* (Charlottesville: University of Virginia Press, 1996).

20. McPherson, *Battle Cry of Freedom*. For more on Cuba during Pierce's administration, see Karp, *This Vast Southern Empire*, 189–98;

Piero Gleijeses, "Clashing over Cuba: The United States, Spain and Britain," *Journal of Latin American Studies* 49, no. 2 (May 2017): 215–41.

21. *New Orleans Delta*, Aug. 2, 1850; *Norfolk Democrat* (Dedham, Mass.), Mar. 3, 1853; *Constitution* (Middletown, Conn.), Mar. 17, 1852.

22. *A Series of Articles on the Cuban Question* (New York: La Verdad, 1849); *Cuestion negrera de la isla de Cuba por los editores y colaboradores de La Verdad* (New York: La Verdad, August 1851); Ambrosio José Gonzales, *Manifesto on Cuban Affairs Addressed to the People of the United States* (New Orleans: Daily Delta, 1853); Lorenzo Allo, *Domestic Slavery in Its relations with Wealth: An Oration Pronounced in the Cuban Democratic Athenaeum of New York* (New York: W. H. Tinson, 1855); *La Crónica* in *Daily National Intelligencer*, July 9, 1853. On *La Crónica* as a "mouthpiece" for slave traders, see *NYT*, July 29, 1853. For suppression of newspapers, see Valentin Cañedo to Presidente del Consejo de Ministros, Oct 6, 1853, 4638/6, Ultramar, AHN; José de la Concha to Spanish Consulate in New Orleans, ca. 1852, 4645/15, Ultramar, AHN. For espionage, see Presidente del Consejo de Ministros to Capitán-General, July 10, 1852, 4637/25, Ultramar, AHN.

23. *Ohio Statesman*, Sept. 2, 1851; *NYT*, Oct. 8, 1851.

24. *New Orleans Delta*, Aug. 2, 1850; *Daily Ohio Statesman*, Apr. 26, 1853; *Commercial Advertiser*, Sept. 13, 1860.

25. *New York Tribune* reprinted in *Pennsylvania Freeman*, Apr. 1, 1852. For pro-slavery position see Drew Gilpin Faust, *James Henry Hammond and the Old South: A Design for Mastery* (Baton Rouge: Louisiana State University Press, 1982).

26. On Africanization see José Antonio Saco, *Ideas sobre la incorporacion de Cuba en los Estados Unidos* (Paris: Imprenta de Panckoucke, 1848), 8–12. On British-U.S. clashes in the Gulf of Mexico, see MacMaster, *The United States*, 387–424.

27. *Daily Ohio Statesman*, Apr. 26, 1853; *NYT*, Oct. 8, 1851; *Cleveland Plain Dealer*, Dec. 16, 1854; Cora Montgomery, *The Queen of Islands and the King of Rivers* (New York: Charles Wood, 1850), 22.

28. From Franklin Pierce, "The Ostend Manifesto Conference, &c.," in *House Executive Documents*, 33rd Congress, 2nd Session, no.93 (Washington, D.C.: Government Printing Office, 1855), 127–32.

29. James Buchanan, "Second Annual Message to Congress on the State of the Union," Dec. 6, 1858, available online by Gerhard Peters and John T. Woolley, *The American Presidency Project:* https://www

.presidency.ucsb.edu/documents/second-annual-message-congress-the
-state-the-union. See also Tex Maris-Wolf, "'Of Blood and Treasure':
Recaptive Africans and the Politics of Slave Trade Suppression," *Journal
of the Civil War Era* 4, no. 1 (Mar. 2014): 53–83.

30. New York *Weekly Herald*, Dec. 11, 1852; *NYH*, Aug. 7, 1853; Hugh
Thomas, *The Slave Trade: The Story of the Atlantic Slave Trade, 1440–1870*
(London: Picador, 1997), 646–47. TSTD2: *Lady Suffolk* (voyage id
4166).

31. *NYT*, May 23, 1860.

32. *New Hampshire Patriot and State Gazette*, May 5, 1858; *NYT*, June
21, July 17, 1854, Jan. 14, 1859, Feb. 16, 1860, June 16, Aug. 15, 1860.

33. Eric Foner, *Free Soil, Free Labor, Free Men: The Ideology of the Republican Party Before the Civil War* (New York: Oxford University Press,
1995).

34. John Nicolay and John Hay, eds., *Complete Works of Abraham
Lincoln*, vol. 1 (New York: Century, 1894), 193.

35. For an introduction to the Slave Power, see Foner, *Free Soil*,
73–102. For Seward's speech, see *New York Tribune*, Oct. 3, 1856; George
Templeton Strong, diary entry of Nov. 2, 1860, in *Writing New York*, 219.

36. *New York Times*, Aug. 19, 1856; *Barre* (Massachusetts) *Gazette*,
Apr. 3, 1857. See also Marques, *The United States*, 227–30, 234–35.

37. New York *Evening Post*, Apr. 14, 1860; *NYT*, Aug. 15, 1854
(quote). On Rynders, see *NYT*, Dec. 22, 1856; Howard, *American Slavers*, 167.

38. *NYH*, Apr. 1, 1857; *Times-Picayune*, Nov. 19, 1854.

39. For Parker's speech see *Liberator*, Feb. 26, 1858. For "Republican newspaper" see New York *Evening Post*, n.d., in Archibald to Russell, Feb. 20, 1860. *Barre* (Massachusetts) *Gazette*, Jan. 9, 1857; *London
Christian Observer* quoted in *The American Church and the African Slave
Trade: Mr. Jay's Speech in The New York Diocesan Convention of the Prot-
estant Episcopal Church on the 27th September, 1860, with a Note of the Proceedings Had in That Council on the Subject* (New York: Roe Lockwood &
Sons, 1860), 8.

40. *Hartford Republican*, ca. Aug. 1851, reprinted in the *National Era*,
Aug. 14, 1851.

41. *Speech upon the Foreign Slave Trade, Before the Legislature of South
Carolina, by L. W. Spratt, Esq., of Charleston* (Columbia: Steam Power
Press, 1858), 6; *New York Tribune*, Aug. 20, 1859; *Charleston Standard*,
Oct. 28, 1856.

42. On the reopening movement see Ronald T. Takaki, *A Proslavery Crusade: the Agitation to Reopen the African Slave Trade* (New York: Free Press, 1971). For Pryor quote see *National Era*, June 3, 1858.

43. *National Era*, July 20, 1854; *Barre* (Massachusetts) *Gazette*, Mar. 12, 1858.

44. *Complete Works of Lincoln*, 206; *New York Tribune*, Oct. 3, 1856; *Liberator*, Feb. 24, 54; *Albany Evening Journal*, May 5, 1856.

45. TSTD2: *Wanderer* (voyage id 4974), *Echo*, also known as *Putnam*, (Voyage id 4284). See also Jim Jordan, *The Slave Trader's Letter-Book: Charles Lamar, the Wanderer, and Other Tales of the African Slave Trade* (Athens: University of Georgia Press, 2018).

46. *National Era*, Mar. 11, 1858; for the convention, see *Liberator*, Jan. 28, 1859; *Commercial Advertiser*, Jan. 31, 1859.

47. *NYT*, Jan. 14, 1859; Marques, *The United States*, 233–34.

48. Buchanan, "Second Annual Message"; Buchanan, "Third Annual Message"; Fehrenbacher, *The Slaveholding Republic*, 188.

49. Slocumb quoted in Robert Ralph Davis, Jr., "Buchanian Espionage: A Report on Illegal Slave Trading in the South in 1859," *Journal of Southern History* 37, no. 2 (May 1971): 271–78; Canney, *Africa Squadron*, 201–6, 233–34. The authoritative source on Africans captured by American cruisers during this era is Sharla M. Fett, *Recaptured Africans: Surviving Slave Ships, Detention, and Dislocation in the Final Years of the Slave Trade* (Chapel Hill: University of North Carolina Press, 2017).

50. For Cuba figures see TSTD2, estimates page.

51. *NYT*, Aug. 25, 1859; Mar. 20, June 16, 1860. For the party platform see *Liberator*, June 25, 1860.

52. "First Inaugural Address of Abraham Lincoln," March 4, 1861, available online at https://avalon.law.yale.edu/19th_century/lincoln1.asp.

53. On the immediate buildup to and outbreak of war, including the Crittenden Compromise, see James M. McPherson, *Battle Cry of Freedom* (New York: Oxford University Press, 1988), 234–75.

54. Confederate States of America, *Constitution Of the Confederate States of America: Adopted by the Congress of the Confederated States, at the City of Montgomery, Ala., March 11th, 1861* (New Orleans: S. S. Callender, 1861); Takaki, *A Pro-slavery Crusade*, 231–43. Palmerston to Russell, Sept. 24, 1861, PRO 30/22/21, John Russell Papers, TNA.

55. Gideon Welles to Abraham Lincoln, Mar. 20, 1861, Abraham Lincoln Papers, LoC; Leonard, entry of June 29, 1861, in C. Herbert

Gilliland, ed., *USS "Constellation" on the Dismal Coast: Willie Leonard's Journal, 1859–1861* (Columbia: University of South Carolina Press, 2013), 318; Somerset to Russell, Sept 13, 1861, PRO30/22/24/44, Russell Papers, TNA.

56. Robert Murray to George Whiting, Feb. 1, 1862, Communications received from Robert Murray & Edward Bates to Sec. Usher, Jan 13, 1863, M-160, NARA. Howard, *American Slavers*, 258.

57. Murray to Whiting, Jan. 10, 1862, Communications received from Robert Murray, M-160, NARA (both quotes); Murray's Memo. on Expenses for Suppression, Apr. 22, 1861–May 30, 1862, Communications received from Robert Murray, M-160, NARA; *NYT*, Aug. 16, 17, 1861; see newspapers in Archibald to Russell, Sept. 5, 1861, FO84/1138, TNA.

58. TSTD2: *Juliet*, 1848 (voyage id 4006); *Erie*, 1860 (voyage id 4653); *Ottowa* (no voyage id). See Archibald to Russell, Apr. 17, 1860, FO84/1111, TNA.

59. E. Delafield Smith to Sec. of Interior, Nov. 22, 1861, Communications rec. from E. Delafield Smith, M-160, NARA. For more on Smith and the Gordon case, see Howard, *American Slavers*, 200–202.

60. Howard, *American Slavers*, 227; *NYT*, Nov. 11, 1861; Smith to Sec. of Interior, Nov. 22, 1861, Communications rec. from E. Delafield Smith, M-160, NARA.

61. For debate see newspaper clippings in Archibald to Russell, Sept. 5 and Nov. 11, 1861, FO84/1138, TNA. Rhoda E. White to Abraham Lincoln, Feb. 17, 1862, Abraham Lincoln Papers, LoC; Gilbert Dean to Abraham Lincoln, Feb. 18, 1862, Abraham Lincoln Papers, LoC; Edward Bates to Abraham Lincoln, Feb. 19, 1862, Abraham Lincoln Papers, LoC. See also Archibald's report to Russell, Feb. 24, 1862, FO84/1172, TNA.

62. Palmerston to Russell, Sept 24, 1861, PRO30/22/21, John Russell Papers, TNA; Lyons to Russell, Feb 11 ("very great change"; "see it with pleasure"), Mar. 25 ("warmly in favor"), 1862, FO84/1171, TNA.

63. Lyons to Russell, Feb. 25, FO84/1171, TNA. Seward to Lincoln, Apr. 24, 1862, Abraham Lincoln Papers, LoC. For more on the treaty, see A. Taylor Milne, "The Lyons-Seward Treaty of 1862," *American Historical Review* 38, no. 3 (Apr. 1933): 511–25. On the Argüelles affair, see Dulce to Ministro de Ultramar, June 12, 1864, 4692/4, Ultramar, AHN; Marques, *The United States*, 219–22.

64. Archibald to FO, Dec. 3, 1861, FO84/1138, TNA; Sanchez to

Archibald, Sept. 30, Dec. 3, 1861, FO84/1138, TNA; Howard, *American Slavers*, 189, 234. On Horn's trial, see *NYT*, Oct. 24, 29, 30, 1862.

65. Robert Murray to Geo. Whiting, Mar. 29, 1862, Communications received from Robert Murray, M-160, NARA; Murray's Memo on Expenses for Suppression, Apr. 22, 61–May 30, 62, in Communications received from Robert Murray, M-160, NARA; E. Delafield Smith to Caleb Smith, Apr. 25, 1862, Communications received from E. Delafield Smith, United States attorney for Southern District of New York, Apr. 12, 1861–Sept. 26, 1867, M-160, NARA; C. A. Munro to Seward, Dec. 16, 1861, Dispatches from United States consuls in Lisbon, 1791–1906, roll 7, 1861–1869, NARA.

66. TSTD2: *Marquita* (voyage id 4829).

67. Tassara Memo, May 1, 1862, 4681/45, Ultramar, AHN.

EPILOGUE. ATLANTIC REVERBERATIONS

1. John Macpherson Brackenbury to Lord Russell, Dec. 30, 1862, FO84/1174, TNA; Alexander Dunlop to Russell, July 29, 1864, FO84/1218, TNA; João Soares Pereira to Julián Zulueta, Dec. 1, 1863, enclosed in Admiralty to Russell, Jan. 7, 1864, Admiralty 123/184, TNA.

2. TSTD2 (General Variables>Rig, tonnage, and guns mounted>Rig of vessel>Steamer).

3. Dunlop to William H. Wylde, May 8, 1865, FO84/1241, TNA; Horace Young to Russell, Jan. 5, 1863, FO84/1203, TNA.

4. John V. Crawford to Lord Russell, Dec. 12, 1863, FO84/1197, TNA; Commodore Wilmot to Rear-Admiral Sir B. Walker, Dec. 31, 1863 in W. G. Romaine to E. Hammond, Apr. 29, 1864, FO84/1228, TNA; Joseph Crawford to Russell, Mar. 8, 1862, FO84/1174, TNA.

5. Tassara Memo, May 1, 1862 in Ultramar, 4681/45, AHN. For the impact of the treaty and the Civil War on the slave trade to Cuba and Cuban slavery, see Matt D. Childs, "Cuba, the Atlantic Crisis of the 1860s, and the Road to Abolition," in *American Civil Wars: The United States, Latin America, Europe, and the Crisis of the 1860s*, ed. Don H. Doyle (Chapel Hill: University of North Carolina Press, 2017), 204–21. For the British withdrawal in 1858, see Murray, *Odious Commerce*, 308. For the rejected proposal, see Dulce to Ministro de Ultramar, June 12, 1864, 4692/4, Ultramar, AHN.

6. For Serrano on piracy, see Serrano to Ministro, Sept. 6, 1861, 3549/3, Ultramar, AHN. For Dulce's expulsions, see Dulce to Ministro

de Ultramar, June 12, 1864, 4692/4, Ultramar, AHN; Memo, Ultramar, 4692/4, AHN. For Serrano quotes see Serrano to Ministro de la Guerra y Ultramar, 25 July 1861, Legajo 3549/3, Ultramar, AHN. For more on these captains general see, Murray, *Odious Commerce*, 309-13; Arthur P. Corwin, *Spain and the Abolition of Slavery in Cuba, 1817–1886* (Austin: University of Texas Press, 1967), 145-49; Jesús Sanjurjo Ramos, "Abolitionism and the End of the Slave Trade in Spain's Empire (1800-1870)" (Ph.D. diss., Leeds University, 2018), 242-45.

7. *Disposiciones sobre la represion y castigo del tráfico negrero: mandadas observar por Real decreto de 29 de Setiembre de 1866* (Madrid: Imprenta Nacional, 1866); *Gaceta de la Habana*, June 7, 1867. On the shifts in Spain and its colonial policy see Murray, *Odious Commerce*, 316-24; Christopher Schmidt-Nowara, *Empire and Antislavery: Spain, Cuba, and Puerto Rico, 1833–1874* (Pittsburgh: University of Pittsburgh Press, 1999), 100-125; Schmidt-Nowara, "From Aggression to Crisis: The Spanish Empire in the 1860s," in *American Civil Wars*, 125-46; Corwin, *Spain and the Abolition of Slavery in Cuba*, 152-88; Sanjurjo Ramos, "Abolitionism," 253-62.

8. For declining disembarkations in Cuba see TSTD2, estimates page. For prices see Laird W. Bergad, Fe Iglesias García, and María del Carmen Barcia, *The Cuban Slave Market: 1790–1880* (New York: Cambridge University Press, 1995), 48-50. For Manzano's report see Murray, *Odious Commerce*, 324-25. On final arrivals also see María de los Ángeles Meriño Fuentes and Aisnara Perera Díaz, *Contrabando de bozales en Cuba: perseguir el tráfico y mantener la esclavitud, 1845–1866* (Mayabeque, Cuba: Ediciones Montecallado, 2015), 241-44. For Cuban planters' positions on local and international changes during the 1860s, see María del Carmen Barcia, *Burguesía esclavista y abolición* (Havana: Editorial de Ciencias Sociales, 1987).

9. José Suárez Argudín, Manuel Basilio da Cunha Reis, y Luciano Fernández Perdones, *Proyecto de Inmigración Africana presentado al superior gobierno de esta isla* (Havana: Imprenta de la Habanera, 1860). For more on Cunha Reis in Cuba, see Expediente de solicitud de Manuel Basilio Reis, June 19, 1861, 4676/64, Ultramar, AHN; *Diario de la Marina*, May 3, 1861.

10. See Gobierno general, Legajo 439/21266-9, ANC.

11. The sale of Africans into the Indian Ocean slave trade continued. For a recent assessment of British efforts to suppress this traffic see John Brioch, *Squadron: Ending the African Slave Trade* (New York: Overlook Duckworth, 2017).

12. Zora Neale Hurston, *Barracoon: The Story of the Last "Black Cargo,"* ed. Deborah G. Plant (London: Harper Collins, 2018), 65–69. For more on Africa Town and a slightly different account of the development of the settlement, see Sylviane A. Diouf, *Dreams of Africa in Alabama: The Story of the "Clotilda" and the Last Enslaved African Brought to America* (New York: Oxford University Press, 2007), 151–81.

Index

Page numbers in italics indicate illustrations.

INDEX

Alcoforado, Joaquim, 138, 143–47, 148
Allo, Lorenzo, 200
Almeida, Francisco Diaz Perez de, 50, 161, 164, 232
Ambriz, 30, 33, 34, 43, 44, 77, 105, 111, 113
Ambrizette, 33, 95, 105, 109, 111, 112, 113
American Colonization Society, 130–31, 193
American Revolution, 2, 16
Anglo-Spanish Treaty (1835), 20, 41, 131
Angola: investors in, 78, 80, 87; slave exporting from, 7, 18–21; suppression in, 28–29, 33–34
Antelope, 67, 68, 167
anti-slave trade laws and treaties, 31–32, 39–40, 186, 245; defiance of, 2–3, 17, 28, 186–92; enforcement of, 26, 192, 211, 217–18; penalties under, 135, 184, 186; prosecutions under, 183–85, 191–92. *See also individual acts and treaties*
apprenticeships, recaptured Africans and, 129–32, 134, 174
Archibald, Edward, 84, 91, *141*, 171–79, 232; correspondence with Emilio Sanchez, 153–56, 160–63, *163*, 166–67; recruitment of spies by, 141, 146, 148, 152, 155
Argüelles, José Agustín, 231
Asia, 171

Backhouse, John, 133
Bahia, 22, 37
Baltimore, 7, 10, 43, 59, 60, 69, 96, 206, 211
Banco Español, 87, 243
Baptista, Augusto Lopes, 49
Barcelona, 235, 237
Barclay, Anthony, 13, 148
barracoons, *37*, 38, 43, 66, 111, 112, 120, 121
Barreto, José, 146, 148, 152
Bates, Edward, 229
Benguela, 29, 44
Bight of Benin, 20, 22, 38–39, 77, 106, 107, 111, 115, 128, 142, 148, 262n19

Bilbao, 235, 237
bills of exchange, 33, 84, 85, 87, 88
birthrate, 40
Blanco, Pedro, 37, 74
Blanco and Carvallo, 74
Borrell, Mariano, 71, 72, 133
Boston, 7, 43, 63, 97, 101, 189
Botelho, Antonio Augusto de Oliveira, 42, 69, 84–86, 98, 154, 168, 235
Botelho, Manoel Fortunato de Oliveira, 50
bounties, 144, 147, 165, 173, 219
bozales, 72, 133
Braman, 78, 93–94, 101
Brand, George, 33
Brazil: coffee and, 19, 26, 27; illicit slave trade and, 19, 20–23, 27, 38, 42, 79–80, 125, 147; suppression and, 25, 29–32, 36, 138, 143–45; U.S. trade with, 3, 15, 23–24, 88
Brazilian and Portuguese Slave Trade Association, 13–14, 42
bribery, 27, 31, 62–63, 70–72, 137, 186
Bridgham, Joseph, 63
Britain: interception of Africans by, 128, 129; legal Africa trade and, 27, 90–91, 242; trade with United States by, 46
British Admiralty, 8, 68, 144, 172–73
British consulate, 47, 142–43, 153
Brookes, 118
Buchanan, James, 187, 198, 199, 204–7, 210–11, 218–22, 230, 234

Cabinda, 3, 20, 33, 105, 173
Cádiz, 63, 84, 85, 86, 142, 148, 235, 237
Calheiros e Meneses, Sebastião Lopes de, 90
Calhoun, John C., 202
Calzada, José de, 165–66
Campbell, Benjamin, 146, 148, 152
cane fields, 131, 150, 202. *See also* sugar
Cangala, 33
captains, of ships, 3, 7, 27, 61, 62, 97, 101, 184
captives: in Africa, 1, 36, 43, 70, 76, 105, 106–12, 120–21; demographics

INDEX